WEEP
NO MORE,
MY LADY

WEEP
NO MORE,
MY LADY

by MICKEY DEANS and
ANN PINCHOT

HAWTHORN BOOKS, INC.
Publishers
New York

WEEP NO MORE, MY LADY

I've been around and seen the sights,
And of this I'm sure:
Yes, you're the one
I've waited for.
You'll be the one to last.
I've had this feeling
Once or twice,
But that's all in the past.
That was then,
And now is now,
For you'll be the one to last.
I've tried before,
I'll try no more,
No need to try again.
You were the one worth waiting for—
I've found my where and when.

—Unfinished lyrics by Judy Garland,
written June, 1969

WEEP
NO MORE,
MY LADY

1

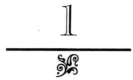

"We love you, Judy!" her audience screamed. "Never leave us, Judy—"

Clutching the microphone, she announced, "This is going to be an interesting performance because I have absolutely no voice. But I'll fake it. Oh, well. . . ." That ingratiating Judy grin, letting you into her private thoughts. "Maybe I'll hit the notes because you're so nice and because it's so good to be home."

It didn't matter whether she was hoarse or in perfect voice. They loved her under all conditions. With a total, fanatic, unconditional love.

"It's okay, Judy," a voice called out tenderly from the balcony. "It's okay. We love you."

"I love you too," she repeated.

Which was absolutely true. I remembered the comment of a playwright who'd once worked with her. "Judy doesn't give a concert. She conducts a love-in."

Now she was singing "I Feel a Song Coming On," and she was really belting it out. You marveled that those powerful sounds came out of that slim, boyish body. Then "The Trolley Song," and pandemonium. "Clang, clang, clang went the trolley," sang Judy, and her audience was fervently keeping time with her. "Swanee" and "Old Man River" followed, the tones simply great. They gave her a standing ovation. She came to the edge of the stage and sat down, legs dangling. When she wasn't singing, she looked touchingly young and scared. I felt the tightness of sympathy in my chest. She sang "The Man That Got Away," and it held all the anguish and yearning of a bruised heart. Many in the audience were in tears. For her? For themselves? I was puzzled, touched, awed, and filled with admiration for Garland, the superstar, and the bright, funny girl with whom I'd spent such an amusing evening a few days earlier.

She needed relief; her energy was waning—and why not, considering the depth and power of feeling projected in her songs? She looked exhausted. Her younger daughter, Lorna, who was then fourteen, came on stage, and Judy introduced her proudly. Lorna did a little dance. She was followed by Joey, Judy's twelve-year-old son, who did a drum solo. Finally, during the last section of the program, a young girl fan could contain herself no longer. She raced down the aisle, a bouquet of roses in her hand, her offering to her idol. Her movement triggered a mass reaction: The aisles were suddenly jammed with fans, offering flowers, gifts, mementoes.

You had to see it to believe it.

She finally sang "Over the Rainbow," which someone in the row in front of me said traditionally marked the end of her performance. And now Judy stood on stage, radiant, exhausted, perspiring, sending kisses from her fingertips and shouting exultantly, "And I made it!"

Someone cried out, "Judy is youth!"

Another, "Judy—the rainbow forever!"

And a cry from the orchestra, "Judy, don't ever go away!"

I was too stunned to move. Finally I went down to the orchestra pit to speak with my friend Bobby Cole, Judy's director, through whom I had met her. I didn't go backstage to see her.

"The critics are underestimating her power," Bobby said as he showed me a clipping from *The New York Times*.

"A raffish, sequin-sprinkled female Lazarus," Vincent Canby called her, "the voice now a memory, her presence colored by those sad and forlorn tales of her personal life, but still one of the most remarkable personalities of the contemporary entertainment scene."

I went back to watch Judy perform on August 26, the closing night of her 1967 four-week New York City engagement at the Palace Theatre. Her daughter Liza Minnelli was sitting in the front row. Again there were the emotional crowd and the immense shock waves of love and the great showmanship and Judy's self-mockery and lancing wit at her own expense. Her audience didn't want new songs, just the sweet old favorites. Finally Liza came on stage, and she and Judy rapped. Then Liza sang, alone, "Cabaret." As her daughter went back to her seat, Judy, brimming with pride, said, "Liza, you've been marvelous all of your life."

The concert was finished by 11:40, but Judy's fans wouldn't let her leave. The loving hysteria of the crowd built up like thunder on a humid night. They waited for her at the stage door. When she emerged from the stage entrance, they were gentle with her, with little of the pushing and shoving you usually encounter in such crowds.

She arrived at Arthur later that evening, exhausted but happy. I made her welcome, and she stayed on, laughing, joking, until it was time for the club to close.

Arthur was not the name of a man but of a club, a discotheque that was a social phenomenon of the rich, fabulous Jet Set sixties. Perhaps if Richard Burton and Elizabeth Taylor hadn't merged under the aegis of *Cleopatra* in a wildly publicized scandalous love affair, Arthur might never have come into being. Richard's wife, Sybil Burton, conducted herself with such taste and dignity that the world doubly sympathized

3

with her. She refused to let herself be pitied, however, and with some of her friends, she opened the discotheque that immediately became the new watering hole for the rich and famous.

In 1967, when I met Judy, I had switched from my work as a musician to the job of night manager of Arthur. The discotheque was at the peak of its fame. Every evening a line of waiting customers stretched around the corner, and limousines and taxis were continuously pulling up to the door. The Pub Room, which provided food, liquor, and talk, had in the right front corner a round table, Number 14, permanently reserved for Sybil, her handsome husband, Jordan Christopher, and their special guests. After Bobby Cole and his wife, Delores, brought Judy to Arthur for the first time when she opened at the Palace, she preferred the quiet Pub Room to the main room, where the chic Jet Setters enjoyed the spotlight. We often chose the far end of the bar, where I could stand in front of Judy— she was so tiny that nobody would see her behind me—and we could talk without the intrusion of strangers, who felt familiar enough to offer her compliments, ask for her autograph, or simply start a conversation as though she were an old, loved friend. Judy generally came to the club when others were about to leave, usually at two in the morning, sometimes even later. It became a habit right after our first meeting in 1967. It continued at intervals during the following year. After the Palace engagement Judy went off on a concert tour of the major cities of the United States, but she often flew back to New York between engagements, and we saw each other then. Sometimes this would happen three or four times a month. Then she might be away from New York for months at a time. She never discussed her personal problems, so I had no idea that in the early part of 1968 she was in grave financial trouble. During the summer and fall of that year she drifted in and out of the city. Finally, exhausted, she checked in at the Boston hospital where she had once recuperated during her Metro-Goldwyn-Mayer period. She called me from Boston, saying that she'd had a fortnight of rest and sleep and planned to remain in Boston, in a rented apartment, for another two weeks. I missed her, but we had no particular understanding. Whenever she was in Manhattan, I thoroughly enjoyed being with her; I never thought, though, "I haven't called Judy in a couple of days." Our dating was casual and spontaneous, but whenever we did meet, it was with warmth and recognition. Two night people, two swingers, recognizing and understanding and gradually learning to love each other's weaknesses and strengths.

Judy and I might have become closer much sooner if I hadn't been so frightened of the Garland legend. I was greatly attracted to her at our first meeting. I remember the way our glances held and her winsome smile and the warmth that developed between us. I had great respect for her. She had marvelous dignity and always behaved like a lady. Moreover, she was delightfully feminine. What impressed me most was that she was so vulnerable, that she so desperately seemed to need protection. Yet whenever I felt a strong inclination to pursue her, I'd back away from the image of stardom, from her reputation and the problems that had been so blatantly spread by international headlines. Still, we could not stay away from each other. I discovered in Judy the small girl who was afraid of the night and who needed someone to comfort her, to keep the ogres away.

When she was in New York, I would either call for her at her hotel or send a car. By the time we were settled at a table in the Pub Room, most customers were gone, and we could sit and talk. She would wait patiently, chatting with the captains while I took care of the final duties that involved putting a busy club to bed. I think she also enjoyed watching me at work, for if she arrived earlier in the evening, I might be talking business over the telephone or perhaps chewing out a waiter who'd overstepped the limits of his professional duties.

Gradually, without our being conscious of it, our meetings began to take on the pattern of a courtship in the closing months of 1968. Judy was under no pressure to conform, so she was at her best, witty and radiant. It was less of a conventional courtship than an easy, relaxed way of being together. There is chemistry, or there isn't. Between us, there was.

If we sat in the Pub Room with some of the staff, we were often joined at four or five in the morning by a couple of policemen from the 17th Precinct, who stopped by to see that all was well at Arthur. They soon became favorites of hers, and she listened, wide-eyed, with that special talent for listening while they related incidents of wild life on Manhattan streets. She had tremendous empathy for the night people, whether they were policemen, bartenders, stars, workmen, or even ferryboat captains.

One of Judy's favorite trips was a ride on the Staten Island ferry in the early hours of the morning. She took her daughter Lorna on the ferry, and Lorna told me later that "Mommy" was known to all the hands on the ferry. A real friendship existed between her and the men who spent their lives on the water. Once when we went to see friends off on the S.S. *France*, she told me how much she loved watching ships take off for trans-Atlantic sailings or freighters leaving for ports with magical, foreign-sounding names. She was incurably romantic. Which may be the reason she loved the sound of the piano.

"Please play 'Poor Butterfly,'" she'd ask me. It was our favorite song, and she never tired of listening to it. Sometimes she asked me how I phrased a song, or she'd suggest earnestly, "Mickey, you should continue with your music. You're wasting your time at Arthur. You're not using your talent. Mickey, I want you to conduct for me. I want you with me on my concerts. Maybe we could do some in Europe . . . Paris. . . . Wouldn't it be fun?" She would be bubbling with wonderful plans.

There was nobody like her.

She was so delighted when her children arrived from the Coast. She brought all three—Liza Minnelli and Lorna and Joey Luft—to Arthur to celebrate Joey's birthday. By some miracle,

6

they managed to create a warm, wholesome little island in that sophisticated atmosphere. Judy was ecstatic when the children were with her; she was tender and loving with them, and whatever mistakes she did make were innocent of the drive and ambition which had marked her own mother's treatment of her. A friend of mine, watching Judy and her trio chattering like birds, laughing in unison, touching and hugging each other, said thoughtfully, "You know, Mickey, to hate the mother is to become the mother."

I misunderstood him. "Judy isn't like her mother at all," I said defensively. "Not from what I've heard."

"You got me wrong," he said. "I didn't mean a girl would take on what she hated in her mother. It's just the opposite. The girl who's had it tough, with a mother who didn't give her love, grows up thinking, 'I'll give my kids what I never had. I'll be a real loving mother.' "

That was Judy.

Lorna often visited Arthur, even when Judy was out of town. Accompanied by her friends, bright teen-age boys and girls, she would drop in early, throw her arms impulsively around me, and ask, "Mickey, can we have a table? Mickey, can we sit at Sybil's table?"

I was always fond of kids and found Lorna particularly delightful. "Well, I'll think about it," I'd say.

"Mickey," she'd exclaim, "why are you frowning? Did I do something wrong? What did I do wrong, Mickey?"

"Ladies don't chew gum."

"Oh"—she clasped the palm of her hand to her mouth—"where shall I put it?"

I held out my hand. "Put it here."

I would then escort her and her friends to the main room.

"Mickey, can I order what I want?"

"Of course."

"Yeah, but no matter what I order, I get ginger ale with fruit in it?"

"That's right, Lorna."

"Oh, Mickey"—her round, pretty face would drop the pout and widen into a huge grin—"you're the most!"

Lorna loved to think she was Cupid, bringing her mother and me together. She had a small girl's sense of intrigue and satisfaction in arranging people's lives to please her fantasies.

When Judy was in town, she'd telephone to check up on Lorna.

"Is she all right, Mickey?"

"She's fine, Judy. Don't worry."

Whenever Judy came to Arthur, she was content to stay until closing time. "I hate the hotel. It's so damn lonely," she said. "Four walls holding in empty space. It's a down."

One evening, Bob Jorgen, with whom I share an apartment when I am in New York, gave a party, and I asked Judy if she'd like to come. Bob and Judy had known each other since the forties, when Bob had been in college and Judy had been the radiant young queen of M.G.M. The party started late and went on until dawn, and Judy, tired for once, wandered into the bedroom and fell asleep. I had an early-morning appointment and left without ever getting to bed, and Bob, who'd snatched some rest on the divan in the living room, got up, showered, dressed, and went in to see if she was all right. Bob is a tall, lean man who carries his Swedish heritage proudly. He has a shaved head and wore at that time a Fu Manchu moustache.

Judy lay on the bedspread with a comforter over her. As Bob came to the door, she opened her eyes cautiously. After a moment she said, "Is it too corny to ask where I am?"

"You're in my apartment."

"Gee, thanks. I woke up and saw the white ceiling, and I thought, God, Garland, it's a hospital. You've goofed again."

"Is there anything I can get for you?" Bob asked.

She propped herself up on her elbow. "Do you have a little bit of peanut butter?"

8

"Yes, I do."

She raised her brows. "And maybe a bit of jam?"

"Of course."

"And a small slice of bread?"

"Certainly."

"Could it be toasted—and spread with peanut butter and jam?"

They chatted like old friends while Bob made breakfast.

Friends affectionately call Bob Doc, and it's not difficult to understand the reason. As an executive in the New York Social Welfare Department, his job is to help troubled people. He has the air of a practical analyst—compassionate and sensitive but objective. Later Judy got in the habit of stopping by the apartment in the afternoon and often staying for dinner. Although they had known each other for years, but only as occasional acquaintances, they now became close.

"This girl really cares for you, Mickey," Bob finally said. "You'd better decide what you want to do."

A decision was the last thing I wanted. I didn't think of Judy in a serious man-woman context. We were both night people, sharing many interests, and I saw her as a warm, vulnerable person who both attracted and frightened me. Yet we always had great times together. We often went to P. J. Clarke's or Elaine's or Max's Kansas City rather than to the obvious spots like "21." We frequently visited a gifted young musician, Charlie Cochran, who lived four blocks from Bob's apartment, and Charlie and I would play the piano while Judy listened, truly relaxed and happy. She was much taken with Charlie's aunt Priscilla. They had a special brand of warmth that made her comfortable with them.

Within the context of my free time, we led a carefree, spontaneous life, always following our impulses. We both detested formality, and we ate whenever we happened to be hungry. One evening Bob was giving a dinner party, with chateaubriand, asparagus with hollandaise—the works. It was a night when I was off from Arthur. When I brought Judy up to the apartment, the guests were still busy with their second rounds of drinks.

Bob found Judy and me in the kitchen with the maid. "What are you eating?" he demanded.

"Tuna-fish sandwiches."

"Dammit," Bob moaned, "you know what a great dinner we're having."

"Yes, Bobby," Judy said, "but we're hungry *now*."

"And if we hurry," I added, "we can catch the nine-o'clock movie."

Judy never ceased to be the superstar to her fans, so shopping was always difficult for her. Yet she hated having clothes sent to her hotel; like all women, she adored going to the shops. Even in her big floppy hat and dark shades, she attracted crowds. I was with her one afternoon when she went to Bonwit's for shoes. The expedition turned into a mob scene. "I don't even know what I bought," she said ruefully afterward as they sneaked us down the back staircase.

We were seeing a good deal of each other, but it never occurred to me that I was possessive about her until she showed up with an escort one night at Arthur. She told me later it was purely a business thing, but it bugged hell out of me. I realized that she was a woman with great needs and that unless I intended to accept the situation, I should end it before either of us was hurt. I tried to be a bit more detached, but she was so damn charming that I lost all sense of caution. I was beginning to realize that we were somewhat alike in our strengths and weaknesses.

She was sometimes as prim as a Victorian lady. I rang her up one day, and she sounded strange. "What's the matter?" I asked.

"Nothing, Mickey."

"Look, hon, you don't sound like yourself."

"I'm okay."

"You mad or something?"

"Of course not."

I was puzzled until later that evening she confessed that she had applied a face mask and had fallen asleep with it on; when I called, her face was so stiff and dry she couldn't talk. She had been too embarrassed to explain. Yet she could be devastatingly candid about other personal things.

It was common talk that Judy had problems with insomnia and that she was taking both pep and sleeping pills, but I saw none of this in the times we shared. She was under no great pressure during that period; she wasn't performing nightly nor working on a film. She was relaxed and happy and in constant gay spirits.

"How did you happen to leave M.G.M.?" I asked her one evening over coffee and sandwiches at Arthur.

She looked at me, her enormous eyes reflecting a wicked gleam. "Leo the Lion bit me."

Then she grew serious, and it was the first time she mentioned her early problems. "I guess you'd call the studio an education, but not for a young girl. I was fourteen when Louis B. Mayer decided to team me with Mickey Rooney. We were working six days a week, ten to twelve hours a day. I had plenty of vitality and endurance, but this was a grind. When I began to sag, the studio doctor fed me and some of the other young performers pills that looked as big as plates. They were supposed to keep us peppy. They sure did. We were wound up like waltzing mice. When I finished shooting, they'd take me over to the studio hospital, where they had a little bed for me. The monkey Cheetah was treated better than I was. At least Cheetah got a banana to eat. All I got was a barbiturate popped in my mouth—until four hours later, when they'd wake me up and put a pep pill in my mouth so I could go back to the sound stage and work another long stretch. And if that wasn't enough, there were always threats. *Watch your diet! You're getting fat!* The doctor Mr. Mayer hired was an ex-abortionist. He didn't know what all those pills were doing to me."

11

Then she smiled with the small-girl gallantry so much a part of her. "I've closed the door on it."

Another time, when we were sitting alone in the Pub Room, she said thoughtfully, "Mickey, I've known you less than a couple of years, and yet I feel you're the only man who understands what I feel—"

I could only guess at what she meant. Surely there had been men in her life who were sympathetic to her unique personality and her problems. David Rose, her first husband, was a sensitive man, but he was a musician, an orchestra leader, and the demands on his time may have made him less aware of her problems. Vincente Minnelli, her second husband, was a painstaking, dedicated director whose life-style—intense, introverted, perfectionist—seems to have alienated her. Sid Luft, her third husband, was primarily an entrepreneur who found her behavior unpredictable and difficult to fathom. When I first knew her in 1967, she was separated from her fourth husband, Mark Herron, whom she'd married in the Orient in 1965, after her ill-fated Australian tour. She said Mark was a nice boy, but he was never around. Yet he had produced her successful Palladium show in London, where she had appeared with Liza, and had chosen the numbers and even written some of the lyrics.

"Afterwards I used to hear from him once in a while, but I think he was in a telephone booth with casters. He left right after our wedding because he had to be back in Los Angeles to work with a little-theater group. I never knew where he was; even his friends didn't. Our marriage ended before it began. I was alone again. I seem to attract people who need to destroy me just to stay alive themselves. If you're considered a living legend, some people just want to hack away at you. Not women, just men."

Sid Luft was back in her life at this time, having arranged for her appearance at the Palace in 1967 and then a series of concerts in large cities. She told me confidentially that she and Sid were at odds again, and she was afraid he might take Lorna and Joey back to California.

What troubled her more than anything else was being alone at night. "I've been alone too often. There's too much of a gulf between the love of an audience I've just sung to and the awful silence of an empty hotel room. Maybe I've got this hang-up about silence, but it makes me feel as though I hadn't been born."

There is no in-between for a star of Judy's caliber. Either masses of adoring fans or an empty, impersonal room. "I'd rather have a few words of love at night than the approval of thousands of people," she said wistfully more than once.

People worship a superstar—from afar. They're either too scared or too awed to get in touch with her, to invite her out. Judy was so often alone in her room after a performance, pacing back and forth, staring at the telephone, and thinking, If somebody would just get the wrong number, I'd appreciate it. Just to hear the phone ring. Around five in the morning, when the night people were going off, she would wonder, Wasn't there somebody in that crowd of twenty thousand who could have come home and had a drink or something?

"I've had mass love," she added with her inimitable grin, "and that's pretty good, I guess. But not individual love, which is so much better."

She told me that when she couldn't pace the floor any longer, she would read her old newspaper clippings or turn on recordings of her Carnegie Hall concerts, which was what Rock Hudson and Marlon Brando had advised her to do. She was devoted to Rock and Marlon. Whenever she was in Hollywood and she was depressed, she knew she could telephone them and they'd drop whatever they happened to be doing and come over. This was also true of Donald O'Connor, whom she'd known since they both were preteen vaudevillians.

One evening early in 1968, when Judy was home in Beverly Hills, alone and crying uncontrollably over her financial plight, she telephoned Rock.

"I'll be right over," he said, and in fifteen minutes he was at the door.

He walked in and asked, "Where's the bar?" and proceeded

to make them a couple of drinks. Then he related some of the wacky things that were going on in his life and coaxed Judy into laughing. Even after he finally left, she remained in good spirits.

Judy sometimes spoke of Marilyn Monroe, whom she had dearly loved. Marilyn once asked her for help, and it troubled Judy not to have been able to give her good advice.

"Marilyn followed me from room to room at a party at Clifton Webb's one night in Hollywood," Judy told me. " 'I don't want to get too far away from you,' she said. 'I'm scared.' I told her we were all scared."

Judy never believed that Marilyn really meant to harm herself when she died from an overdose of sleeping pills. And while we were sitting at Arthur in the early-morning hours, when the club was empty, Judy said something that turned out to be tragically prophetic. "You shouldn't be told you're completely irresponsible and then be left alone with too much medication on hand. You take a couple of sleeping pills, and then you wake up in twenty minutes and forget you've taken them. So you swallow a couple more, and the next thing you know, you've taken too many. It's happened to all of us. It happened to me. Luckily, someone always found me and saved my life.

"There are times when I have deliberately tried to take my life. And once I cut my throat with a razor blade, but I don't really think I wanted to do it. I just wanted not to get up and try to get through the day. A week later I was glad I'd failed. Committing suicide would mean robbing too many people. Including myself. When my number is up, I want a new one."

She was riding the crest of the Judy Garland boom in 1961. She had just done forty-two concerts in forty-two cities. The tour must have grossed more than a million dollars, and it paid off most of the debts she had run up in England, France, and the United States, with a little left over for her too. But suddenly she noticed such a decline in the money she had accumulated that she realized funds had been attached for bills that hadn't been paid. She was in trouble.

I'd read, like the rest of the world, about Judy's troubles, but everyone felt she was indestructible. And as she sat opposite me, talking in her husky voice, taking sips of her vodka and tonic whenever she thought of it, I felt the strength of this small, frail woman. Her life may have been peaks and valleys, ups and downs, but she sounded as though she were back on the comeback trail.

To cheer her up I said, "Jack Paar said you'll always be Dorothy—"

"He's not the only one," Judy said wryly. In England, after a command performance, the queen mother told Judy that she felt her throat tighten whenever she heard "Over the Rainbow."

"Ma'am," Judy replied, "that song has plagued me all my life. You know, it's hard to be remembered by a song you first sang thirty years ago. It's like being a grandmother in pigtails."

2

I knew in a more modest way the loneliness, fatigue, and boredom of being on the road: the anonymous hotel rooms, the sameness of cities. Before taking on the job at Arthur, I was a performer. I played the piano with a trio behind me and also conducted a show band for two years. I knew firsthand the rejection of an apprentice entertainer. I learned my profession by performing, but the climb to recognition was tortuous.

There were no musicians in my family. I was born Michael De Vinko in Garfield, New Jersey, on September 24, 1934. All of my family have this fantastic talent for working with their hands. They can build, repair, construct. As a matter of fact, my parents still live in the house that my grandfather built.

Friends have said I was the love of my parents' life, being the youngest of their three children, two boys and a girl. They expected me to be a professional man, to settle down to marriage, and to raise a brood of grandchildren for them.

I puzzled them. A musician? What future was there in music? But I yearned for a piano. The only way to get one was to earn the money. So my fourteenth summer, I worked for a friend, Nick Macadonia, in his appliance store, handling refrigerators and washing machines. Even after giving my mother money each week, I had thirty-five dollars saved by Labor Day, and I traded my wealth for an old upright with fourteen broken keys. There was a professional tuner in Garfield, and I hung around his workshop, doing odd jobs without pay for the privilege of watching and learning. Meanwhile I continued working at odd jobs after school and weekends to pay for piano lessons. The structure of an act gradually took shape in my mind. This need to set a goal and steamroll toward it remains one of my present compulsions.

My professional career was launched at the Club Lee in Fort Lee, New Jersey, in 1956, and from there I went on a circuit of small nightclubs. It was a gypsy life—casual hours, sketchy meals, many disappointments, a few achievements—but I was young, resilient, and fiercely ambitious. People moved in and out of my life. After a while, however, I learned to chop things off, not to become attached to people, and also to keep my eye firmly on tomorrow. Meanwhile I did my stint in the army, attended Emerson College in Boston, and came back to music. I went to work at Jilly's in New York, which is famous because of the proprietor's friendship with Frank Sinatra, who makes the bar his New York headquarters. I alternated at the piano with Charlie Cochran. The customers gathered around my piano bar were stars like Frank Sinatra, Dean Martin, Sammy Davis, Jr., Peter Lawford, Sarah Vaughan. From Jilly's I went to the Tenement in New York, to clubs in St. Croix, Antigua, and Miami, and finally to Harold's Club in Reno. But I wasn't keen about life on the road or the lack of a permanent pad and my own possessions.

I knew a good deal about the pill scene—not hard drugs, but ups and downers. They were everywhere. I used them sometimes to get a buzz. At the close of my run at Harold's Club, I realized that as much as I loved music, my work had become increasingly pointless to me. I was downcast and depressed.

About this time a friend, Murray Drucker, told me of the new discotheque Arthur, which was hiring young actors and musicians as waiters. He suggested I give it a try.

I was appalled. "Murray, me a waiter?"

"Why not? These kids are making three, four hundred a week, and mostly they don't even pay taxes on the whole thing."

I laughed at him.

"What about captain, then?" he suggested, evidently recruiting for Sybil Burton. "All you gotta do is say hello to people, and they'll slip a *schmear* in your palm. Give it a try. You don't like it, you lose nothing."

Playing a kind of host appealed to me. I had always gotten on well with people. Before long I became night manager. It was a job that called for tact, common sense, and a feeling for organization. The mechanics of running Arthur appealed greatly to me. Whenever I'd worked in other nightclubs, I listened to the managers talk about how to tighten their organizations. I discovered I had the mental muscle to deal with crises and personnel. Arthur soon developed into more than a tide-over. I spent three years at Arthur, and I felt that somehow I'd stumbled onto my destiny. Recently, however, I'd begun to feel anxious. It seemed to me the phenomenon of Arthur was beginning to run its course.

What originally had made Arthur a success were the celebrities who dropped in each night and the people who came in to see the celebrities and still do their own thing. But the party seemed to be over. All we could do now was keep Arthur running without too great a loss. I wanted to get out but not while Arthur was sliding downhill. Pride egged me on to stay until hopefully I could leave with a winner. Meanwhile it was a twenty-hour-a-day ordeal, and by December, 1968, I was beat.

Judy arrived in New York well before the Christmas holidays, and our feelings moved into high gear. Somehow we allowed ourselves to be in love, ignoring the consequences. Judy was feeling well, but she complained about her helplessness, a trait that made her enormously appealing. Her problems were so poignant and she was so feminine and helpless that you wanted very much to take care of her. We were back in our carefree pattern. Judy would meet me at the club. Some mornings, having decided to breakfast at my apartment, we'd go shopping in an all-night market. Judy was so tiny that she would sit in the basket like a happy child, and I'd push her up and down the aisles, the two of us laughing like crazy kids. She so enjoyed the small pleasures that had been denied her.

In the New York apartment I shared with Bob Jorgen, Judy made scrambled eggs, toast, and fresh grapefruit juice. Her appetite was slight, but she seemed to enjoy her food. She was in a reminiscing mood and regaled me with some of the incidents of the Hollywood Rat Pack, of which Humphrey Bogart and Lauren Bacall, Frank Sinatra, Sammy Davis, Jr., and Judy and Sid Luft had been members. Irving Lazar, the movie agent, had bought a Rolls-Royce and was inordinately proud of it. "He fussed over it like an overprotective mother," Judy said. "Not an ash visible anywhere. It was showroom perfect."

He offered a ride one evening to Judy, Frank Sinatra, and Dean Martin. Lazar was at the wheel, and the three of them were in back. While he raved about the car's style and engine ("At sixty miles an hour all you can hear is the tick of the clock"), his three guests busied themselves with a project of their own. They built a small, lively fire in the back seat. It took Mr. Lazar a long time to forgive them, and Judy still chuckled at the memory of his apoplectic rage. She used to join her anti–Hollywood Establishment buddies in deflating anyone or anything pompous.

We attended a few formal events the last week in December. Among them was the opening of a Hollywood girl singer at the Plaza's Persian Room. Judy wore a big wide-brimmed black hat trimmed with coq feathers. Whenever a waiter passed, he would jar the hat slightly, and feathers would drift through the air. He would then apologize profusely.

"It's perfectly all right," Judy said proudly. "It's just something I whipped up myself."

3

She was as proud of her simple skills as of her dramatic talents and her extraordinary voice. As a matter of fact, she was completely objective about her reputation as a superstar. She was deeply touched, though, when Noel Coward, whom she adored, once wrote about her, "Whenever I see her before an audience now, coming on with the authority of a great star and really taking hold of an audience, I know that every single heartbreak she had when she was a little girl, every number that was taken away, every disappointment, went into the making of this authority. But that, of course, is the way to learn theater."

She was thin-skinned, abnormally afraid of a rebuff from her friends and fans and even from her children. She longed to see them, but she wouldn't pick up the telephone to call them. She worried about them, often needlessly. I remember one night in 1967 when the kids were with her in New York while she was playing the Palace. She called me at the club, absolutely hysterical. "Joey is sick. My poor baby, he's going to die!"

"What's the matter with Joey?" I asked.

"He has a cold—"

"Did you take his temperature?"

"No, but he's *terribly* hot. He must have a temperature of a hundred and four. I can feel it. Oh, what's going to happen to my poor baby?"

"Hon, look, don't get uptight. Phone downstairs and get a thermometer from the drugstore. Then call me back. If he's got a fever, I'll get hold of a doctor right away."

It turned out that Joey's temperature was 100°, but the doctor came and reassured her. Thinking about it later, I realized why she was so frantic. The terror that she might lose him was another part of the fear with which she constantly lived.

As I grew to know her, I realized Judy was afraid of the slightest rejection. The reason for it was a puzzle to me then, although it became clear later, when she told me more about her childhood. But Bob told me of an incident that happened to him. It was after we had all been partying for a couple of nights and Bob had had no sleep. The telephone rang at the apartment just as he was about to fall into bed.

"This is Lorna Luft," the small girlish voice said. "Miss Garland would like you to join us for Tony Bennett's opening tonight."

Bob asked to speak to Judy and explained that he couldn't make it.

"I guess you've had enough of me," she said quietly.

Yet once when I was playing for friends in the apartment and I missed a note and apologized for it, she said fiercely to Bob, "Why does Mickey denigrate himself?"

Judy was planning to leave for London and a five-week appearance at the large cabaret Talk of the Town. Talk of the Town had once been the Hippodrome Theatre and is comparable to Manhattan's old Latin Quarter at its peak. Needing money, she went back to her old agents, Creative Management Associates, who arranged for the engagement. Before her departure she was to take over as hostess of Merv Griffin's talk show for one night. There was a party for Merv at Arthur, and we arrived rather late, obviously bursting with a secret.

"Shall we tell them?" Judy asked with a giggle.

Just then Earl Wilson telephoned, and John Springer, Judy's press representative, went to talk to him.

"Why don't you come over, Earl?" he suggested. "I think Judy and Mickey have something to tell you."

Actually, it was all quite spontaneous. Judy and I were really grooving, and when I thought of her leaving for London, I got uptight. Almost without volition, I had heard myself saying, "God, hon, we ought to get married."

And Judy's humorous, happy answer: "You'd better not be kidding."

When I brought her back to her hotel that night, she said, "I feel different about you than anyone I've known, Mickey. I don't feel alone anymore. . . ."

Her voice was poignant. I felt the need to protect her, to keep her out of harm's way, safe from rejection and humiliation and disappointments. We did have a chance. There was hope for the future. I've always made my own judgments. I never listened to others. I saw Judy as a fine human being, and I cared enough to want to marry her.

I wasn't exactly naïve. I knew that in our profession love has about as much chance of enduring as a snowball in hell.

But sometimes love begins with an unspoken cry for help.

And a response.

4

The next week was for us a wild, swinging, loving time. Both of us were fighting the Hong Kong flu, but no virus could interfere with our hectic around-the-clock activities. Judy was getting ready for the trip abroad, and I was looking after my obligations at Arthur. Neither of us got much sleep, but it didn't seem to matter. Excitement carried us to a high. Everyone knew of our plans to marry, which were carried the morning after Merv Griffin's party in Earl Wilson's column. We planned to marry in London.

We were scheduled to leave for London on December 27, 1968. Judy wasn't quite ready, so it was a last-minute rush to get to Kennedy Airport on time. We were fortunate to have Henry, our driver, take us through the dense holiday traffic. Henry was much more than our driver; he was our friend who had lived through our courtship and who was kind and discreet, as well as available at all hours to ferry us wherever impulse happened to take us.

As usual, Henry was waiting. As usual, we were late. I remember that wild ride as a portent of the future. Judy, Charlie

Cochran, and I were sandwiched together in the back seat, packed in among countless pieces of bright-red leather luggage, all initialed "J.G." Charlie was one of my best friends. He had the right background, had attended the right prep schools and college, but music was his bag. Charlie was accompanying us to London to be best man at our wedding. He was clutching two magnums of Dom Perignon against him like rare jewels. Judy was giggling, her enormous eyes filled with humor at our plight, for we were inundated by most of her twenty-eight suitcases and a few of mine and Charlie's. The rest of our belongings were hanging precariously from the overloaded trunk compartment.

"Do we have everything?" Judy asked. She seemed to thrive on the confusion, and she was ecstatic with happiness. She kept brushing our cheeks with her lips and nearly dislodged the champagne from Charlie's arms.

Despite the polished gray limousine, our arrival at Kennedy was somewhat like that of a gypsy caravan.

The Pan American public-relations staff was waiting, as well as some onlookers. Judy's brown hat was askew on her head. Two hours before we had left for the airport she had said, "I absolutely must have a new hat. I simply cannot leave for London without a new hat." She had a thing about hats, so she dispatched Charlie to buy her one. Poor Charlie went on a mad, confused safari through Saks and Bergdorf's, and finally, just as we were loading, he arrived, carrying a big floppy hat. Judy was enchanted. She put it on, and it promptly fell over her eyes. This didn't disturb her at all. She loved the hat and planned to use it for laughs.

The crowd was thickening around the Pan Am staff. People —I was to discover—seemed to become aware of Judy's presence without its being verbalized, and the whisper grew: "It's Judy Garland. It's Judy Garland."

We made our way to the private lounge, all of us laughing, Judy happily signing autographs. Once in the lounge we were greeted by Fred Reisert, one of my oldest friends and a mem-

ber of the New York police force. Fred's left arm was trying to
guard two bottles of champagne, while his right hand presented Judy with a bouquet of lovely flowers. We were overwhelmed by this deluge of champagne, since neither Judy nor
I cared for it, but it didn't matter. During our trans-Atlantic
flight, it would be put to good use.

Judy and I were in a state of manic happiness. Our feet
didn't touch the ground. Every incident—as well as the fact
that we were together—seemed wonderful and highly amusing.
If we were slightly mad, it was the most marvelous form of in-
sanity.

The flight was airborne at eight-thirty in the evening. It
wasn't crowded, and after we were seated, Judy noticed a
young girl, attractive and alone, opposite our section. I think
Judy was a born matchmaker. She nudged me. "Tell Charlie."

I did. But Charlie had qualms. "She looks about sixteen."

"I'll find out," I offered. Judy was watching us, enormously
amused.

"Hi," I said. The girl looked up. "We were betting on your
age. My buddy says you're twenty-one, but I said, No, you're
about twenty-four."

"Twenty-one," she corrected me with a smile. "Today, as a
matter of fact."

"That calls for a celebration," I said, and she agreed to join
us. She turned out to be a hell of a fine card-player—good, but
not as good as Judy, who played poker with a man's courage
and a woman's bluff. The two girls teamed up against Charlie
and me for low stakes and loose change. When I ran out of
change, the stewardess relieved the other passengers of their
silver, but the girls did beat us, which pleased Judy no end.

When our plane landed at seven-thirty in the morning, we
were all suddenly depleted. I figured Heathrow Airport
wouldn't be crowded this early, and Glynn Jones, a member of
Bernard Delfont's staff, would be meeting us with a car to
take us to the hotel and some sleep. Thinking back, I am surprised at my naïveté. A Pan Am representative escorted us

right through customs. Glynn Jones was at my side. (I would be seeing him every day during Judy's engagement at Talk of the Town. He was considerate and dedicated.) I was accustomed to photographers and members of the press, but not to the degree we encountered that morning. London has twelve daily newspapers and three television channels, plus private news services and free-lance photographers. All of these had sent representatives to cover Judy's arrival, and there were also the fans and the amateur photographers. My need for sleep disappeared quickly. I never woke up so fast, and that includes my basic-training days in the army with my platoon sergeant blowing the whistle.

Judy was accustomed to this kind of publicity melee, but to me it was as though this mob were pushing its way through the front door of my home. We were blinded by blazing lights from the newsreel cameras and the flashbulbs of the still cameras. Microphones were shoved in our faces as we tried to edge our way through the crowd, with everybody shouting and asking questions all at once.

It was not my first trip to England, but this time the soft-spoken, courtly Englishmen didn't seem to be present. As we went ahead from customs, a man walking backward alongside us handed me a brown envelope. I assumed he was one of Judy's middle-aged fans with a gift for her, but it turned out that he was a private detective, serving her with legal papers.

London was beautiful that morning, covered with a thin layer of snow that had fallen during the night, and was for the most part untouched except for tracks in the streets. "It looks so fresh," Judy said happily, linking her arm through mine.

The drive from Heathrow to Piccadilly seemed short, and at the entrance of the Ritz we were greeted by more members of the press. We were welcomed at the front desk and ushered into an elevator and to our suite. "I'm always so happy here," Judy said. "It's not like a hotel. I feel more like a guest in a home."

Felix, a middle-aged Englishman, was assigned to be our butler, but he did so much more for us than his role suggested.

He thought of everything we might wish or need and took care of us with great kindness and grace. (I returned to the Ritz last autumn—alone—and Felix greeted me in my suite. As I reached in my pocket for a cigarette, he handed me a fresh pack of my brand of menthol cigarettes, which aren't normally stocked, and apologized for not having them on my tray. It seemed as though I had never left.)

But during the morning of this visit with Judy, I ordered coffee and breakfast for us while the housekeeper supervised the maids doing the unpacking. Glynn checked with us about the time schedules for the orchestra rehearsals to make sure they were convenient for Judy. The telephones started ringing and rarely stopped from that moment on. We remained in a state of keyed-up exhaustion. During all this well-organized confusion I noticed there was no piano in the suite. Stan Freeman, the talented young composer, had come up with an opening number for Judy, "I Belong to London," in about an hour's time before we left New York. Now Judy needed a piano to rehearse. Stan had given Judy the piano copy, but no orchestration had been written. It was now Saturday morning. Where, Judy asked, could we get a piano? Glynn Jones did not fail us. He located a new spinet somewhere; it was probably the only one ever delivered by limousine instead of van. This kind of piano is not a favorite with me. I've always felt spinets were designed for an unmusical housewife who wanted something to fit in the corner of her living room. Judy blossomed amid the confusion. She walked around the room, a cup of coffee in her hand. "There's enough caffeine in one cup of coffee to blast you awake," she remarked.

"Hon, do you know why the English drink tea?" I asked.

Judy made a delightful straight man. She even managed to look confused.

"Because they can't make a goddamned pot of coffee," I said.

Before we knew it, the time to rehearse with the orchestra was upon us. Judy begged off; she needed a nap.

"Mickey, will you make the first one? Please."

Two more rehearsals were scheduled before the Monday opening, so I agreed. Charlie Cochran, Glynn Jones, and I went off to meet the conductor, Bert Rhodes, and we discussed the tempos. More than once I discreetly asked Charlie's opinion of the tempos, among other problems. The rehearsals over, we ventured back to the hotel. The gentleman who was to do the arrangement on "I Belong to London" was conferring with Judy. She wasn't too happy, so after he left, I sat down at the piano with her, and we rehearsed until the song started falling into place. There were a good many lyrics to this number, and in spite of her fatigue, Judy was patient. We were justified in having great hopes for this engagement.

5

"Whenever I'm happy, something awful happens," Judy said, staring at the writ. Judy was previously under contract to Group V, arranged by Sid Luft, but evidently her contract had been turned over to a couple of strangers. This was all very confusing to me, since the judgment claimed that Group V owned Judy and that she had no right to appear anywhere without the monies she earned being paid over to them.

"You've got to fight this," I told Judy, who was hysterical with anxiety.

I spent most of Sunday consulting with her lawyer and at the same time trying to keep Judy calm. It was painful to see the disruptions that threatened her peace of mind. The Talk of the Town engagement was important for her both professionally and financially. We wanted all to go well so that her recent reputation for illness and instability would be wiped out and she could arrange for a successful continental tour.

Monday was tense. Mr. Justice Megarry heard the arguments by Judy's lawyer and those of the two American businessmen, Howard Harper and Leon J. Greenspan. They were trying to stop Judy from appearing without their consent, so their writ was against not only Judy but also Theatre Restaurants, Ltd., which ran Talk of the Town; Robert Nesbitt, producer of the show; and impresario Bernard Delfont. Judy didn't appear in court. She remained at the Ritz, shut off from calls and messages.

Stanley Waldman, the London lawyer for Judy and her co-defendants, explained to Judge Megarry that Judy had entered into a contract with a company named Group V, under which she had given them her exclusive professional services in return for the "vast salary" of one thousand dollars a performance. Moreover, she had agreed not to work for anyone else during the period of the contract. Group V had the option of extending the contract by four one-year periods. That option had been exercised on the previous June 8.

The counsel for Mr. Harper and Mr. Greenspan claimed that if Judy appeared at Talk of the Town, it would be a "flagrant breach" of the agreement. According to them, Group V had assigned the contract to them in order to secure a loan of $18,750. Since the loan was not repaid, the contract for Judy's services now belonged to Mr. Harper and Mr. Greenspan. Their lawyer said that Judy "was a woman of considerable experience in the entertainment world who must have entered into many contracts for her personal services. But now she comes along, without specific allegations, to say this was not the bargain she entered into."

Judy's written testimony revealed that the first thing she knew about these proceedings was when she came to England. "I never heard of either of the plaintiffs," she indicated, "or knew any assignment of contract had taken place."

Stanley Waldman said there was no evidence that Judy had agreed to be "pawned" by Group V. She had been "pledged as collateral security for a loan"—a transaction not envisaged, the press reported, by her contract.

Judy herself explained that the Group V contract came about in an unusual way. Group V was formed to set up trust funds for Judy, Sid Luft, and the children, and it was also to have tax advantages for her.

"Sid told me about it as I was on my way to a performance," she explained. "It was just one page, and I signed it."

Later, when she saw the contract, about fifteen pages had been put in front of the page she had signed. She was emphatic about having been misled about the Group V setup.

The press reminded their English readers of a similar case heard in London. That was the Warner Brothers suit against Bette Davis in 1937, when she fled Hollywood for London and signed a contract with another film company.

"I won't stop Judy," Judge Megarry decided. "Slavery is no less slavery if the chains are gilded."

The legal decision was popular. Judy was given permission by Mr. Justice Megarry to appear at Talk of the Town restaurant that night. He stipulated his refusal to grant an injunction applied only to that first appearance. The news came about five hours before her performance. Judy veered from gloom to joy. She had won her professional freedom for the first time, and it gave her a tremendous booster shot of confidence.

Unfortunately, this wasn't her only problem. Just before we left for London, Judy couldn't locate her musical arrangements. She was notified that someone was holding them and wouldn't release them to her unless she paid thirty-five thousand dollars. Without them she couldn't give a performance. She lacked money to ransom them.

Time was short. Luckily, I was able to have the arrangements lifted from her previous recordings. Now I began to realize how helpless Judy really was. I found myself taking over for her in a way I hadn't ever planned to. You take for granted that when a star of Judy's caliber gives a performance, all behind-the-scenes business is carefully structured to run serenely. In Judy's case it seemed that she not only lived but also performed in a whirlwind.

I helped write arrangements. I took over orchestra rehearsals when she was too upset by the injunction to attend them. I dealt with the business affairs that she wasn't prepared to cope with. I was drawn against my will, and by the exigencies of her need, into the maelstrom of her professional life. I was Judy's manager, business adviser, producer, lover—all the roles that were essential to keep her functioning.

Under the circumstances, it was impossible for me to get back to my job in New York. The sorry news about Arthur caused me considerable concern, and I kept hoping to be able to fly back and square things there, but the demands of Judy's engagement kept me in London. I wrote them at Arthur, explaining my problem, and two weeks later, I received a kind and understanding letter from the board of directors. Yes, it was kind. Yes, it was understanding. And yes, I was fired.

6

Much information was carried by the press about Judy's appearance at Talk of the Town, and much of it was either biased or inaccurate. Since I was constantly present behind the scenes, I can attest to the fact that it was in the main a standing-room-only success.

Naturally, she was nervous before her first appearance. She paced around our rooms at the Ritz, too jittery to sit still. She was always tense before a performance. Although she was happy to be free of Group V, she was definitely uptight.

Judy never did any vocal warm-ups before she went on stage, but she went through some physical exercises and she did the yoga headstand to help her relax. Then she took a long warm bath and a shower. She didn't eat before the concert, but earlier in the day I had coaxed her to have some scrambled eggs. Her hairdresser arrived to arrange her hairstyle. When it came to makeup, Judy could apply it better than any makeup man.

She was nervous in the limousine driving to her first performance. "Give me a cigarette, Mickey. Talk to me." Anything to keep her mind off the ordeal ahead.

As we drove through the crowded London streets, I hid my concern. The hassle with Group V had drained her, and even though it was a legal triumph for her, the strain was telling. She was walking a perilous wire between a high that would enhance her performance and the low of complete exhaustion. Her fingers tapped nervously against the car's window.

"You'll be great," I promised her.

"If you say so," she replied with a wan smile. Then she bestirred herself. "You know, Mickey, things were a lot worse a while back. I didn't have a cent. The Internal Revenue Service threatened to take away my house because I was behind in tax payments. My car was repossessed. I wondered if I would be able to pay my grocery bills. I was flat broke." She clutched my arm. "I never saw much of the money I earned." Her laugh was filled with irony. "Mickey, when I was one of M.G.M.'s biggest money-makers, I didn't have a petticoat without a rip to it."

I knew how important the success of this engagement was to her. "Don't think about it now, Judy. You'll have money again. This time it won't go to anybody but you, I promise."

For the concert she chose a bronze Beau Brummel trouser suit glittering with sequins and gold beads and an emerald-green chiffon scarf. She was nervous in the dressing room while the hairdresser arranged her hair. She fussed with her scarf, tying it over and over again.

"Do you like it this way?"

"It looks great, Judy."

I reported to her on the guests sitting out front. Some of her friends were there. Zsa Zsa Gabor, Ginger Rogers and her husband, William Marshall, Johnny Ray, Beryl Reid, Danny La Rue, David Frost. The orchestra started the overture, and we were in the wings. She was trembling, petrified—as she was, I discovered subsequently, before each performance.

"Mickey"—she was clutching my arm, and I could feel her tremble—"tell me a funny story—make me laugh." Laughing would relax her so she could go on stage smiling.

And there she went, a small, slim girl-woman in her glittering pants suit, her head high, microphone in her hand, singing her new number, "I Belong to London." Dinner, the revue *Fine Feathers*, all that came before her act, were wiped out. Judy was to treat the whole night like a private party.

I heard later that those who hadn't seen her since her Palladium appearance with Liza two years previously were apprehensive. "She looks so frail," a stagehand said in an undertone. The air was charged. The overture, composed of her hits, built up the tension. One of the staff had questioned its length. "It's apt to give the guests a feeling that something is wrong backstage—that Miss Garland is missing," he suggested. But Judy had purposely wanted the overture to be prolonged. She began to sing, still offstage, her voice pure and strong. The audience, in a state of emotional expectation when she finally appeared, exploded into hysterical applause.

There is no logic in the phenomenon of Judy Garland.

"Something extraordinary for me," she said on stage in a quizzical aside; "not only have I appeared but I am singing a new song." Her trembling vanished. The joy of being with an audience transformed her. She gave them a medley of old Garland favorites. In the middle register the voice was sometimes off, but the voice was only a part of the Garland magic. When she sang, "Just in Time," "The Man That Got Away," "I'd Like to Hate Myself in the Morning," the audience's response fascinated me. It wasn't only loyalty or nostalgia or even sentiment but a fusion of all that was the Garland legend: the vulnerable, the lost, the lonely girl who clung bravely to her dreams. It was again a kind of mass love-in, which charged Judy to a virtuoso display that astonished and awed all of us.

Sometimes she wielded the microphone cord like a lion-tamer's whip. She did little dance steps. She strutted, arms akimbo. Her movements were suddenly grotesque, like a marionette's. She threw her arms up stiffly, her legs came together at the knees, she walked uncertainly over to the conductor, she leaned down to speak to him, she blew kisses to the audience,

35

all the while singing out her heart for them. The pants suit
with its brilliance emphasized her little-girl body, and the
small boy's haircut made her eyes look large and haunting, like
a starved waif's. Halfway through the performance she started
to sag. The physical strain was telling on her. She was wet with
perspiration. The handful of ups she'd swallowed in the dressing room weren't enough to restore the flagging spirit.

She appealed to Danny La Rue, the English entertainer, to
come up on the stage. "I know it's my night," she said, "but
I'm tired." No one seemed to mind the happy disorganization
of Judy's program, and later I heard guests remark that they'd
not forget the evening in a hurry. The pathos, the self-mockery, the flashing wit, were part of her charisma.

At the climax of the evening she sat quietly, cross-legged at
the edge of the stage, and with a single spotlight on her sang
"Over the Rainbow." I'm not licked yet, she told them with
her heart. I'm still searching for that bluebird. . . .

They gave her a standing ovation. She reprised with "I Belong to London."

Backstage, wrapped in a toweling robe, perspiring, her
makeup running, she collapsed in a chair. Yet she happily
greeted the well-wishers who stormed her dressing room. The
adoration was champagne. In an hour the dressing room was
clear. Judy was ready to be driven back to the Ritz. She never
liked to go out to dinner. It made her self-conscious to know
people were watching her while she ate. She nibbled just
enough to exist.

This was the hour she used to dread. The post-performance
blues. The high of the concert plunged to zero, when you are
alone with your moment of truth and the doubts begin to
creep in. Do people like you for yourself or because you're
Garland the superstar? Do they latch onto you for their own
selfish purposes or because they truly love you?

Sitting curled up in the back of the limousine, my arm
around her, Judy said in her tired, hoarse voice, "Whenever
I'm onstage, I have a love affair with my audience. I always

have." Her hand clutched mine. "I can live without money, but I can't live without love. Nights have always been difficult for me. A man can always find a girl, but a lady can't do things like that. And I'm an old-fashioned lady. Very proper. I can't pick up a man and become his lover." She raised her small, valiant face. "I'm not alone, am I, Mickey?"

"No, Judy," I said. "You're not."

7

Only two other American performers inspired such adoration in the English—Lena Horne and Danny Kaye. But English audiences, for all their impeccable manners, can show an overt anger when a favorite star lets them down. Yet few criticized Judy. When she sang "I Belong to London," there was no quieting them. The rapport between her and her audience approached the abandon and mystery of an orgiastic peak and yet sustained a kind of communication that went beyond the six senses.

Over coffee I read to Judy Derek Jewell's review in the London *Sunday Times:* "No logic, no analysis, no judgment in the world can completely explain the phenomenon of Judy Garland's performance at Talk of the Town. She walks the rim of the volcano each second. Miraculously she keeps her balance. It is a triumph of utmost improbability." He conceded that time had flawed her voice. He added with awe, however, that "within a certain range and volume, it survives—most beautifully in the downbeat of 'Just in Time.'"

At the beginning of her engagement Judy was "talking"

more than singing "Over the Rainbow." She told me she couldn't make the notes anymore. I discovered she was still singing in the same key she'd used when she first sang it in the movie. I lowered the key in her orchestrations and suggested that with her sincerity and ability, she'd be able to carry it through. She believed me. And from that night on she sang it as beautifully at Talk of the Town as she had on the Yellow Brick Road.

But in this period of her life Judy's performance was not exclusively in her singing. It embraced her nervous gestures, the tremulous lips, the image of being lost, all suddenly belied by the sincerity and power of the voice, the innate yearning that aroused a similar response in the listeners. They knew she was molded in an age of innocence when our values weren't threatened by urban revolt, guerrilla warfare, and all the hazards of a nuclear age. They knew that her troubles were theirs. They knew that life had been both generous and tough to the farm-fresh little girl. It seemed to me from what I saw and heard that Judy's fans felt for her because she was so human, because she had suffered as they suffered.

At Talk of the Town one evening, she stopped by a table to speak to a girl in the audience. "How old are you?" Judy asked.

"Eighteen," the girl replied.

"Nobody is eighteen anymore," Judy said wistfully. She turned to her orchestra leader, smiling, and her smile was an affirmation of her life credo. "We've been through a lot," she said. And someone backstage said, almost unbelieving, "It's nearly thirty years since she was Dorothy singing 'Over the Rainbow.'"

The first weeks in London were a happy time, supercharged with excitement for us. Judy worked well for the most part, and she was the toast of the town, as well as the talk of the town. We charged through the days and nights at a frenetic pace. Often we got home with the sun. Judy would fall into a fitful sleep that would last into the afternoon, but I'd usually be up before noon because there were business matters to attend to—the press and many activities connected with Judy's disorganized affairs. There was no one else to look after her, so I was elected. In spite of the furious pace, we found this was the sort of life we understood and enjoyed. We laughed, we sang, we yelled at each other—we made up, and we loved each other. After the performance we were often obliged to go out with promoters or business people. Judy never liked to join large groups. She had good insight, but out of bitter experience she often mistrusted everybody. Now, however, she was beginning to feel more secure. She was no longer alone, wondering whom she dared trust.

"I don't have to live for applause any longer," she repeated to an interviewer. "I could give it all up tomorrow without a single regret or heartache. I'm happier than I've ever been—and the future promises that I will be happier still. I want to be loved by one man, and Mickey is that man."

What made her feel good, she added, was that she didn't have to fight anymore. "It's a great feeling. No more pressures or decisions. I can sit back and be a lady. I don't even have to answer the phone or worry about who is calling or what they want. Mickey takes care of everything. And of me."

This was an exaggeration, but I realized that Judy meant it. And I was damned sorry for all the years that this little girl turned superstar had had to withstand the buffeting from the voracious men around her.

The informality of her stage presentations seemed to charm her fans. She often invited the audience on stage; one evening there were about twenty-five male admirers on stage with her. She climaxed every performance by singing "For Once in My Life," which she dedicated to me. She insisted that I be in the wings or at a ringside table where she could see me. Each night she would pull me on stage and introduce me to her applauding fans. Once I refused to come on stage with her, so she walked out airily without her microphone. She knew damn well I'd have to step out on stage and hand it to her. When she introduced me, I'd pick her up and hold her in the air, which she loved.

In spite of the exciting time, I couldn't help but notice that Judy was not looking well. She was sleeping fitfully and scarcely eating. She was almost skin and bones, and the effort it took to belt out those songs of her youth surely drained her. Watching her from the wings, listening to the poignant strains of "Just in Time," I thought, So much of what has happened to her has been cruelly misrepresented by the press. Much that was written about her is erroneous. How many times I heard people say, "I saw Garland last night, and was she stoned!" Meaning that she was drunk.

Actually, the fact that Judy was not always steady on her feet / was not the result of any stimulants. When I knew her, Judy was not a drinker. Most of the time, she would hold a glass until the ice melted, and then she'd ask for another drink. The world did not know then (nor did I, for that matter) that Judy's tendency to stumble slightly seemed to stem from some genetic trait in her mother's family. Her inability to sleep perhaps helped to aggravate this condition. She may have drunk too much once in a while, but such occasions were exceptional.

Her real problems had started in her M.G.M. days, when she was put on an inhuman schedule in order to fill her commitments for films that were making a pile of money for the company. The amphetamines that woke her up, the barbitu-/ rates that put her to sleep, created a health hazard. Later on she began to rely on ups to tide her over long hours of travel, rehearsals, performances. Even then she might have saved herself had she respected her body more, but she was careless about herself; after all, no one had ever emphasized to her the importance of caring for her health. She kept performing until she was exhausted, then she rested until her strength returned, and once again, she started. Yet Frank Marcus wrote in a London paper, "She is talented enough to bury her own legend—if only the audience would let her."

Judy had no control over this problem. To the public she

was still the adored Dorothy of *The Wizard of Oz*. Her fans demanded that she retain the image that L. B. Mayer and her mother had fostered. The public thought of her as a little girl. Always Dorothy. Never Judy. They would forgive Dorothy anything. But Dorothy was a sixteen-year-old girl, and Judy had the problems of a mature woman. As a result the world was shocked by her behavior, and her slightest faults were magnified in the press. All of her adult problems made headlines. Judy lacked the strength of Elizabeth Taylor, who said, "Screw you," to criticism. Judy had a fantastic respect for her public.

8

Variety, reporting Judy's five-week stay at Talk of the Town, called it a "troubled success." It was more than that. It was a troubled triumph.

Judy in a loose white silk blouse and black tights. Each night the dramatic intensity of her performance caught her audience and held it enthralled. She was in the third week of her engagement, and if sometimes her voice cracked, if she forgot the lines—either deliberately or otherwise—if there was a trembling vibrato, it didn't matter. Because she was what show business is all about. When she sang "Just in Time" or "Rock-a-Bye" or "The Trolley Song" or "You Made Me Love You," her audience was mesmerized. "We love you, Judy," they shouted, giving her a standing ovation.

And Judy returned their love. "I love you, too," she reaffirmed. "I love you, too."

Judy had the most extraordinary spiritual effect on some of her fans. One night at Talk of the Town one of the managers told me about a young woman who was eager to have a picture of Judy autographed. "She seems somewhat handicapped," he explained. I went out to speak to her. Her name was Patricia Peatfield, and she was an attractive young woman in her early thirties. When I introduced myself, she said, "It would mean so much to me if Miss Garland would sign this photograph. You see, I was partially paralyzed and confined to a wheel-chair, but when I heard her sing 'You'll Never Walk Alone,' something impelled me to try and walk again." Miss Peatfield had spent her savings on the visit to Talk of the Town.

"Wait here," I suggested and went to Judy's dressing room. When I returned to the table, holding the still-unsigned photograph, Miss Peatfield looked so disappointed. I took her by the hand.

"Judy says if you want an autograph, you'll have to come up and get it."

I'll never forget her radiance.

One evening while we were still living at the Ritz in London and after our secret marriage, we went to visit our friend Johnny Ray, who was appearing in a cabaret, Caesar's Palace, in Luton. We had a table near the stage. Halfway through his act, Johnny received a package from an usher. He opened it and read the enclosed note.

" 'This is a pullover I borrowed from you,' " he read aloud. " 'My wife washed it.' " It was signed "Mickey." He then held up a sweater so shrunken it might have fit a small child.

"This sweater has been washed by the most expensive laundress in the world," he said thoughtfully, "Mickey's wife—Judy Garland." The audience adored his announcement.

Whereupon he invited Judy on stage, and they sang a duet together amid hysterical cheers. Afterward we gambled a bit—craps, dice, blackjack—and returned to the Ritz, where Brandy was waiting for us. Brandy was a brown-and-black Alsatian dog who was originally a vicious police-trained guard dog at Talk of the Town. The first night we saw him backstage, he was wearing a muzzle and was on a strong chain leash. I asked his keeper if I might pet him. "You'll lose your hand," the man warned me. He was wrong. It was instant love between us.

We "kidnapped" him one night. He became the third member of our family, as sweet and loving as he once was vicious and snarling. Bernard Delfont, who owned Talk of the Town, was amused by our outright thievery and made us a gift of the dog, pedigree papers and all. Brandy belonged to us legally. The security chief explained wryly, "We gave the dog to Miss Garland. Well, she sort of assumed the right of ownership."

For Judy too had fallen wildly in love with him, and he was now living in luxury at the Ritz. Later, when we had to fly back to New York on business, we left Brandy in the care of Johnny Ray.

There were evenings when Judy's rapport with the audience was less sound than usual. She sang one song, then another, but with the high frequency of her perceptions she knew there was no real contact. Finally in a burst of feeling she started to go. This was Judy letting out the hurt, the suffering, the yearning, which we all shared with her. And when she finally sat there, singing "Over the Rainbow" with infinite pathos and longing, her audience invariably jumped to their feet, shouting and cheering. "We're with you, Judy, baby!"

I had never seen anything like Judy's performance in my years around. Her fans included every age, young and old, and they were ecstatic about her. "I didn't know she still had it in her," an elderly staff member said in awe.

"Sometimes you can't go on," Judy confided during that crucial period, the last fortnight of her engagement, when her nerves and physical strength were showing signs of exhaustion. "Either your voice gives out or you injure yourself or there are personal considerations. When it happens to other singers, nobody makes a fuss. But when it happens to me, it's a great scandal. Garland is drunk, a drug addict, an atheist, a fiend—who never had any talent and who simply has been passing for a human being—"

"Hon, you're blowing it up," I said, but her state of mind gave me concern. Once on stage, however, her winsome smile would disperse any doubts.

Of Judy's fan clubs throughout the world, the London branch seemed the most dedicated. Lorna Smith, its head, proved to be not only a devoted fan but a resourceful and obliging friend. She rang Judy at the hotel after our arrival and offered any assistance that might be needed. Judy was deeply grateful and said she would very much appreciate it if Lorna could help with her costumes before and after each performance for a few days until a professional dresser could be found. Lorna arrived at the Ritz each night after her own job was finished and arranged Judy's clothing, makeup, or whatever else was needed. She was very helpful, but she often said apologetically, "Few people could be less suited to the task."

"We make a team," Judy said good-humoredly. Lorna remained, loyal and devoted, for the first four weeks of the run.

In the beginning Judy dressed at the club. There were so many interruptions from well-wishers, however, that it was tiring for her. I had a talk with Glynn Jones. Suppose Judy were to make all her preparations at the hotel and then proceed to the club and go directly on stage. We would eliminate the wait in the dressing room and perhaps ease her preperformance apprehension. This worked out well. To give us more leeway, it was arranged to have a comedy act precede Judy. The drive from the hotel to the cabaret took about five minutes. When Judy was ready to leave our suite, I would nod to Glynn, he would telephone the stage door of the club, and then he'd buzz past me to hold the elevator. Frank, our London driver, was waiting punctually downstairs. Lorna Smith grabbed Judy's makeup kit, I put Judy's coat over her shoulders, and off we went. Judy waved to people waiting outside the hotel, sometimes signed an autograph, and stepped into the car. As we pulled up to what was the stage door of the old Hippodrome Theatre, Reggie, the doorman, was as quick as though he'd been alerted by radar.

"Good evening, Miss Garland, Mr. Deans," he said, opening the stage door. A pause at the full-length mirror next to the wall telephone. (The comedy team had been signaled as we left the hotel.) Judy checked her hair and the big bow she wore with one of her three pants suits. I bounced down the four steps and nodded to the conductor, who lowered his baton. The overture started.

The inevitable question from Judy: "How do I look?"

"Great." Or if the bow was crooked, I righted it. Then I helped her down the stairs. Judy shouted to the boys in the brass section, "Yea—hit it!" A fast hello to Michael, the stage manager, who was wired into the men in the lighting booths on the balcony. Judy was singing, and off she went, dispensing charm and melody.

"I'm here, aren't I?" she often said to her audience. "That's a remarkable thing in itself." It was a standard ploy. She laced her performances with self-castigating remarks, pronounced with gamine humor.

"I haven't learned a new song since 'The Covered Wagon.' Not since Andy Hardy met Deanna Durbin. Now what do we do?"

Or, "I've been through a lot. People ask, 'Is she going to appear? Is she dead?' Well, I'm here. You couldn't keep me away."

Or, "They say I'm a legend," with a laugh.

She was often unpredictable. For instance, she had a feud with the orchestra leader. He was very good, but not an extrovert, and when she was on stage, Judy needed a straight man. "He makes me think of a Gestapo agent," she said, grumbling. She decided to hire a conductor of her choice. She was obstinate about it. I talked privately with the orchestra leader and with the fellows in the band and convinced them the new man would conduct only for one evening. I wanted to protect the performance. The new man went on, but the following night, Judy was in good spirits, and there was no further objection to the regular orchestra leader.

"Don't believe what you write about me," she told reporters. She had a rare wit, but it was so often at her own expense that I wondered if it wasn't a form of cutting herself down. I'll make fun of myself before anyone else can demean me—that kind of thing. Aren't comedians always suffering with under-developed egos?

She'd stroll out, shake hands with ringside guests, and say, "I'm supposed to say a lot of words, but all I can think of is 'Hello.'" Sometimes her voice was rich and clear. Other times, as she explained in an aside to the audience, "My voice was left at the hotel."

She asked a reporter, "Did you come here to say nasty things —or to pay me a compliment?"

"A compliment," the young man replied.

"Make it a long one," she suggested with her gamine grin. "It will be nice to take with me on my honeymoon."

Each performance took so much out of her; she was physically drained but emotionally high. Her feelings surfaced on stage, revealing the inner woman. If not for the act of singing, those intense, unpredictable feelings might have sent her to a sanatorium. No human being could remain in tune with life for long with such intense feelings bottled up in her.

"She's wound up tighter than a watch spring," one of the musicians said, sounding concerned.

Sometimes she was almost too ill to hold the microphone, but she confessed that singing then gave her a good feeling. *See, I'm so sick I can barely stand, but I'm singing my heart out for you.* Perhaps it revived memories. There was so much stored in the attic of her mind. She was playing an old, old tape, the little girl singing to please Mama and Mr. L. B. Mayer.

I suppose it had to happen. Everything had been tranquil for too long. Judy's fans increased in number and applauded her with emotional frenzy. In spite of our efforts she was late occasionally, but not so late as to antagonize her audience.

Judy was daily growing more tired. The recurring bouts of the flu which started in New York had weakened her. Sometimes she could hardly pull herself together to appear. Her mental anguish at the moment was terrible. I understood how

48

she felt, but I thought she should have rested for a few days. Her health was worse than on our arrival. The doctor finally insisted that she stay in bed until her strength returned.

"I have to show up," she fretted. "They won't believe me."

And then on January 23 she faced a belligerent audience. Their anger was triggered by her being an hour and twenty minutes late. The cabaret show usually started at 11 P.M., but Judy's starting time had become erratic; one night, perhaps before eleven, another time after midnight.

That evening our carefully arranged timing from hotel to cabaret lagged. We telephoned the management to say Judy would be late, but she would definitely show up. The show began at eleven, and the dancers performed, but the audience was restless and began to show its restlessness by clapping slowly, ominously.

"What're we waiting for?" someone shouted.

As she walked out at twelve-twenty, singing "I Belong to London," the audience didn't react with its usual affection. Here and there, scattered among them, were small islands of rude people who were perhaps less offended by Judy's late appearance than involved in a need for sadistic horseplay. They tossed empty cigarette packs at her and increased their shouting.

She couldn't be heard above the uproar. I was upstairs in the sitting room, very upset because she had insisted on going on. It was the one time I should have been in the wings.

"Oh, dear, oh, *dear—*" Judy cried, making a futile effort to pick up the bits of paper scattered on the stage. A breadstick sailed through the air, following by a drinking glass that shattered on the floor. One uncouth man rushed up to the stage and grabbed Judy and the microphone, yelling, "If you can't turn up on time, why turn up at all?"

Judy, stunned, replied that at least she was a lady and that he was showing no respect for her. She walked offstage in tears.

The audience was shocked into reality by this man's lunatic actions. Mr. Delfont had evidently neglected to inform them

49

that Judy would be late, and they took out their frustration in this ghastly display.

"Judy Garland had the flu, and she was told not to go on," we informed the press in answer to the following morning's headlines. "But she did go on, and it was an obvious strain."

Mr. Delfont asked Judy not to return to the cabaret until her doctor passed her as fit. He also insisted that she henceforth start her act on time.

This episode was a great trauma for Judy. She had made a genuine effort to perform in spite of being ill. She had hoped to be received affectionately, to be applauded and loved for a brave try. Instead she was rebuffed and rejected. She locked herself in her room and refused to take calls or see visitors.

Judy remained locked in our hotel room for twenty-four hours. All I could do was to comfort her and listen when she chose to talk. Gradually, in spurts at first, she began to unburden herself. Painful memories that she'd stifled for years were coming up now, demanding to be reassessed. Mostly she talked about how she hated her mother.

"Judy," I said, "I learned the hard way. It isn't the one you hate who's the problem. It's the one you love."

"My father?" she exclaimed, startled. "Why, he was the *only* thing in my life!" She recalled his gentle manners, his charm, his quick Irish wit (which she had inherited). "But he was no match for my mother," she said. "*She* overwhelmed him." Then she added, "He always called me Baby."

As she told me this, Judy broke down. Deep, quiet sobs shook her frail body. I let her cry, knowing there was no comfort for any girl who'd lost her father too soon. I held her to me, and after a while she began talking about those early days, perhaps not from her own memory, but from hearsay.

She knew something of her mother's background because

her Aunt Irene Milne was proud of the family genealogy. Judy's maternal great-grandmother, Mary Elizabeth Harriot, was raised in a convent in Dublin, Ireland. After she emigrated to the United States, she married Hugh Fitzpatrick, who was a first cousin to General Ulysses S. Grant, the famed Civil War hero and later President of the United States. They had thirteen children, and one of the elder girls, Ena (Judy's grandmother), married John Milne, a railroad engineer who was a confirmed atheist. The entire family had some degree of musical ability.

Judy was the daughter of Ethel Milne, a small, pretty woman, according to turn-of-the-century provincial standards. Ethel had musical pretensions and fantasies of a career on the stage. Her ambitions, unfortunately, were greater than her talents, and she settled for playing the piano in a movie house in a small Wisconsin town called Superior.

America in the early 1920's was a land of bucolic innocence. Its heartland was a world without radio, television, or modern transportation. Girls like Ethel Milne had to rely on the church social, vaudeville at the local opera house, or movies for communication with the outside world. It was still an era of vaudeville, more dreary than glamorous. Except for the top performers, most vaudevillians were rather inept self-taught entertainers who traveled from one small town to another and earned scarcely enough to feed themselves. Actors in general were regarded with suspicion, child actors with tolerance. But as D. W. Griffith and other creative directors gradually upgraded the quality of films, America's life-style was remolded by the influence of the motion picture. There remained, however, room for the vaudeville acts, which now appeared as a supplement to the movie being shown.

Ethel Milne was typical of her times. Movies were an obsession with her. Her dream was to reach Hollywood and become a movie star. It happened all the time, according to the new movie magazines she devoured. The poor girl deluded herself; her voice was commonplace, she lacked personality, and she was not photogenic in the style of the beauty of the period, which demanded huge eyes, a small, inconsequential nose, a rosebud mouth. Still, self-delusion is often a strong crutch for ambition. Ethel compromised by getting a job in a movie house as the pianist, playing suitable melodies to synchronize with the action on the screen while her eyes devoured it. And when her Prince Charming inevitably came into her life, it was proper to the script that he should be young, attractive, affable, and Irish. Frank Gumm had recently graduated from Sewanee University; he was in Superior on vacation when he found work at the theater where Ethel played the piano. He had a sweet tenor, and his job was to sing a few songs and lead the audience in a community songfest. He and Ethel met, fell in love, and married. What made Ethel particularly happy was that now she too could become an entertainer. They started an act called Jack and Virginia Lee, Sweet Southern Singers. They were always hoping for a break, but evidently they were so mediocre that it never came. During this time their family grew. Their first child, Sue, was born in 1916, the second, Virginia, in 1919, and finally Frances, on June 10, 1922. Before Frances was born, they had given up the road and settled in Grand Rapids, Minnesota. Frank Gumm managed the local theater, and the family put down roots—temporarily, according to Ethel's still unsatisfied ambitions. As the girls grew up, Ethel coached Sue and Virginia and presented them as a singing team. She wasn't much of a coach, and their voices left much to be desired, so Ethel's dreams faltered until Baby Frances made them reality.

Frances, as Judy had been christened, was not the boy her family had hoped for after two girls, but she had something the older girls lacked, a lively personality, a sense of mimicry, and for so small a child, a big voice. One evening while her sisters were performing at Frank's theater during the Christmas season, Baby Frances was sitting on Grandma Gumm's lap, straining toward the wings. Grandma was obliging, little Frances being her favorite, and she deposited the child on stage. Frances was born with the instincts of a performer. She was not yet three years old, but she belted out "Jingle Bells" like a clarion, ignoring her mother's anger, her sisters' distress, her father's signal to come offstage. "Jingle bells, jingle bells!" she sang, and when she finished the verses, she started all over again.

"It was the first time I held the center of the stage, and I loved it," she said later. "I sang the chorus again and again, and even when I was out of breath, I wouldn't stop—until Dad came out from the wings and marched me offstage."

Dad. Baby. Between Frank Gumm and his youngest daughter was something unique, something missing from his relationship with Sue and Virginia. Perhaps he sensed in this small chubby dark-eyed mimic a quality of character, a lusty love of life that was part of his genes, too. The mysticism, the fey nature, the romanticism, the wit—all the endearing, baffling traits of the Irish.

Ethel Gumm was impractical but had a shrewd sense of reality. Sue and Virginia were adequate. None of her efforts on their behalf, the primping, grooming, cajoling, coaching, ever produced a performance that she, as well as theater managers, conceded was more than mediocre. But this funny little one— she was money in the bank. She was Ethel's golden opportunity.

The movies created a whole new world and gave birth to many new types that might have languished forever in their small hometowns if not for the magical camera and the wide screen. One type was the child actor, another, the stage mother.

Judy was a natural child actor. Her mother was born at the right time and at the right place. She became the prototype of the stage mother. That's how it all started.

When the play *Gypsy* opened in New York City to critical acclaim, audiences were fascinated by the character of Gypsy's mother, the brash, thick-skinned, adroit, devious, conniving woman who was determined to make stars of her children at whatever cost to herself or their personalities. Judy told me that she wanted to play the mother in *Gypsy*. It was a role she understood from her childhood conditioning. Nor was she surprised when Milton Berle announced that he couldn't understand why the mother was so maligned and criticized. Weren't all mothers like her? Milton himself had had a stage mother, as had Jackie Coogan and any number of child performers.

One of Judy's friends who had known Mrs. Gumm told me later, "Ethel Gumm confused love with ambition. She was convinced that her efforts on behalf of her children, particularly Judy, were signs of her devotion to them. What she never realized was that she was living out her own thwarted ambitions through Judy's talent, and as a result she really swallowed Judy. Her husband was no doubt dear to her, but he too was relegated to second place in her grand design. From the time Judy was three years old, the child was robbed of her life. She became a pawn."

Ethel Gumm was not the only mother who burned with Hollywood fever for her offspring. All America was child-actor conscious. It was after Jackie Coogan had his fantastic success with Charlie Chaplin in *The Kid*. A horde of maternal prospectors trekked westward, seeing the new gold strike in the little town of Hollywood. They dragged their kids to casting studios, to talent scouts, to agents. Hal Roach said that each year at least a thousand ambitious stage mothers stormed his doors. Most of them were frustrated actresses who saw their children as extensions of their own thwarted ambitions. They tried to teach the poor kids to dance, act, and speak like elocutionists. They adorned them with fancy clothes, fancy curls, and a false sense of values. Those youngsters were like monkeys on a string.

"Nobody ever taught me what to do on stage," Judy told me with a kind of bemused objectivity. "Everything Mother did was awful. Everything I did was right. I think it made her furious, but she saw her salvation in me. I never learned to read music, but I had a true ear."

Judy took a sip of vodka and grapefruit juice to ease her

parched throat. "She used to complain she couldn't teach me to sing or dance. I guess it was because she was no teacher. She had a genius for mismanagement, and whenever poor father objected, she silenced him. She waved my hair and manicured my nails and made my costumes. God, what costumes—fussy atrocities, that's what they were. They made me look fatter than I was. I was awkward too, which drove her crazy. She was furious because my older sisters, who were slender and pretty, didn't have talent. Well, she never let me forget my inadequacies."

Ethel Gumm finally persuaded Frank to sell their possessions and make the westward trek. "Baby Frances must have her chance," she said sanctimoniously.

"I guess what she really meant was that Mama would have her chance. Poor Dad, he tried so hard to please her. Along the way we played small vaudeville houses to help pay expenses. Don't let anyone tell you that trouping was romantic. We lived in dumps and were poor. It was awful, dreary, and depressing, and everybody loathed it."

Hollywood was jammed with ambitious mothers who'd got there earlier. Hollywood was cold and inhospitable to the Gumms. Their money ran out, but Mrs. Gumm was adamant. They were not leaving California. To appease her Frank Gumm found work in Lancaster, California, located some eighty miles north of Hollywood. The town was quiet, proper, with rigid middle-class standards of behavior. Frank became operator of the local movie house. Lancaster did not approve of the Gumms.

Baby Frances was a gregarious little girl of about five or six years old who longed to be with the neighborhood children, but they were forbidden to play with her. "Child actors," mothers said, sniffing. "You stay away from them, hear?" Her sisters ignored her; they were allied in years and interests, and perhaps they recognized her genuine talent and like siblings, resented it.

She was lonely, not by temperament but by circumstances.

"The only time I felt accepted or wanted was when I was on stage," she told me. "I guess the stage was my only friend, the one place where I felt equal and secure."

There it was, of course. It didn't take a psychiatrist to discover the seeds of Judy's compulsion to sing, her frantic belief that only across the footlights could she communicate and receive love.

She was crying when she talked about her childhood, and I lifted her in my arms and cradled her back and forth, like a child. She was so tiny, so like a starved bird, that I found it hard to imagine the plump, jolly child who was so hurt by rebuffs. Until I saw her eyes. It was all still there.

"My mother didn't know when to let well enough alone," Judy said. "She parked my sisters with my father in Lancaster and took me out alone on the vaudeville circuit. We were third rate, make no mistake about it."

It was probably during that period that Ethel perpetrated a cruel form of punishment on Baby Frances, one that might have come out of a Dickens novel. If she was "naughty" in her mother's eyes—that is, if she didn't obey implicitly—Ethel would take her own suitcase out of the hotel-room closet, pack it with her own clothes, snap the lock, and get her coat and hat while the little girl watched, at first paralyzed with horror and then finally reduced to hysterical tears. Then Ethel would announce she was leaving Frances alone in this strange room in this strange town because Frances was bad. Nothing terrifies a child of this age more than separation from the mother. Frances would plead, sob, promise to be good, but Ethel was adamant. Suitcase in hand, she would leave the room and lock the door behind her, leaving a crushed child. The fact that after a suitable interval Ethel would return and the little girl would beg her forgiveness did not ever alter the circumstances. The trauma was to remain with her forever, through nightmares and psychoanalysis.

During their life together in Lancaster, they did some family bookings. Whenever the Gumms played in vaudeville,

Frank would introduce Ethel as a "tiny, pretty lady with tiny, pretty hands."

Judy choked up as she remembered it. "He used to sing 'I've Been Saving for a Rainy Day.' Sometimes he played his own songs."

The girls sang together, but each had her specialty. "We weren't very good," Judy added. "If we'd been on during amateur night, they probably would have used the hook on us. . . ."

Her father did have an aptitude for business, which together with his warmth and charm paved the way for a growing success in the movie business—not in acting, nor directing, but in running a movie theater. Business in Lancaster improved, and in time he opened theaters in two neighboring towns.

It looked then as though they could be a family again. No more breakups while Ethel guided the children through a series of small, dreary towns. He could take care of his family. Ethel, forget the crazy dream. Settle down to life. Let the girls go to school.

For the growing Baby Frances this was indeed a dream come true. It meant that she would be with her father more. She loved him with passionate, undeviating devotion; he was the fulcrum in her life. When she was separated from him, she always dreamed of her return, when they would be together again. She loved him, and yet she was angry with him. Why did he allow Mama to take her away so often? Didn't he know that he was all she loved and that when Mama took her so far away, she was alone and scared and waiting for him to come and rescue her?

Already the little girl was divided between the life her ambitious mother imposed on her and the life she longed for. The stage child sat on a trunk in the wings of a theater, waiting for rehearsals, making friends with other kids on the road, with the stage doormen, with the hangers-on. It was a life beyond the understanding of a child, but she was stoic, accepting what was meted out to her, torn between love and hate for her mother, and always, always waiting for the magic moment when the automobile would be heading back to Lancaster, that hot, miserable little town that she loved because her father was there. But Lancaster was unfriendly, and since her father had little time for her, she was wretched once home again, but still stoic. She did whatever she was supposed to do without complaint or protest—which made her such a great trouper in her later days at M.G.M.

All the ebullience and the high spirits that went with her enormous brown eyes, her uptipped small nose, her wide smile, were revealed now only during performances. At home she was quiet, intimidated by circumstances, for it was evident to the sensitive child that the family life was breaking up. But Frank was determined to keep them all together, and when Ethel issued an ultimatum that Lancaster was out, he followed her to Los Angeles. Here his experience in managing a movie house enabled him to buy a local movie theater.

Baby Frances, now nearly ten years old, plump and a bit awkward, was sent to Mrs. Lawlor's School for Professional Students. But Ethel had no scruples about taking her children out of school whenever an engagement beckoned.

While the Chicago World's Fair was in progress in 1933, Ethel Gumm received an offer to appear at the Century of Progress exhibition. The people who hired the Gumm sisters disappeared when it was time to pay the act, though, and Ethel and the girls were broke. The life of an itinerant vaudeville team had made Ethel resourceful. She heard of a canceled booking at the Oriental Theatre and persuaded the theater-owner to use her trio. "This is your big chance," she goaded the girls. But misfortune seemed to be their shadow. True, they were to see their name in lights that night, but the electrician had spelled it Glum. "The Glum Sisters." It was too much. In tears they rushed to Georgie Jessel, who was headlining the bill and always had a sympathetic ear for pretty girls.

"Tell you what," Jessel said helpfully. "Why don't you take the name Garland after my friend Bob Garland, the drama critic?"

Baby Frances had never liked her first name either. Hoagy

Carmichael had written a song called "Judy"; she adored the lyrics. "If her voice can bring ev'ry hope of spring, That's Judy, my Judy./If she seems a saint and you find she ain't,/ That's Judy/Sure as you're born." And so, out of a run of bad luck, Judy Garland was created out of the stocky, rather clumsy little twelve-year-old who had beautiful stage presence and a lovely voice.

Ethel Gumm was weaning the girls away from family life, although without obvious intent. The lines of communication between her and Frank were no longer open. Frequently they separated and made up. He disapproved of her dragging the girls around, making them victims of her inordinate ambition. He knew intuitively that this kind of life was creating emotional problems for his daughters, particularly the youngest, his baby. Ethel was obstinate, however, with the single-minded purpose of a stage mother. Frank gave in again. He bought a theater in a suburb of Los Angeles. Life in Lomita was no different. In 1933 Ethel wangled a job for her girls at Cal-Neva Lodge, at Lake Tahoe, Nevada; the following summer they returned for an engagement there, again without much success. But through Judy's appearance at the lodge, Harry Akst, the composer of "Dinah" (which was one of Judy's favorite songs), took an interest in her and brought her to the attention of an agent, Al Rosen. Rosen was impressed with Judy and took her on the rounds of the studios without much success, since all of them had seen her before. Yet through Rosen, she got an audition with Metro-Goldwyn-Mayer.

Fortunately, Ethel was away from the house when the call came. Judy happened to be out in the back-yard garden. If Ethel had been present, the next hour would have been a time of hysteria. Curl your hair, change into a frilly white dress, polish your Mary Jane slippers, stand up straight, smile, tell them you're a professional—

Her father said only, "Take it easy, Baby. They'll like you as you are." She was in slacks and a middy and sneakers; she looked like a middle-America girl-next-door—friendly, wholesome, natural. After all the previous little baby-dolls who appeared at auditions as their mothers' versions of baby screen stars, Judy was a relief. Her father played the piano for her, which made her very proud, and naturally, since she was feeling secure just because he was there, she sang well. She sang "Zing! Went the Strings of My Heart," and the talent chief, Jack Robbins, was so impressed that he was able to reach Louis B. Mayer through Mayer's autocratic secretary, Ida Koverman. She was evidently the only one who could manage to summon Mayer at such brief notice, and he arrived, looking annoyed and impatient. Judy sang for him too. Mayer was a difficult man, but he had a divining rod for talent. Both Frank and Judy were left abashed as he stalked out of the audition room without comment. What they didn't know was that he ordered a contract for her. He didn't even ask for a screen test. No doubt he sensed that here was pure talent, a voice and an acting potential which would not be handicapped by a lack of the assets of a conventional starlet. Here was a genuine gold mine.

Thus Judy justified a *Variety* review that suggested, "The youngest . . . handles ballads like a veteran and gets every note and word over with a personality that hits audiences."

Ray Bolger said, "She planted the seed of love in your heart."

Spencer Tracy once said, "A Garland audience doesn't just listen. It feels. It wants to put its arms around her."

This was how they greeted Judy on her return four nights later to Talk of the Town. Bernard Delfont, manager of the cabaret, had asked her not to appear on stage without her doctor's permission. Dressed in a flame-colored dress, she walked on stage, waving a medical certificate that reported her to be fit for work. The welcome was tumultuous, and the finish of her performance was greeted with a wildly affectionate standing ovation. She left them shouting, laughing, crying. Backstage I heard someone say awed, "And this is how a legend is created."

Meanwhile, Judy's engagement at Talk of the Town was

coming to a close. On the farewell night she was showered with bouquets of lovely flowers from the audience, even though she was twenty minutes late in starting her program. She left the stage in tears, so deeply touched by the standing ovation.

"I guess when you are well known or famous, people tend to be frightened of you," she told a reporter after the final performance. "Or in awe of you. Either way they put you in a different category altogether. Either they think you are great and they worship you—which is rather silly—or they think you are a freak and treat you like one, which is just as ridiculous."

She went on to say she'd had problems. And tempers and tantrums. But who of us hasn't? "If you want fame, you have to pay for it. And I have. Even from my earliest days at M.G.M., when I was a child star with the great Mickey Rooney."

Sometimes she grew introspective about her adolescence. She told me that she regretted the fact that her growing pains were made public domain, exploited by M.G.M., and reported by the press. They left scars that would never disappear. She tried to contrast her youth with that of the typical American small-town girl, but the difference left her speechless and thwarted.

"I felt like a prisoner at Metro. Sure, I got a big pay check, which I never saw, and I was supposed to be a coming star, but if anyone reaped the joys out of my job, it wasn't me. They used to starve me whenever they thought I was putting on weight. A starlet was supposed to be slim, like Ava Gardner and Lana Turner. Not that the food I got in the commissary at Metro was worth eating, mind you. All they ever gave me was chicken soup. Chicken soup at M.G.M. was supposed to be a great delicacy, because it was Mr. Mayer's favorite—he had this hang-up from his mother's kitchen."

Sometimes Judy spoke well of Louis B. Mayer, other times with scarcely controlled anger. There was an incident she enjoyed recounting. One day she was invited to lunch with him. The other guests were producers and directors. Plates were filled with tasty food and passed to everybody but Judy. She was given her usual midday ration of chicken soup—without noodles. Even teen-age starlets were supposed to be sylphs.

"I had baby fat," she explained. "Everybody can have baby fat; it's no criminal offense." So while her nostrils were tantalized by the succulent aromas, her stomach rebelled against the chicken soup. Judy passed her cup of soup to the man on her right, Harry Rapf.

"The bigshots were all flattering Mr. Mayer. 'Oh, this is the best food, Mr. Mayer.' " Meanwhile Judy was slowly dying of hunger.

Finally a beautiful apple pie was passed around. Harry Rapf was perspiring (from Judy's chicken soup). He was obsequious that day, perhaps because his contract was coming up for renewal or because he had incurred Mr. Mayer's displeasure. He said, "Mr. Mayer, this is the best apple pie I've ever had in my whole mouth."

Nobody smiled, but Judy cracked up. She was never invited to the royal table again.

When she spoke of those days to me, Judy added, "There were good times too. Mickey Rooney and I clung together, like two on a lonely island. I guess that's when I learned to laugh at myself. It's the fun that gets you through the heartache and tears and misery."

She added that she was always laughing, which was not quite accurate. But her sense of humor was truly her lifesaver. "Without it," she often said, "you may just as well give up."

10

Judy was a prude. She was at heart completely Victorian, and nothing worried her as much as the fear she wouldn't be considered a lady. She needed respect so much.

Judy didn't approve of our living together as lovers. It offended her strong sense of morality. She even felt that every tap on the hotel door might be a policeman, come to arrest us for violating the code of British decency.

One evening while Judy was resting in bed, I, clad only in shorts, happened to lean against the wall, accidentally setting off the service buttons that brought two maids, a valet, a butler, and a housekeeper to the door. They all arrived simultaneously, resulting in embarrassment and apologies all around. Judy was genuinely upset at what she considered the revelation of our "illicit relationship."

I was still unsettled about marriage. I took marriage seriously, no doubt because of the solid pattern set by my parents. Since my own career had kept me on the road, which didn't make for a stable family life, I had carefully avoided any permanent relationships.

But my love for Judy outweighed any remaining fears. From

the beginning of our stay in London, we discovered that we were essentially good for each other. We shared a growing confidence that our life would improve. What was important was the fact that we truly enjoyed being together. Liking one another, we discovered, was an integral part of loving one another. There was reason to be optimistic.

Meanwhile there were problems. Nothing in Judy's life was ever uncomplicated. Technicalities in the California divorce laws left her still a married woman. Neither Judy nor her fourth husband, Mark Herron, had picked up the final divorce decree. I didn't know this until I called her California attorney, Godfrey Isaacs, and instructed him to send Judy's divorce papers to us. When they arrived, I discovered the papers were not final. The technicality required that either party must sign a last form to be registered with the California court clerk. Only after the clerk received confirmation that the final decree was entered would we be allowed to marry.

Knowing this setback in our plans would disturb her, I waited until after the performance that evening, when we were finally alone, to give her the news. I managed to convince her that a few more days of waiting wouldn't matter.

"Mark will sign the decree," said Judy optimistically. "He is a nice guy." She wasn't angry with him, just philosophic about the strange marriage that ended so abruptly. She told me about the circumstances of this marriage, which came about as a result of her terror at being left alone after a performance.

"In spite of a successful concert tour, I was broke again," she said, "so my agents booked me for a tour of Australia. An entourage of twenty-six people came with me, some absolute strangers to me. The tour was a disaster. I was exhausted and depressed, so I flew to Hong Kong for a rest. The doctor there discovered my collapse was due to a heart attack. After I recovered, he suggested a sea voyage. I took off two months and traveled around the world with Mark Herron, who became my fourth husband. I did make one stage appearance—with Liza— at the London Palladium. Mark produced it.

"Mark came into my life in the most unexpected manner. He arrived at my house one Sunday night with a group of people. He came back the next weekend too. Everybody else would finally leave, but Mark was still there. So I said to myself, 'Well, I guess he's okay.' He was always there in the background, quiet but comforting, and never saying anything. He just drifted into my life as though I was a kind of terminal.

"After I married Mark, I couldn't find him. Isn't that wild? He left shortly after the wedding ceremony because he had to be back in Los Angeles to work with some little-theater group. He'd promised them."

She added wryly that it hadn't been too bad to fight with Sid Luft. "Sid could stand up and fight back. But often I never knew where Mark was. I couldn't trace him through his friends; even they didn't know. It was over so soon."

Her smile turned bitter. "That happened just when I was finding it harder and harder to earn a living. I had two servants in the house who'd been with me five years. They worked without pay for a long time, but finally they left too. Mark filed for divorce. And then, to cap it all, I heard somebody was writing a story called 'The Death of Judy Garland.' "

With the abrupt change of mood that was such an endearing trait, she leaned over and kissed me. "Don't ever be jealous, Mickey. After I met you, I never had a date with another man, unless it was simply an escort to an event."

We waited a week and a half until it was all settled. The Reverend Peter Delaney, a close friend of ours, had gone to Caxton Hall with me so we could establish residence and make application for a license. Although meanwhile Judy learned it was against British law for a divorced person to be married in a church, nothing would satisfy her until we were positively, legally married. In a church.

I was obliged to scout around until I found a priest in London who agreed to perform the marriage. For obvious reasons I do not feel it would be right to reveal his name. But on January 9, 1969, while Judy was appearing at Talk of the Town, we found an elderly cab-driver who, fortified by spirits for the wintry night, drove us to the church and agreed to wait for us. If he thought our visit was at an odd hour, he was probably too befuddled to remark on it. The young priest, waiting by the back door of the ancient church, let us in. The dim lights, the dark woods, the lifetime of tradition and ritual of the old church, gave us an eerie feeling. Judy was like a fey child in the delicate gray chiffon under her fur coat. She was shivering, whether from excitement or the strange setting I wasn't sure. I held her small hand in mine. Outside a clock chimed the hour —it was 4 A.M., the middle of the day by Judy's time clock.

We had neglected to buy a ring and were in a sudden panic. But the young priest, knowing the circumstances, perhaps anticipating our anxiety, and touched by our needs and love, had brought his grandmother's wedding band. It was old and worn, much too big for Judy's small finger. She curled her fingers into her moist palm to keep it safe. She thanked him, gentle-eyed and deeply touched.

There at the altar, lit by flickering candles and feeling infinitesimal in this cavernous gloom, we were married. We shared a glass of sacramental wine with the priest. Then, abruptly, Judy panicked. What about witnesses? Was the ceremony legal? The priest assured her that God would be sufficient witness, which she found most comforting. She had never been married in a church before, and I think she truly believed at that moment that none of her previous marriages counted, the past was wiped out, and we were starting life afresh as man and wife.

That night on our return to the hotel, Judy and I initiated a new habit. We said a prayer that would no doubt amuse many of our friends. It was not the kind of prayer one would associate us with, either, but every night thereafter we repeated it together with growing comfort and conviction. "Dear God, please treat us tomorrow as we treated others today." Judy was never more lovely and childlike than when she repeated this prayer.

We kept the ceremony secret and arranged for a civil marriage to take place later.

11

During her Talk of the Town engagement I came to realize how much Judy was depending on ups and downs. Even then it didn't seem like a monumental problem. I had heard rumors of Judy's dependency on amphetamines and barbiturates, but all during our friendship I'd seen little evidence of it. It was Judy at her best whom I knew then—she was getting plenty of rest, eating enough to sustain her strength, and was not exposed to the awful tension of performing.

In the entertainment field almost everybody has at one time or another resorted to pep pills to keep going or barbiturates to get some sleep. It's no big deal. Nobody worries about them because few people go off the deep end. At Arthur our waiters were often approached by customers asking, "Have you got a diet pill I can have?" I mention this simply to show that when I saw at first hand how Judy was taking ups and downers, I wasn't too disturbed. What really bothered me was the reckless way she squandered her strength. She turned day into night, not by intent but by conditioning. After finishing a performance, she was overstimulated. It took her hours to calm down.

She was jittery, restless, and eager to keep going until dawn, when she would finally take a barbiturate, which gave her at most four hours of sleep.

Judy's basic problem was not pills but insomnia. She found it impossible to get a restful night's sleep. She often went forty-eight hours without sleep. As a result her life-style contributed to her failing health.

"Nobody can understand what films are all about unless he worked for Mr. Mayer in the 1940's," Judy once said to me. "You got up at five in the morning. Maybe you didn't sleep because you got to bed too late and were too stimulated to simmer down. The studio gave parties, and you were expected to attend. And the long, tedious hours before the camera. You were always playing roles—"

Role-playing for an adolescent girl. The crazy schedule of making films, with the amphetamines to keep you awake, barbiturates to put you to sleep (that's when the four-hour sleep span began). And this routine while a girl's glands are changing, while the stress and strain of approaching womanhood are in themselves enough to make it a critical emotional and physical period. To work on this wild schedule, to try and study at the studio schoolroom, to placate the bosses, to keep her mother calm, to deal with the death of her adored father. . . .

"I had a childhood that never was. I would make two or three pictures for M.G.M., take ten minutes off to learn a bit of French or a snatch of arithmetic. How's that for a life? Tell me."

She was conditioned to a future of amphetamines and barbiturates. By the time I met her, she was accustomed to tranquilizers, energizers, and sleeping pills. Like Linus with his blanket, she had to have a bottle of Ritalin in her purse, even when she wasn't taking many. She had not only built up a tolerance to the drug, but she actually also took more than she needed. During the last two weeks of the Talk of the Town engagement, when she was physically so drained by the flu, she took enormous amounts of Ritalin in order to perform and large doses of Seconal to lull her to sleep. When she suffered from a kind of malaise of the spirit, the combination of the two drugs taken together produced an instant high.

Ritalin, I discovered, is suggested for the treatment of mild depression. Judy had for years suffered from depression—chronic fatigue and apathy. Used also to combat the drug-induced lethargy produced by Seconal, Ritalin wakes you up, peps you up.

Doctors are usually cautious about giving Ritalin to emotionally unstable patients, particularly those with a history that may include alcoholism. These patients are apt to increase the number of pills taken on their own initiative. Nervousness and insomnia are the most common adverse reactions to the drug, but they can usually be controlled by reducing the number of pills and also by not taking them in the afternoon and evening.

Judy, of course, took ups early in the evening before a performance and more if she was sagging physically during the performance. The drug killed her appetite, made her sick to her stomach, and increased her pulse rate. She sometimes took another drug when she felt her heart was beating too fast. One of her doctors was worried because she had developed a digestive problem and found it difficult to eat.

At other periods in her life, whenever she felt herself at the breaking point, she would take a couple of weeks of self-ordered cure. That is, she'd leave the city, taper off of Ritalins, sleep or rest in bed, eat six small meals a day; since she had great recuperative powers, she always bounced back. But she never learned her lesson. She had a kind of blind spot where health was concerned, and you couldn't blame her. After all, her childhood didn't follow the normal patterns, nor did her days as a movie star encourage a healthy life-style. As a growing girl she was fed gallons of black coffee and encouraged to smoke a couple of packs of cigarettes a day—anything to keep her sturdy body in sylphlike contours. So she kept going at a wild pace until she broke down. Once she felt better and strong, the crazy hours and partying started all over again. Whether it was her way of fighting the demons that tormented her I never found out. It was a fact of life I had to accept.

"You'd do better smoking a joint," I once suggested. The thought of marijuana horrified her. She simply couldn't rid herself of her guilt feelings. She needed to see that her problem was not a great sin.

Once I realized how much Ritalin she was taking, I was deeply upset. She had built up an incredible tolerance for all pills, swallowing amounts that would have been fatal to others. Judy explained that she couldn't function without these crutches. The prospect of running out of pills made her hysterical. Fortified by them, she could face the showbiz pressures, the promotions, the incessant demands, as well as the strain of the performance itself, the fear that she might have lost the touch, that her voice was betraying her, that the magical communication between her and the audience had been broken.

12

As the five exhausting weeks at Talk of the Town came to an end, Judy and I decided to lease a small house in London, although we were not yet legally married.

Judy had rented many houses before, but they were always big, impersonal, servant-run mansions. In November, 1960, she lived for a time in the house owned by Sir Carol Reed in King's Row. It was a house of beauty and tradition; Ellen Terry, Gwen Farrar, and Peter Ustinov had all lived there at various periods. Her children, Joey, then five, Lorna, eight, and Liza, fourteen, were living with her.

Joey and Lorna attended Lady Eden's School in Kensington, and Liza was enrolled at a tutorial school on Victoria Street. A friend remembered that before Christmas their nanny took them over to what was then the Chelsea Gaumont, and they brought prettily wrapped presents to place at the foot of the Gaumont's Christmas tree. The presents were for the National Society for the Prevention of Cruelty to Children's party.

I was concerned that Judy wouldn't like the modest little mews house I had found, but with her bountiful enthusiasm, she fell in love with it. It was small and snug, six cozy, intimate rooms, rather impersonally furnished but promising comfort and warmth once we added our possessions. A white stucco house with a yellow door and a cement flower box that ran its length, it was tucked into Cadogan Lane. On the other side was the garage, with a bright-blue interior. The front door opened directly into the living room, which had white walls, gray carpeting, and white sheets covering the furniture. Judy wrinkled her nose in a gamine grin. "It looks medicinal."

The shrouds hid rather attractive black-and-white ticking upholstery on the chairs and sofa. We moved the furniture around. This was the first improvement. We removed the naked light bulbs with their white painted sconces and replaced them with handsome gas lamps. We brought our piano, which neither of us could do without, from the Ritz.

Judy was mad about flower porcelains, and whenever she found a piece she liked, it was added to our collection. The living room blossomed with exquisite china florals. To the right was a small powder room, papered in full-blown cabbage roses and with the smallest sink in the world. Whenever we turned on the hot water, the faucet became so hot that we had to warn our guests about the danger of scalding their hands.

The dining room had red walls, a round table under a skylight, and a matching buffet and sideboard. "Noel Coward must have written *Fumed Oak* after seeing this furniture," Judy commented.

Central heating was a joke. Judy complained always of being cold. The gas furnace in the corner of the kitchen was supposed to provide central heating. Judy said it spoke to me, which it did, with friendly, bubbly sounds. Judy decided it didn't like her, which also seemed true, for once when I was on a business trip to Scandinavia, it began leaking gas. Fortunately, an old friend of Judy's, Bumbles Dawson, was staying with Judy while I was away. She had to get up early, which saved them both from asphyxiation. Bumbles thought she was experiencing the after-effects of the previous night's Scotch until Judy walked into the kitchen and was hit by the full impact of the escaping gas. Judy flung open the front door, raised the windows, and called for a plumber. She wrapped herself in a fur coat and perched on the cement flower box in front of the house until help arrived. Afterward she turned on the large gas heater in the living-room fireplace. Why the house didn't go up in flames I'll never know, except that some guardian angel was surely watching over her.

The kitchen was large and pleasant, with the usual facilities, including a very temperamental washer-and-dryer unit. I could make it work; Judy couldn't, which exasperated her. "Everything comes so easily to you," she'd say half in complaint, half in pride.

"It's because I have a mechanical thumb," I said.

"Okay, I've got a green thumb. Wait until you see my flowers in the spring."

The master bedroom, located above the living room, had a large window overlooking Cadogan Lane. There was a double bed, a chest of drawers, two small chairs, and a dressing table, as well as a couple of fairly spacious closets. For contrast with the off-white walls, we added lamps, colored sheets, and a bright-blue chintz bedspread. And everywhere fresh roses in vases, as many roses as I could buy for Judy. She loved them, I think, not only for their beauty as growing things but also as a symbol of the success of her concerts, when she was often pelted with beautiful bouquets of flowers.

The small bedroom alongside, which would be Judy's dressing room, I painted a warm pink. We installed a light-green Tiffany lamp, operated by a dimmer, and rose-colored carpeting.

A third, rather nondescript bedroom was destined to be my den. I hoped to panel it, and Judy planned to buy a bright cover for the bed and turn it into a couch by adding throw pillows. Across from our bedroom, through the hall, was a large sallow-green–tile bathroom, containing a window through which you could see the skylight in the kitchen. The bathroom had matching green fixtures, and we pondered what to do short of changing the unattractive tile.

We didn't want to get involved in the expense of permanent alterations until we were certain we'd be keeping the house. Just a few days prior to Judy's death, we knew we wanted it and decided to make an offer to the owner.

From the time we moved into the mews, Judy's forward steps toward health began to exceed the steps back. Progress was slow sometimes, painful, and disappointing, but we were confident that with the love and understanding between us, possibilities could turn into probabilities. Judy never before appreciated what it meant to be a housekeeper. Now we went shopping together at the supermarkets and loaded up on fruits, meats, and staples. English fans were singularly courteous, and in general they left Judy pretty much alone, but she preferred to eat at home. She felt self-conscious with strangers watching her eat.

She was always aware of people watching her, perhaps judging her—that was the Victorian part of Judy Garland. But what helped her—and our relationship—greatly was that she was learning not to be ashamed of her problems. I realized that she carried a greater burden of guilt than anyone I'd ever known. Nobody else was so guilt-ridden. She felt she was the only one in the whole world afraid of the dark, afraid of sleep, afraid of death, or taking pills. She believed that her very human frailties were unshared. Her eyes were always fixed blindly on a kind of perfection in human relationships. In the long, empty nights she often totaled up her assets and liabilities and found herself lacking. I hope I helped her understand that she was no worse than anyone else and far better than most.

Judy had been bullied. She was bullied by her mother, her producers, her husbands, a myriad of agents, and business associates.

She was only five feet tall and weighed less than one hundred pounds, but when I knew her, she could fight like a tigress whenever she felt herself crossed. I am not without temperament myself, so we fought each other and then took on the world together. Once my wife realized I could outshout her any time, we were able to sit down and talk things out. It took time, of course. Then there were also many hours in the early dawn when my wife and I found a love that had never existed before for either of us.

I want to repeat—Judy was a tremendously moral person. An American Gothic in her attitude toward sin, she could never entirely shake off the belief that she was the only sinner. Primitive fears rise in the night, and Judy faced them with what she considered her guilty ghosts. She never wanted to blot herself out entirely because of her inherent terror of death. She was always in flight from her fears, and in order to exist, she was obliged to build a world of fantasy. But I truly want to believe that the flashes of beauty and harmony in our marriage made reality more attractive to her and allowed her to begin for the first time in forty-six years to face life.

In Judy the self was cruelly divided. She had three faces for me: the wildly unreasoning, utterly polarized star; the scared, guilt-ridden, immature small girl; and the warm, glowing, maturing woman who was my wife.

As time passed, I was able to reduce the triple images of Judy by one. The small girl was disappearing as the woman who was my wife gained strength. That was my Judy, the Judy that was real, the Judy I remember.

There were so many small, endearing ways in which she showed change. Previously she used to listen to Judy Garland records all day and night. Now she often turned off the record player and asked me to play for her. She could sit curled up in an easy chair for hours while I practiced and played. She listened intently, noting improvement. While I was still at Arthur, there had been predawn gatherings with my friends at my apartment, when Judy sang and I played the piano. Now it was I playing, whether I was practicing or simply entertaining my wife. Judy just listened.

76

Please don't misunderstand. I'm not picturing a miraculous change, nor am I saying that any kind of a totally new Judy Garland emerged from these experiences. Superstar into housewife? That was impossible. Mostly, I believe, there was more progress than retrogression. Common sense told me that neither of us could remedy in a short while the emotional conditioning of our lifetimes, particularly Judy's, but it was definitely hopeful.

Our marriage was always in high gear, which is how we both wanted it. We liked movement and excitement. We wanted to go everywhere and see everything. But we really enjoyed just staying home. Here we played new and different roles. Judy the housewife, Mickey the carpenter. Mr. and Mrs. Mickey Deans, finally installed in their mews house, planning the future.

We ate when we were hungry. We slept when we were tired. We were creatures of impulse, and this pattern suited us. And yet Judy started to give recognition to tomorrow's obligations. If I had a morning meeting, she realized I had to get some sleep in order to be fresh, that we couldn't always be playmates for twenty-four hours a day, which was her wish.

I got several business offers during our London period and was trying to decide which would be the most suitable. Judy was very much upset. "You can't accept them." Her voice was peremptory. "I need you. I don't want to be alone."

"But Judy, I have to work."

"Then why don't you use my name? Take advantage of it. Everyone else has."

Her retort, half loving, half hostile, did not appeal to me. I'd been earning my own living since I was a kid. I wanted to help Judy, but in order for our marriage to survive it was important for me to be head of the family. It was also important for Judy's future that her manager be devoted to her cause, patient, understanding, and a good businessman. Judy often started a business relationship with high hopes that ended for her in disillusionment. She would be furious if she wasn't consulted on business matters, yet whenever she did get involved in contracts and productions, the result was a disaster. A friend had warned me that it was in Judy's nature to wheedle and cajole until she persuaded the man she was presently involved with to take over her life. Yet she needed looking after, and for the moment I was elected.

Judy had a campy sense of humor. A large rubber tree stood in a tub at the turn in our staircase. Whenever I was in a hurry, taking three steps at a time, I'd be apt to brush the leaves. Judy would utter a warning cry: "Here he comes, Herman. Watch out." She was very fond of Herman, wiping down the thick green leaves and tying up the heavy branches with bright ribbons.

There was a poignant Chaplinesque quality to her humor, most of it being turned in on herself. She had the gallantry of the small tramp, which may be the reason why her portrayal of the tramp in *Easter Parade* was so fetching. Let's laugh, she seemed to be saying, before the world does us in.

She came down into the living room one evening while I was still working on correspondence, wearing my gold-and-purple bathrobe (we had identical robes to protect us against the hazards of the central-heating system). She was completely inundated by the robe, my slippers, and a Sherlock Holmes deerstalker cap. She was imitating Carol Burnett, and she was hilarious.

Later, I showed her a business letter. She refused to read printed matter. "I can't see without my glasses," she alibied.

"Where are your glasses?" I asked, even though I knew she hated to be interrogated.

"I don't know."

"Did you lose them again?"

"Of course not."

"Then where are they?"

"How should I know?"

What might be a simple problem for most of us loomed up

as a crisis for Judy. She was always misplacing her glasses. I needed to have mine repaired, but I hesitated because I couldn't persuade Judy to get her eyes checked. Had I gone ahead, she would have complained, "Oh, why didn't you get mine too? You don't care about me." This was the part of her nature that could drive one up the wall. She could twist any situation adroitly to her advantage. I soon learned that it was shattering for her to accept blame of any sort. This may have been a throwback to her M.G.M. days, when she was blamed for everything. We finally went to an oculist together, and we each bought two new pairs of glasses. She was pleased with the results, but after a lifetime of being ordered around, she resented it even when she needed direction.

"No one ever listened to me," she said. " 'Shut up and sing.' That's all they said. 'Shut up and sing.' "

She wasn't much of a reader, but she had a treasured Bible that her old friend the Reverend Peter Delaney had given her ten years ago, and she carried it with her in her train case and read it frequently. Sometimes when she couldn't sleep, she would read her favorite verses aloud to me and it seemed to give her comfort:

> Though I speak with the tongues of men and of angels and have not Charity, I am become as sounding brass or a tinkling cymbal. . . .
>
> Charity suffereth long and is kind; Charity envieth not; Charity vaunteth not itself; is not puffed up.
>
> Doth not behave itself unseemly, seeketh not her own, is not easily provoked, thinketh no evil;
>
> Rejoiceth not in iniquity but rejoiceth in the truth; Beareth all things, believeth all things, hopeth all things, Endureth all things,
>
> And now abideth faith, hope, charity, these three, but the greatest of these is Charity.
>
> 1 Corinthians 13

Where painting and sculpture were concerned, she showed neither interest nor knowledge, but she passionately loved the theater, and we saw many plays. Mostly, however, she enjoyed staying home, sharing in the plans for decorating the mews cottage. Her emotions swung to extremes. One day while I was putting up new lamps, I got an electric shock. Judy was hysterical, clinging to me afterward like a badly frightened child. All of her nesting instincts were blossoming. At the Ritz she'd taken the antimacassars from the chairs and arranged them on a marble tabletop as a tablecloth. She liked to take a bright scarf and tape it over the bed. She loved pretty fans, and I started her collection. We went shopping together in the markets. Flowers were her joy, both the exquisite porcelains and fresh ones, particularly red roses. I think she equated flowers with love and adulation. In the spring she planned to have a flower garden in the outside cement boxes.

The less amphetamines she took, the more her appetite returned. I've never known anyone who loved mashed potatoes and chicken gravy as she did. Because I drank lots of milk she gradually picked up the habit, although she hadn't touched milk in years. There were other signs that she was gradually relaxing. She would soak in a warm tub and then take a shower and spray herself with Ma Griffe. No appointments, no performances—and how she responded to the easy, casual life!

As a housewife she made a valiant stab at cooking. When she failed, she was desolate until I reminded her that while other girls were learning housewifely arts, she was winning accolades from *Variety* as a promising Sophie Tucker. One evening she made some popcorn. She poured a generous amount in a pan, turned up the heat—and we were barraged by the kernels. Once she made a meat loaf, and it took a week for my stomach to recover. "Look," she said apologetically, "I don't expect to be the best damn cook in the world, but it's nice to be able to fix a few dishes."

I was fairly good in the kitchen myself, the result of having been a bachelor all those years. Judy did learn to prepare excellent bacon and eggs, and she was sweetly proud of her skill. The small chores involved in making a home out of the mews cottage expanded her sense of accomplishment. Here was Judy, who could hold an audience mesmerized, expending her scant energy in learning to be a housewife. And loving it.

Father Peter Delaney was a frequent visitor. One day he saluted her blithely: "How's Gladys?"

She laughed, obviously amused. "Gladys, eh? *Gladys?*" Pointing a finger at me, she added with relish, "And he's George, naturally."

"Naturally," he said.

I had grown tired of hearing my name repeated endlessly at Arthur, with everybody demanding, "Where's Mickey? Get Mickey. Mickey, where are you?" So when Judy began calling me George, I rather liked it. It seemed a fun thing.

"Gladys, are you ready?" I'd call up to her if we were going out.

"In a minute, George."

If we had an engagement, Judy would insist that we drive to our destination, even if it was only around the block. She would insist on being very formal. I had the devil's own time backing our car out of the cottage garage, but we would drive properly to the party. When we left, Judy sometimes got into the driver's seat, but she really preferred me to drive. She told Reverend Delaney quite earnestly that she had a driver's license. She didn't add that it was considerably outdated, being a relic of her M.G.M. days. Nobody could be more precious and lovable than Judy.

Judy romanticized everything. She hungered for security yet did not know how to gain it. Her financial problems were staggering. She earned more than almost anyone in the profession, except perhaps Frank Sinatra, yet she was broke and in hock to Internal Revenue. As a matter of fact, she was terrified of returning to New York because of the I.R.S. She was totally impractical, since she never handled her income, and the people around her shrewdly encouraged her to be dependent on them. She told me she was always being hounded by bill collectors, even while she was earning fantastic sums. While she had been playing to sell-out houses at the Palace, those who were reaping financial gains from her performances were notoriously lax in paying her bills. She had no notion of what had happened to the vast sums she'd earned.

Before we'd left New York for London, she'd confided to Bob Jorgen, "I think it would be wonderful if I didn't have to work—if Mickey could get a job playing in a little club—I wouldn't care if they paid him twenty-five dollars a week." She was sincere. She was content to be my wife. Delores Cole, who'd been her companion during the abortive filming of *Valley of the Dolls*, told me that being a wife rather than a star was now Judy's dream.

The little white house with the picket fence was nearly in sight.

13

Much has been written about the condition of Judy's health. It was even reported in the press that she was suffering from cirrhosis of the liver and had already expended her lifespan. Nothing could be farther from the truth. She did have hepatitis, which incapacitated her for a half year, but her recovery was good. All during our London stay after her Talk of the Town engagement, her energy was focused on regaining her strength. The superstar was offstage most of the time. Her inexplicable tantrums, which were part of the legend, were diminishing. She was docile and winning. During the day she rested a good deal. She tried to eat three small meals. I'd heard that one could trigger an outburst with the suggestion "Judy, try to eat," but this never happened at the mews cottage. She was doing her best. And as her ration of Ritalin decreased, her appetite did improve.

Another thing: Judy didn't always mind being alone. It was the night, particularly after a performance, that held terror for her. Her managers, perhaps trying to get her to rest, used to tell her it was unseemly for her to go off in a party. So she usually returned alone to her hotel and waited for the sound of a human voice. That's where the trouble started. But in London she loved to go off by herself to window-shop, perhaps, or browse in a shop, or go to Fortnum's for afternoon tea.

All the time we were married, Judy was never left alone. If she felt ill and I was obliged to go out on business, I would hire a nurse, or our friend Bumbles would come over to be with her.

Judy assured me with a winsome smile that she was truly changing. It took a while before I realized that under her influence I was changing too. She gave me more strength than anybody ever did, simply by depending on me.

Before knowing Judy, I was apt to be careless, leaving my clothes around. This was also true of Judy. But gradually we both learned to pick up after ourselves. On tour and in the studio, Judy'd had a dresser to assist her. At home she was well intentioned but inexperienced. So much was missing in our everyday upbringing. We were both careless of health.

Bright colors appealed to her, red and orange—particularly orange, the color of life. Hats were her special joy. She designed the floppy, wide-brimmed hats she favored. Whenever she was overweight, she used to wear slacks and a loose shirt to rehearsals. "To disguise the flab," she would explain wryly.

There was no need now for such disguises. She was thin, much too thin, her bones showing, but she liked herself like that. She was also naïve in a charming, unrealistic way. For example, she suggested, "You know, Mickey, I'd like to open a boutique. I could design clothes."

She had the flair but not the training. The red chiffon dress she wore the final week at Talk of the Town was one of her designs. Attractive clothes appealed to her. She was dressed for her films and concerts by outstanding designers, but in the world we now moved in, it seemed to me her clothes were oddly out of date. Wouldn't it be fun, I suggested, to be with the times?

She admired white boots. "Why don't you get a pair?" I suggested.

"Oh, Mickey, I just couldn't. They're not for me."

Taking one of her slippers for size, I went shopping on Carnaby Street and returned with a pair of knee-high white boots and a mod dress. She was ecstatic. Now, with a changed image, she brightened. I rewired her makeup mirror, putting dimmers on the lights so she could use it not only for her stage makeup but for making up for a dinner party in a restaurant or a private house.

She wanted to look young for me, since she was unduly sensitive to the difference in our ages. Her feelings were evident when we were out on the town. Nightclubs and discotheques exploded with beautiful young girls with smooth faces and long, shining manes of hair. A wistful look would come over Judy's face.

"Can you imagine being married to one of them?" I'd say. "You'd have to bring home comic books for her." Put all together, none of them could touch her.

Judy and I never pretended to be anything but what we were—two highly geared, non-Establishment human beings. Yet we entered a union in the best and most complete sense in the little mews cottage. And Judy had an endearing way of pointing to her wedding ring, to prove we were indeed married.

Still, there was a perpetual tug of war within her. She was Gemini and I was Libra. We often discussed the supernatural, not really believing in it, yet wanting to believe there was a pattern in life that brought us together. She was always a surprise to me. In the grab bag of her emotions there was a mercurial range of behavior. Even though both of us had confidence in our marriage, she was forever testing me: Do you love me? Do you love me as I am? Will you still love me if I'm bad? Both of us were filled with a thousand indecisions. Many of Judy's were simple: What shall I wear? What shall I do about my hair? These I was able to help her solve easily. Mod clothes. Wigs, so a hairdresser needn't be underfoot all the time. But there were more complicated problems, such as her habit of signing contracts without first reading the fine print.

85

Then too we were both loathe to see where we did wrong. Sometimes we'd fly into a tantrum that had no relation to the subject we were arguing about, and we drove each other wild until we realized it was our way of saving face. In order to follow our reasoning, you'd need a private road map, created out of our own characters.

When the tension built up, we fought. Loud, angry, wild *Taming of the Shrew* battles. We were cruel to each other as only lovers can be. Once I slammed out of the house and finally returned, contrite, only to discover Judy had locked me out. I forced the door and shut myself in the guest room for two days, refusing to talk to her. When I finally came out, she was standing at the door, screaming hoarsely.

At such moments of crisis, we learned a good deal about each other. We learned also to face the realities of our marriage. Both of us had always found it simpler to live in fantasy. Now we were discovering, somewhat painfully, that only through truth could we find ourselves and each other.

Judy was deeply sensitive to malicious gossip, particularly any attack on her private dignity. "Mickey, I am a lady, aren't I?" she would ask.

She was indeed a lady, and through the worst of the scandals she walked tall, often self-deprecating but with her unique pride. Few critics realized that her unprofessional behavior, the star syndrome, the temper tantrums, and changeability were the result of the extreme pressures that were poisoning her. When she was not on a performance schedule, she was warm, considerate, and charming.

We were playing games, of course. I learned to handle Judy's temper tantrums by ignoring them. She learned that when I got angry, the storm would blow over quickly if she pretended it never happened. Sometimes, in a moment of extreme anxiety, she would assume the superstar role, but eventually she would retreat from the pedestal.

"Mickey, don't be mad," she'd whisper. "It was the other one—not me." This was the key to Judy's problems.

"Hon," I'd remind her, "I'm your husband, remember? Not a member of your fan club."

Whenever her behavior simply made no sense, I tried to understand it within the context of her career, as well as her nature. Her tendency to blow hot and cold, to go into tantrums, her bursts of rebellion, probably had their origins in the very tragedy that made her a superstar—the driving mother, the callous father-substitute, the mercenary hawks around her, and her own desperate will to survive in the face of so many destructive forces. Disappointment in love, failure in marriage, disillusion, despair, loneliness, instability—since she was a small girl, she had lived in a climate of terror or emotional upheaval. When I thought about it, my anger would melt.

She tried to dominate me. I tried to dominate her. Each time our absurd efforts failed, our marriage took a healthy stride forward. She admitted being a little afraid of me, which evidently pleased her. When we had our fights, we each laid out our boundaries. She knew there was a step beyond which she'd best not venture.

"My old man has one helluva temper," she told friends, sounding proud. Or, "Oh, I'd like to, but Mickey wouldn't let me." Or, "I wouldn't dare do that; Mickey wouldn't like it."

Her moods followed the cycles of her life force. Just as her health seemed to be deteriorating, she'd astonish you by a sudden, amazing resurgence of vitality. At such times she managed to sleep for longer periods; on awakening, she made a valiant effort to eat, and then she'd go back to sleep again. This fantastic recuperative power surely saved her from an earlier death. She would live it up for a few weeks, making the rounds of parties, drinking a bit, keeping high with pep pills. Finally, when total exhaustion set in, she'd collapse, rest for a few weeks, eat and keep (for her) regular hours. Then the wild pursuit of escape would begin all over again.

Judy seldom slept more than three or four hours at a stretch unless she was utterly beat. Then she curled up on her bed under a canopy of blazing lights and blaring music. But she was gradually learning to rest without these crutches. Our being together served as a kind of mutual security blanket.

The fact that I could sleep for a long stretch at a time annoyed her. So finally we made a deal, I to sleep an hour less and she to try to sleep an hour more. That made sense to her. I stopped taking the barbiturates that I needed in order to get some rest in our hectic routine, and she agreed to make an effort to cut down on her dosage. She always responded best to gentleness. The fact that her fears were often irrational didn't make them any easier for her to accept. She needed a shoulder to lean on that was sturdy but yielding. Nothing made her dig in her heels more stubbornly than a dictatorial order. Instantly it brought back the days at M.G.M. and the horrendous threats by Louis B. Mayer and his cohorts.

Often, just as you saw the superstar, she would suddenly become an irrepressible gamine. "I'd like to have the ability to handle men and be a swinger," she confessed to me during those last days in London, "but I really don't know how." Then, as the humor of her statement struck her, she burst into laughter. Nobody could laugh like Judy. It was a sound coming from deep within her chest, genuine and full-bodied, such a big sound for a little girl. Like her songs, it was bigger than life.

"More than any city in the world, I love London," she told Bumbles Dawson one afternoon as we were all having a drink in the living room. Judy was curled up in an easy chair, with the once-ferocious Brandy lying at her feet.

"I have such a sense of well-being here. London has tradition and good manners, and everyone is so kind. I shudder, for instance, whenever I have to take a cab in New York. I once asked a driver to go a little slower and he got so mad he practically threw me out of the cab—and had the nerve to make me pay for the fare as far as we'd gone. In London I feel as though I belong."

"They love you here, Judy," Bumbles said.

"The English audiences are the warmest and best in the

These two photographs were Judy
Garland's favorites. The one with
President John F. Kennedy always
traveled with her, as did the picture
with her son, Joey, and her
daughter Lorna.

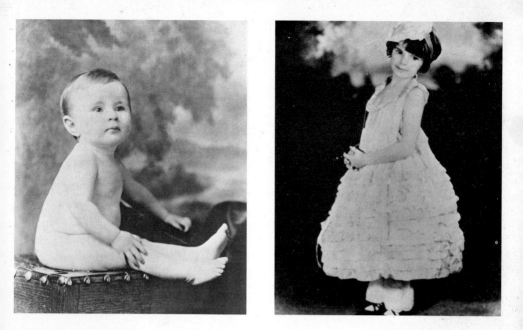

Judy at one year old (above left, The Bettmann Archive, Inc.), at four in 1926 (above right, Wide World Photos), and two undated photographs (below, Springer/Bettmann Film Archive and Steve Young)

Left: Johnny Ray, Judy, and Mickey at the Chelsea Registry Office before the marriage ceremony on March 15, 1969 (Photo courtesy of London *Evening Standard*)

Judy made her stage debut at 3 years old, and her daughter Liza followed in her footsteps at 2½. Here Liza rehearses a scene with her mother for *In the Good Old Summertime*, a 1949 film. (Photo courtesy of Wide World)

Judy Garland and her mother, Ethel, in a publicity photograph of the 1940's (Photo courtesy of The Bettmann Archive, Inc.)

Judy Garland was married to five different men. On the left-hand page at the top she is shown with David Rose at the Brown Derby in 1940. In 1945 she was married to Vincente Minnelli, who is shown with Louis B. Mayer in the center picture. At the bottom Judy is seen with her third husband, Sid Luft. Actor Mark Herron married Judy in 1965 in Las Vegas (top right). The author, Mickey Deans (bottom right), married Judy in London in 1969. (Photos courtesy of Wide World)

Judy and her two sisters as they appeared in their first professional stage appearance in Los Angeles. Judy is on the left, Virginia in the center, and Sue on the right. (Photo courtesy of The Bettmann Archive, Inc.)

world," Judy said. And then she continued on what was a familiar theme. "All these years, without my audiences, I'd be nothing. I always felt that if I pleased them, it was my justification and my happiness. But it's changed for me now. Professional happiness doesn't last through the night. You can't take it home with you after the curtain rings down. It doesn't protect you from the terror of a lonely hotel room. And in a way, it destroys your soul to feed off of applause. I know. I've tried to draw strength and security from it. But in the middle of the night, applause becomes an empty echo and you think, God, how am I going to make it until morning? When you're that scared, you need another human being to save you—somebody who cares about you and what you stand for. Fame isn't enough. It doesn't give you companionship and the feeling of possessing and being possessed. I've gone through the mill." There was a quiver in her voice. "I've made plenty of mistakes —and paid for them. But now Mickey and I have found what we've been searching for. Life's a lot easier to face when there's someone to face it with you."

14

Although Judy seldom spoke about her father, I knew the scars were only barely healed and the shock of his death had shattered her so completely that her being was never completely whole again. It was not only that her emotions were so blocked that she couldn't cry at his funeral. It was something deeper and more vital. I had the feeling that with her father's death, Judy reached another crossroad in her life.

Had her father lived, it is possible that her tenure at M.G.M. would have been less traumatic. Although Frank Gumm did not often stand up to his wife, he loved his youngest child dearly, and it might have been that if he were present during the threats and indignities heaped on Judy, he would have protected her.

About a year or so after Judy's death, my wanderings around town left me beat. I dropped into a flick, picked up a bag of popcorn, and saw a new film, *I Never Sang for My Father*. It brought back memories of Judy, as nearly everything did. Her relationship with her father had been good, as far as it went. How she had longed to spend more time with him, to confide in him, to receive from him the love that would assuage the hunger in her heart.

"My father was a handsome man," she often said, "and so friendly." Judy had inherited his hearty laugh. But where the family was concerned, he was always in the background, deferring to her mother. Ethel, the "tiny little lady" he'd fallen in love with, had an obstinate and aggressive streak. She rode roughshod over obstacles, including the objections of her husband. As a result Judy had had little time with her father. She didn't know what he was like under the veneer of being a husband and a father. What was he as a human being? She had never tapped her father's unspoken thoughts or dreams. Was he happy managing a movie theater, or did he want something more of life? She used to hope he'd take a positive stand against her mother, that he'd say, "Now, Ethel, I will not allow you to chase Baby Frances all over the country. I want you and my girls at home, where we can live like a normal family."

But if he did speak up, Judy never knew about it. She couldn't help but feel acute disappointment in him. The first man in the small girl's life had let her down, and the result filled her with an empty and lonely hunger. Later the residue left from her early needs often colored her choice of husbands and lovers, and she was usually disappointed.

Judy did sing for her father, however. All her childhood was a tacit song for her dad. And that first day he brought her to M.G.M., she sang not for the men watching her and listening with the cold dispassion of horse traders but for her father.

Two weeks later Frank and Ethel signed the contract with M.G.M. which was to bring Judy swift and permanent stardom. Judy was excited, for by this time she was indoctrinated by her mother's ambitions. This was the big break. It made her mother happy, which helped Judy's frame of mind. It wasn't often that she could please her mother.

"You're a lucky girl," Ethel repeated endlessly. "D'you realize how lucky you are?"

Thus she was forced into early blooming.

In Judy's case innocence did not triumph.

Nobody gave her credit for talent, ability, discipline, in

those days. She was a bouncy, friendly, trusting child with the vocal chords of a natural singer and the emotions of a vulnerable little girl. During those thirteen years at M.G.M., where her most popular films were made, the studio and her mother kept a tight rein on her. There was always the reminder and the threat. "At M.G.M. they never told you how good you were," she once said. At her peak she was threatened in a subtle way that June Allyson would supplant her. It was part of Louis B. Mayer's policy to generate fear and insecurity among his players. When he thought a star was showing signs of independent thinking, he'd bring in another, who could be groomed to supplant her. This happened earlier when he'd signed Greta Garbo as a threat to Lillian Gish.

Each day Judy was greeted by threats. If she didn't obey the studio, which had made her, the studio would break her.

"No one can possibly imagine what happened at the studio. My mother actually threatened me that if I didn't behave and do what the studio told me to do, they'd have a lobotomy done on my brain, and then I'd be a vegetable who had to obey what they wanted me to do. It sounds like a horror movie, but it was true." She could somehow talk about it as though it hadn't happened to her.

Her childhood was spent in a climate of fear. And even the M.G.M. contract was not total happiness. Shortly after she signed with the studio, her father became ill with what was finally diagnosed as spinal meningitis. In the days before antibiotics it was nearly always fatal. Judy knew he was in serious condition, but as usual, they told her little. No one involved in Judy's life ever sat down and gave her facts that might have cleared the air. Lack of communication was one of the terrors of her youth. That's when it started, the "Don't talk! Sing!" syndrome.

The night she participated in a radio show with the great and difficult Al Jolson, her father had a radio by his bed. Judy sang for him that night. She never knew if he really heard her. By morning he was dead.

She didn't cry for her father. Not immediately. Her first re-action was that of a terrified child: He can't do this to me. My father won't do this to me.

The shock of his death left her numb. She went through the motions of the bereaved during his funeral without any feeling. Finally, a week later, the grief surfaced. She locked herself in the bathroom (the only private place for her), and she cried for what they had been to each other, for all they should have been, for all they had missed. It took a long time for the ache to ease. Forever after, Judy would be seeking the love and under-standing she and her father had sometimes shared. But it wasn't only the father image she yearned for. It was the love she knew she'd never get from her mother.

"I was born at the age of twelve on the Metro-Goldwyn-Mayer lot," Judy often said. "I missed the gentle maturing most girls have."

The big break turned out to be a tragic turning point in her future as a human being. Whether another studio might have discovered her worth, had M.G.M. passed her by, is difficult to speculate. Mrs. Gumm would never have shelved her dream. If the movies hadn't picked her up, there's no doubt Judy would have continued in vaudeville and eventually made it big. (Sophie Tucker once prophesied Judy would be the next Sophie Tucker, and as Sophie had the highest opinion of her own tal-ent, this was a great compliment indeed.) Now Mrs. Gumm was in her element, the fully established stage mother. She pos-sessed Judy while inwardly rejecting her, and the early days at the studio initiated a kind of schedule that eventually wrecked the girl and the star.

One of the studio portraits taken thirty years ago was a great favorite with the fan magazines. It shows Judy sitting, with her mother standing behind her. Judy is looking up eagerly at her mother. Her mother is staring into the camera.

In most families love and adulation are given to the most gifted child, but not in the case of the Gumms. Judy had a deep hunger for family ties, and she loved to hear from her mother's sister and her cousins. Her aunt, Irene Milne Mathias, recalls a visit that she and her son paid to Detroit, where Judy was playing at the Michigan Theater. Ethel came down to the stage door to bid her sister and nephew good-bye. Judy was upstairs at a party to which she had invited the Mathiases but which they'd decided not to attend. Ethel sent Judy downstairs to make her farewells. They had the uncomfortable feeling that Ethel didn't want Judy to grow too attached to her relatives. "But she loved us," Mrs. Mathias averred, "and we loved her."

As a child Judy shut her mind to any criticism of her mother or any doubts that swam into her own mind. Children are fiercely closemouthed about their parents' faults. They are apt to blame themselves rather than their parents. So when she was informed that whatever went wrong was her fault, Judy believed it. *I must be no good.* Her inner world was growing cold and introspective. Sometimes she felt invisible.

She never adjusted to the studio. Where life at M.G.M. was concerned, she said, "It's like being a wildflower in a hothouse."

Where her talent was concerned, however, Judy happened to be at the right place and the right time. Hollywood, the original world of the dropout, was in the first third of our century in the hands of self-made, often illiterate, but immensely shrewd operators who parlayed the American dream into a billion-dollar industry.

Louis B. Mayer, head of Metro-Goldwyn-Mayer, was typical of this new breed. The son of immigrants, his father a junk dealer in a small Massachusetts town, he was hungry, shrewd, with a crude and ruthless will to survive. Young Mayer's future was bleak and unpromising until he stumbled onto the new American craze, the nickelodeon. Moving pictures were especially popular with the immigrants who had recently arrived in the country and found the English language an obstacle. Silent films were a great source of communication for them, giving them insight into the new land. When D. W. Griffith produced his epic *The Birth of a Nation*, Mayer managed to procure the New England rights. He was on his way to riches and power that would be unchallenged for two decades in Hollywood.

As a father surrogate for the vulnerable, sensitive Judy, he was a disaster. He was a man of tremendous strength and monumental weakness, contradictory, unpredictable, a ruthless manipulator, a sentimental weeper. Gratitude was unknown to him. Tantrums were among his weapons. Whether he overreacted because of a weak character structure or because histrionics helped him get his way, it didn't matter. It gave him tyrannical power over his stable of actors.

Like a chameleon, he changed his role to suit the moment. He used fainting spells as a ploy to get out of difficult situations. His private weeping spells suggest that his emotional balance was always precarious.

Judy, who had been exposed to her mother's unhealthy drives, to the life-style of a child vaudevillian, found in the new father image a man who was often unpredictable, demanding, threatening, and then unexpectedly kind, the sort of behavior she was used to in the adults around her. She was afraid to protest.

Mayer usually paid court to the young actresses through their mothers, but he evidently did not consider Judy another pretty starlet to be chased around the desk. Where sex was concerned, Mayer, like most men of his caliber, divided women between the madonna and the whore. Judy was the nice little all-American girl that you held in respect. She was also a big money-maker, and he was determined that her innocent image would remain intact. It is quite possible that he thought of her also as he did of his own two daughters: chaste, dutiful, obedient, an innocent young girl. Even when Judy was nineteen, he did not want her to attend the premiere of her tremendous success *Babes in Arms*. It was only after Hedda Hopper, the columnist, practically shamed him that he allowed Judy to appear.

Mayer had a youth syndrome after a fashion, not only for his own needs but also for business reasons. He loved stories about children and was hopelessly sentimental about them. The fantastic success of Jackie Cooper in *The Champ* reaffirmed his hunch that the studio would do well to build up a stable of young talent. Among the future stars to be groomed were Deanna Durbin, Lana Turner, Judy Garland, Elizabeth Taylor, Mickey Rooney, Ann Rutherford, Kathryn Grayson, and Freddie Bartholomew.

These youngsters would in time replace the reigning stars of the era, the abundant beauty and talent in the studio—Greta Garbo, Joan Crawford, Myrna Loy, Norma Shearer, Jeannette MacDonald, Nelson Eddy, Clark Gable, Spencer Tracy, Robert Taylor, Walter Pidgeon, William Powell. Movie patrons adored the M.G.M. movies because they were so glossy, so handsomely mounted, so totally involved in the fantasy of the American Dream. Mayer didn't need the sociological study *Middletown*, by the Lynds, to understand the needs of the average American. He believed in the simple, elemental virtues. He believed in stories with a moral. He loved wholesome, sentimental tales that brought a tear to the eye and a good feeling in the heart.

But what could he do with a plump little thirteen-year-old girl? She attended the studio school, studied musical arrangements with Roger Edens, who had great faith in her talent, was asked occasionally to sing at a studio party, where, she said, she was treated like the help, and that was it, for $150.00 a week.

Judy's first movie, filmed on the M.G.M. lot in 1936, was a two-reel short called *Every Sunday*. It served as a showcase for her and another young singer, Deanna Durbin. Judy sang the swing numbers while Deanna warbled the classical arias. Joe Pasternak, then a producer at Universal, saw the film and was greatly impressed with both youngsters. When Deanna Durbin's option was allowed to lapse at Metro, Universal signed her up, and her musical films rescued Universal from incipient bankruptcy. Judy remained at Metro by a fluke. Arthur Freed, who had great faith in Judy, dissuaded Mayer from dropping her, but the studio did loan her to Fox for a college-type film called *Pigskin Parade*, which was produced by Darryl F. Zanuck. The cast included Betty Grable, Patsy Kelly, Jack Haley, and Stuart Irwin, but none of them made a great impact on the movie fans, although *The New York Times* did mention that Judy was "cute, not pretty, but a pleasingly fetching personality, who certainly knows how to sell a pop."

That was the last time Judy was allowed to stray off the M.G.M. lot for thirteen years. At Universal, Joe Pasternak wanted Judy for a script called *Three Smart Girls*, since the lead required a singer who could sing "swing." Mayer, who had just signed Judy for another year, refused to loan her out, so Pasternak changed the script to conform to Deanna Durbin's classical talents. On its release Deanna became an international star.

Movie fans followed Judy's career and devoured news of her private life in *Photoplay, Motion Picture*, and other fan magazines, as well as in movie columns in the newspapers. The private life disclosed was mostly the fantasy creations of the press agents, but once in a while in an interview, Judy's candor and a suggestion of her wit shone through. She spoke of her dismay when she first saw herself on the screen in *Pigskin Parade*. She had secretly hoped makeup and the technique of the photographer would perform a miracle, but she was still little Frances, whom the family called Pudge.

She was also Judy Garland, a gifted young singer, M.G.M.'s answer to Universal's now spectacularly successful Deanna Durbin. In *Broadway Melody of 1938* Judy's talents won recognition among such able young performers as Robert Taylor, Eleanor Powell, Binnie Barnes, George Murphy, Buddy Ebsen, and the late great Red Hot Mama, Sophie Tucker. Judy was obviously a young girl in ankle socks and Mary Jane slippers, just getting into adolescence, round with baby fat, but with that winsome smile and vivacious manner which already prophesied the later charisma. In the movie fifteen-year-old Judy sang a song addressed to Clark Gable, pensive and yearning over his photograph: "Dear Mr. Gable, You Made Me Love You."

The lyrics had an interesting beginning. To celebrate the birthday of Clark Gable (Mr. Mayer's studio was big on birthday celebrations), Roger Edens wrote a fresh verse to the song "You Made Me Love You," and Judy sang it to Gable while he and Myrna Loy were filming *Parnell*. It was evidently a memorable moment. Gable, who was basically a decent man and cynical about his title, The King, was deeply touched by the emotion Judy projected and later sent her a gold bracelet, engraved "To My Girl Friend, Judy Garland, from Clark Gable."

The same year she made *Thoroughbreds Don't Cry*, with Mickey Rooney, Robert Sinclair, Sophie Tucker, C. Aubrey Smith, and others from the stable at M.G.M. The story of two young boys—Mickey Rooney and Robert Sinclair—trying to train a horse was familiar, reassuring, wholesome, family-type entertainment. This was Judy's first movie appearance with Mickey, although they had known each other since childhood. On the screen they registered well together. Mickey was brash, funny, a natural clown; Judy was quiet, sensitive, and at times withdrawn, but she felt comfortable with Mickey. She remembered, no doubt, the casual acting tip Mickey Rooney had given her: "Let yourself go, kid."

In 1938 she made a third picture, *Everybody Sing*, which unfortunately was what nearly everybody in the film did. She received praise as a "superb vocal technician," and since her song to Gable, "You Made Me Love You," was heard endlessly on radio throughout the country, Judy Garland was already a personality. In the ads Judy received second billing (Allan Jones received first), and Fanny Brice, the great stage comedienne, received third billing.

Another film followed shortly, *Listen, Darling*, with Mary Astor, Freddie Bartholomew, Scotty Beckett, Alan Hale, and Walter Pidgeon. This was again one of the studio's wholesome family films, the story of a young widow whose two children decide to find her a husband. Judy belted out "Zing! Went the Strings of My Heart," "Nobody's Baby," and "On the Bumpy Road to Love" and acquired more admirers.

To use the fresh, youthful talent of the young actors, the studio created a series of low-budget films, the Andy Hardy series. The Hardy family was soon to find its place in the American scene, as familiar to most movie fans as the people next door. There was a fine father figure in Judge Hardy, a typical American boy in Andy Hardy. Lionel Barrymore was excellent in his role, and Mickey Rooney was indeed the all-American boy. The first film of the series was *Family Affair*, which made no great impression on the critics. Audience comments were all favorable, however, and some theater-owners even suggested another picture using the same characters. The second was called *You're Only Young Once*. There was something in the air that suggested a great future for the Andy Hardy series. After the first film Barrymore was replaced by Lewis Stone, who was superb as the judge, and Fay Holden was cast as the mother to replace Spring Byington. By this time the studio realized it also had a great property in Judy and introduced her into the series as Betsey Booth. She was the visiting girl next door, a role she was to play in three of the subsequent Andy Hardy films. *Love Finds Andy Hardy* had all the warmth and identification of the earlier films, and the characters were now familiar to the audiences, who fell in love with them. Lana Turner was in the movie, but one of the critics suggested she already had too much glamour for this kind of film.

The simple, everyday problems of the Hardy family now captured Louis B. Mayer's interest. This was the ideal American family as he envisioned it. Judge Hardy was a fount of good sense laced with the Puritan ethic, Andy was the mischievous American boy, exposed to the tribal rites of young manhood. Lana Turner was in contrast to Judy already beautiful and sexually provocative. Naturally Mickey Rooney had eyes only for Lana.

But Judy, as the girl next door, the pal, the confidante, was so endearing that their public thought of Mickey and Judy together as a pair. Judy was cast in two more Andy Hardy films—*Andy Hardy Meets Debutante* and *Life Begins for Andy Hardy*. The press was papered with the usual sunny, optimistic reports on and interviews with the young star, all in harmony with L. B. Mayer's notion of what a proper young girl singer, already an American idol, should be. No gossip stained her reputation, no suggestion that this warm, spirited youngster was already the hapless victim of men who considered her a piece of highly marketable real estate and had no awareness or compassion for the small girl who, in the process of growing up, was losing herself.

And when *The Wizard of Oz* was finally released in 1939, seventeen-year-old Judy Garland became an international idol. *The Wizard of Oz* is still seen on television and according to a recent Nielsen rating drew sixty million viewers.

Mervyn LeRoy, a gifted and imaginative producer, was eager to do *The Wizard*, but the property was held by the equally astute Samuel Goldwyn. After five years Goldwyn finally gave up trying to cast it, whereupon he sold it to LeRoy. Arthur Freed and LeRoy were both determined to have Judy in the role of Dorothy, although the businessmen wanted to borrow Shirley Temple, then America's darling. Fortunately, this was impossible; Shirley's cuteness would perhaps have ruined it.

Dorothy, the lively, sturdy young orphan living with her aunt and uncle on a Kansas farm, is upset by an obnoxious neighbor, played by Margaret Hamilton, who complains that Dorothy's beloved dog, Toto, bit her knee. The neighbor demands that Toto be put away. Dorothy, terrified that she will lose her dog, runs away—straight into a tornado. By the time she turns back to the farmhouse, the rest of the family is locked in the tornado cellar, and Dorothy, running upstairs to her room with Toto, receives a stunning blow on the head. In her dream she is now on the road to the land of Oz.

Along the way she meets a Straw Man, who was Ray Bolger, artfully done up as a scarecrow, a Tin Man, who was Jack

Haley, and a Cowardly Lion, impeccably performed by Bert Lahr. The three join Judy and Toto on a trip through a perilous forest to the Emerald City, where hopefully the Wizard will grant their wishes. The Straw Man longs for a brain, the Tin Man for a heart, and the Cowardly Lion for courage. Dorothy wants only to return home to her beloved aunt and uncle.

"The Straw Man, the Tin Man, and the Cowardly Lion had to have lots of makeup," Judy once told me, "and they were always complaining about it and making bets, each one being sure *his* was the most cumbersome. In the little dance up the Yellow Brick Road I was supposed to be up front with Ray Bolger, Jack Haley, and Bert Lahr," Judy added with a rueful smile, "but I always trailed after them because they managed to push me in the back. I was too scared to complain. But Victor Fleming, sitting on the boom, yelled, 'Hey, you three dirty hams, let's have the little girl in there.' "

The Emerald City was populated by tiny people, the Munchkins, so the studio was obliged to scout for midgets all over the world. The little people were all housed in a hotel in Culver City. Judy recalled with her inimitable chuckle, "They got smashed every night, so they were picked up in butterfly nets."

So many little people were needed for the mob scenes that the studio hired children to play the older midgets in the background shots. The studio spared no effort in turning out this film, using magical tricks that previously had been only in the grasp of cartoonists. Nearly all of M.G.M.'s twenty-nine sound stages and sixty-five sets had been exhausted before Victor Fleming, the seventh director, finally finished it at a cost of two million dollars.

The results more than justified the frenetic work, anxiety, and tensions. The combination of fantasy and reality, impeccably turned out by a cast of superior actors, brought an avalanche of critical acclaim and box-office returns. For a studio known for its syrupy dramas, *The Wizard of Oz* was a milestone in creative effort.

The film's lyrics were by E. Y. Harburg, and the music by

Harold Arlen, who were to write many of Judy's top hits. Harburg, writing the lyrics for "Over the Rainbow," had a vision of the bleak Kansas plains and a little girl's wistful dreams. Judy made the vision come true. Forever after, the world thought of her as the little girl who watched the bluebirds wistfully and sang, "If happy little bluebirds fly . . . why, oh, why can't I?" Judy went on to a series of fabulous movie successes, but *The Wizard of Oz* was a turning point in her career and her life.

Judy and Mickey Rooney flew to New York for a personal appearance at the premiere of *The Wizard of Oz*. Fifteen thousand fans, for the most part children with their parents and teen-agers, swarmed to the Capitol Theater, starting their loving vigil at five-thirty in the morning. From then on Judy drew crowds wherever she appeared. Even when her talents had a showcase of music, lavish sets, and attractive leading men, the image of the serious, wholesome Judy remained. Whether she was painfully thin or on the buxom side, it didn't matter. She was the embodiment of the nice American girl. She was what Norman Rockwell painted. A whole generation of parents thought of her as a loved daughter, while her own peers identified with her.

The studio now had the magic formula: Judy and Mickey. No longer Judy the quiet, wholesome girl next door, but Judy slimmed down, dressed by the top studio designers, made up to accent the dark, expressive eyes, the wide, friendly mouth. Not Lana's sex appeal, but enough in her own right and, one critic noted, the most beautiful legs in Hollywood. Somehow her devoted fans never stopped to analyze Judy's figure or features in terms of symmetrical beauty. She was uniquely Judy, a rule in herself.

The studio began to mine its lode with a series of smashing musical comedies, starting with *Babes in Arms*. All was in high gear. Mickey Rooney was, in 1939, the number-one box-office attraction. Judy profited by their association, both emotionally and professionally. They were devoted to each other but on a platonic level. Mickey was already involved with a series of tall, slender, ravishingly beautiful starlets. Judy remained wistfully the girl next door in private as on film.

They were still in adolescence and were the two outstanding young stars of the time. Seasoned by vaudeville and by the apprenticeship in the studio, they had poise, vitality, and showmanship. They were inspired by each other, by the adulation of the world, by the heady response that their appearances triggered. They were adored. And thousands of fans, reading about Judy Garland, attending her movies, thought she was surely the luckiest girl in the world.

Judy and I spent many dawns in our bedroom in the little mews house, Brandy in bed with us, keeping us warm as we talked. I suggested that she spend about fifteen minutes a day putting on tape some of her memories, but she never got around to it—a deliberate lapse, I suspect, to keep from reliving pain.

Years earlier she had told an interviewer, "When you have lived the life I've lived, when you have loved and suffered and have been madly happy and desperately sad—well, that's when you realize you'll never be able to set it all down. Maybe you'd rather die first." Yet she liked to talk about her early years at M.G.M., and at times she could even laugh about them.

The studio had a schoolhouse of sorts for its gilded young hopefuls. "Can you imagine us—Mickey Rooney, Lana Turner, Elizabeth Taylor, Deanna Durbin, Freddie Bartholomew, and me—packed in one small room? We were supposed to be learning something, and we had a teacher who wouldn't quit. She was a terrifying woman, like my mother. Mickey Rooney always wanted to smoke, so he'd raise his hand to be excused to go to the boys' room. Then Lana would raise *her* hand to be excused, and she'd go out to smoke. Me, I just burned inside."

She added, "Have you ever tried playing hide-and-go-seek with midgets in the mens' rest room?"

She recalled Elizabeth Taylor as a girl with a chipmunk

called Nibbles and a passion for horses. She remembered her first impression of Deanna Durbin as having one thick eyebrow that went across her forehead. She was intensely competitive with Deanna.

The studio heads didn't encourage any friendship among their young players. "They didn't want us to know we were big stars," Judy said. "We were kept under wraps. But when we had a hit, we knew. There was a grapevine."

The studio was a gilded guardhouse, and its future royalty was guarded zealously. Once Judy began making films, the studio used her as impersonally as an inanimate object or a piece of real estate. Judy was by nature a joyous youngster, full of innocence and good will. The musicians loved to work with her. She was a quick study—as a matter of fact, she never learned to read music, but her ear was faultless. Her acting was an outpouring of intuitive feeling, for no one had ever taught her how to act, except for her good friend Mickey Rooney, who advised her to sing and act as though she believed in what she was doing. But her genuine talent was shaped and refined by doing rather than learning. She was always somewhat unsure of herself. Perhaps it was this heartbreak quality that added something rare and precious to her singing.

She always felt inferior to the young beauties on the lot. Yet Lana Turner once admitted wistfully she would trade her looks for Judy's talent. When Judy sang, her whole being was illuminated. In those days she was delighted to sing when anyone asked her. She was kept unaware of the high stakes she was winning in her life. Studio officials, as well as her mother, were always denigrating her in order to keep her subjugated. They cultivated the feeling of unworthiness in her. She was constantly reminded of her good fortune and how much she owed the studio, whose bosses could break her if she didn't cooperate with their plans for her future. Her future was already in the hands of the money men.

Judy's flight toward stardom was not rapid enough to satisfy her mother. Judy's appearance was to blame, she decided. How could Judy compete with the young beauties on the lot? She was short, and the extra weight made her look pudgy. She walked pigeon-toed. (Later, a critic said, "Judy has a walk nobody can duplicate.") A movie face need not be fantastically beautiful. Some of our superstars are quite ordinary-looking in actual life, but they have the bone structure that turns magical under the camera's eye. Judy's bone structure was not remarkable. She was sturdy, wholesome, and spirited, but when she sang, she had moments of radiance. And later, when pills, suffering, and despair whittled down her body so that she was like a slight, trembling bird, there was a luminous beauty about her that defied definition. But in those early days she suffered from competition with ravishing Elizabeth Taylor and Lana Turner.

Mrs. Garland, as Ethel now called herself, was determined to remake Judy. Toward this goal she was abetted by Louis B. Mayer, who wanted Judy thin. Although the young girl resented her mother's voracious ways, she accepted the threats, the sarcasm, the criticism. Like most youngsters she took into herself not the loving parent but the rejecting one.

Judy was to be transformed into a slim beauty. They started on her diet first. All carbohydrates were forbidden. The craving for sweets in adolescence is fairly normal. The young body is growing, the glands are making new demands. Besides sweets to a deprived child are a substitute for affection, for rewards, even a symbol of happiness.

Judy drank black coffee or the detested chicken broth and dreamed of hot-fudge sundaes. Whenever she tried to buy a sweet, the commissary warned her it was forbidden, "at Mr. Mayer's orders." Judy worked and starved and obeyed. And once she was on her way, in 1938, there were the diet pills, ordered by the new studio doctor.

Kids need time to do nothing, to dawdle, to confide in friends, to daydream. Judy never was granted this leisure. When she wasn't performing or attending the studio school, she was being driven home in a studio car. "Metro was a prison that ruined most of its child stars," she once said. Yet she was one of the child stars who made good.

Kids need privacy. She never had it. When she was at the studio, people were always barging in and out of her dressing room without knocking. The only place she found privacy was in the bathroom, which was the reason that even in later years she insisted always on locking the door. She was offended also by the crass way the studio brass treated her, as though she were simply "flesh."

She confided to me that a producer once summoned her to his office, where a visitor was seated. The producer put his arm around Judy and brought her over to the man. "This is Judy," he said matter of factly. "Touch her breast—" And he refused to let her draw back. "Pretty well developed, eh?" It was enough to sicken her. It strengthened in her a lifelong need for respect.

She was seventeen when she played Dorothy in *The Wizard of Oz*, and she looked fourteen, with the help of the makeup department. They strapped down her budding breasts and encased her in a straitjacket of a girdle. She already had the plaintive, lonely cadence of a gospel or blues singer, and when she poured out the golden notes, the hurt and pain showed. But there was also the promise of a dream. With the big waif's eyes, the urchin grin, she crept into the world's heart. She made us feel that out there was a world bigger than ourselves where dreams could come true.

"Judy sang not just to your ears but to your tear ducts," E. Y. Harburg said. In his opinion she had the most unusual voice of the first half of our century.

Money? She heard talk about it, but she never saw it. She was in bondage both to her mother and to L. B. Mayer. In 1940, she signed a contract that guaranteed her $2,000 a week for the next three years, $2,500 for the following two years, and $3,000 a week for two years after that. But she never saw the money. This was during the period when parents or guardians were allowed to do as they saw fit with the earnings of their offspring until the young actors turned twenty-one. Mrs. Garland was busy spending the income without plans to protect her daughter. Shirley Temple's family salted away her earnings for her, and Shirley was a rich young lady. Mrs. Garland unfortunately had a genius for mismanagement, her daughter said, and it included investments in silver mines instead of Los Angeles real estate, as Judy suggested.

Judy's mother and the studio now redoubled their efforts. The new doctor had a miracle drug, amphetamine, to cut down on appetite and release energy. The pill worked, except for one side effect. Insomnia. She was fed barbiturates, the little red devils. People didn't know much about pills in those days, nor that they were habit-forming. She would be high on pep pills, having a great time, and then on schedule the nurse would feed her sleeping pills, and she would fall asleep until it was time to awake again. Friends who knew her at that time are convinced that her inability to sleep for longer than four hours at a time started then, as did her awful fear of the dark. She fought sleep because it was like death.

Over the years Ethel had played on Judy's nature, encouraging her sense of competition. The fantastic success Deanna Durbin was experiencing at Universal chipped away at Judy's ego. It was taking Judy longer to gain recognition abroad. Since she was so obviously the image of the nice young American girl, she was accepted less warmly than Deanna in Europe and South America. In many of her early pictures she was the girl next door who always lost the hero to the glamour queen. Quite possibly this constant climate of rejection played an unconscious role in her personal life, when she found love was easy to come by but hard to retain.

The small child, nearly crushed by the voracious, indomitable mother, found the door marked survival in her talent for singing. So there was Judy at seventeen, the popular young star, adored by young and old, already on amphetamines and barbiturates for three years, her nervous system showing the first signs of faltering. She'd never had a natural moment when she could be herself from the time she was a toddler. Now it was too late. She was on a skyrocket; she was such a valuable property that the studio would go to any means to keep her quiet, passive, and obedient. No one really looked at Judy the person. No one ever listened to Judy the person. L. B. Mayer was terrified of any scandal touching his young star.

The one close girl friend she cultivated and with whom she shared an apartment after her mother's second marriage to a William Gilmore turned out to be in the pay of the studio, reporting what Judy ate, whom she saw, giving a complete dossier of her life. It was little wonder Judy grew progressively more paranoid and shied away from personal relationships. There was too much pain and disillusionment at each betrayal.

Her early attacks of anxiety were a warning signal, ignored by the world around her, either out of ignorance or indifference. Anxiety was a concomitant of the drugs she was taking, and the ups were usually followed by wells of depression. Sometimes she looked at you without focusing. Sometimes she stayed in bed for days at a time. The constant nagging about her weight problem didn't help either. When she was underweight, she looked attractive enough to please the studio brass and her mother, but she actually felt much better with a few pounds of flesh padding her bosom and hips. During the years when she was first the darling of the movie audiences, while crowds were spilling into theaters when she and Mickey Rooney made guest appearances, she was already on the verge of a serious emotional crisis. The constant juggling of weight and the addiction to pep pills and sleeping pills were enough to play havoc with the young girl's nervous system. Added to it, the tension of making one movie after another, traveling for personal appearances at the studio's behest, giving interviews and cooperating with the press, and yet always being alone in a crowd—all this was making visible inroads on Judy's health. Sensitive and fantastically aware of the people around her, she withdrew into herself. Her feelings were verbalized in perceptive poems that revealed the quiet side of her. Otherwise she was on stage all the time, and those who remember her during that period suggest she was generous and loving, a born clown with a sharp, funny wit.

"Somewhere behind every cloud, there's a lot of rain," said Judy.

"No matter how bad things are, they will be worse," said Judy.

They laughed. Funny Judy. Good Judy. If she showed any signs of rebellion, you had only to say, "I'll tell Mr. Mayer," and she quieted down. People were all around her, but they were jailers with whom she could not communicate. Her inner life was like a waking nightmare or a Kafka story.

"To the very talented, stardom comes fast," said Jack Paar about Judy. "Learning to live with it takes a little longer."

Judy certainly didn't have much chance to rebel or grow at the studio. Next to Mickey Rooney, the enormously gifted, amusing, and cocky young king of the box office, Judy was Metro's most valuable property. The decade from 1940 to 1950 saw Judy, sometimes slim, sometimes plump, but always dancing, emoting, and singing from her heart, in a series of fabulously mounted musicals that made the studio a fortune: *Strike Up the Band, For Me and My Gal, Presenting Lily Mars, Girl Crazy, Thousands Cheer, Meet Me in St. Louis, The Harvey Girls, Till the Clouds Roll By, The Pirate, Easter Parade, Words and Music, In the Good Old Summertime, Summer Stock.* Mickey Rooney was often her leading man. They were superb together—two tiny ex-vaudeville kids who'd made it big and who complemented each other. Mickey, always full of bounce, larger than life, hugging Judy, grinning, "Come on, Toots, we'll knock 'em dead."

Like Judy, Mickey Rooney was a natural. Fortunately, he had a thick skin that enabled him to survive. He treated Louis B. Mayer with an offhand insolence that both irritated and amused the tycoon. "Uncle Louie," Mickey would begin whenever he wanted a favor. He was a genius at stealing scenes from the older actors who were considered the aristocrats on the lot. And he was the best friend Judy ever had. He was astonishingly generous with all those he was fond of, and his kindness to Judy made her life bearable. In spite of his obsessive way of life, he always found time to help her, and it is doubtful if she could have survived that decade without his support.

Mickey's talent, like Judy's, stemmed from the child within him. Like Judy also, he realized soon enough that the child could create, but when it came to dealing with the studio, the child was threatened and vanquished. This disparity between talent and reality was the cause of so many heartaches even before disillusionment caught up with them. Judy was frank and admitted she was crazy about Mickey, but Mickey, with a prescience beyond his years, had the grace not to involve her in what he considered his "mixed-up life."

Among her leading men in that fabulous period were Gene Kelly, George Murphy, Richard Carlson, John Boles, Tom Drake, Robert Walker, John Hodiak, Van Johnson, and Fred Astaire. The songs she made famous were to become favorites of the Judy cult forever. Who could ever forget Judy singing "Zing! Went the Strings of My Heart," "I Cried for You," "I'm Just Wild about Harry," "For Me and My Gal," "After You've Gone," "Embraceable You," "Biding My Time," "I've Got Rhythm," "But Not for Me," "The Trolley Song," "The Boy Next Door," "Have Yourself a Merry Little Christmas," "On the Atchison, Topeka, and the Santa Fe," "Look for the Silver Lining," "Be a Clown," "A Couple of Swells," "Get Happy"?

Judy Garland movies of that decade were musicals at their peak. Audiences stormed the theaters to worship their youthful favorites. Judy's films reflected not only the times, including the World War II years, but also the Hollywood dream factory at its best. If the musicals were fantasies, the feelings she projected were touchingly real. "We believed in Judy," a critic wrote, and the world shared his feelings. Frank Sinatra, a warm and loyal friend, as well as a great admirer, said she could make the most banal lyrics sound like a hymn to life.

Judy was money in the bank for M.G.M., and Mayer was determined to keep her under his thumb. He was convinced her public loved her best when she was performing in musicals, and his decision was law. Meanwhile she bitterly resented the fact that the men around her handled her like so much meat. Even now, a full-fledged star, she wasn't consulted or allowed to participate in plans for her future. There was nobody to protect her, except Mickey Rooney, and he was too busy dealing with his own life problems. She made it so fast that she never got to realize how great was her success. She experienced only the heartache and grief.

By the end of the forties, when she was a superstar with an entourage—agents, studio men, so-called friends, and hangers-on—a reporter asked her what she wanted of life. "I don't know." She was frank, as usual; admitting her stardom was enough to turn a girl's head. In a low, thoughtful voice she added, "Things happen to me. Or I bring them about. I don't know which, and I could care less." A rather melancholy confession for the adored Judy Garland.

In Judy's scrapbooks were photographs of a 1949 M.G.M. version of the play *The Shop around the Corner*, retitled *In the Good Old Summertime*. Judy played opposite Van Johnson in the kind of musical the studio did with such commercial aplomb. The plot was sentimental and predictable. The young lovers became pen pals, never guessing they were co-workers in a music shop, and they suffered through the conventional misunderstandings. Judy looked well, with none of the nervousness which had been so evident in *The Pirate*. Only when she sang "I Don't Care," the old Eva Tanguay hit, was one aware of the tension in the stark, jittery way she used her hands. The lyrics pouring out of her throat seemed an affirmation of her wild inner turmoil: "Don't try to rearrange me/'Cause nothing can change me./I don't care,/I don't care,/I don't care.

What I recall most is that the pen pals of the film mention the poetry of Elizabeth Barrett Browning. Later I would have poignant reason to remember Elizabeth and Robert Browning.

The migraines, the backaches, the throat troubles, were a testimony to the perilous drain on Judy's emotional and physical health during those glittering years when she was one of M.G.M.'s biggest money-makers. Sometime in those years she became accident-prone, always stumbling, falling down, and injuring herself. Once when she had a sore throat, she told me, they gave her cortisone, and her face swelled up like a small pumpkin.

As the expensive star-mounted musicals came off the studio assembly line, elevating Judy's professional status, her insomnia worsened, so that she was existing on a schedule of ups and downers. She was overstimulated, underfed, overworked, but nobody worried about killing the young golden goose.

Recently researchers at Stanford University's Sleep Disorder Clinic have discovered that sleeping pills can be dangerous for people with insomnia. They can have the reverse effect, and they can lead to the kind of sleep that may be harmful over long periods. Whatever interferes with the normal sleep pattern may cause mental changes, as well as abnormalities in the sleep pattern. The individual is apt to have nightmares. He may become tense and excitable. It is suggested that withdrawal should never be sudden, as the result may be severe anxiety and terrible nightmares.

If withdrawal is slow, the patient usually will sleep better than before he began taking the pills.

Judy was much too overwrought to consider doing without barbiturates. Her work schedule was so demanding that she was terrified of trying to sweat out a completely sleepless night. Fears in general rose in the night, bringing back memories of the days when her mother deserted her in a strange and lonely hotel room. The unperceptive studio brass didn't realize she was tottering on the verge of collapse. They saw only an ungrateful girl who was putting on the airs of a movie queen and whom they decided to cut down to size. These executives had no awareness of their star's immense emotional needs. "Producers and directors can grow old and fat," Judy once said, "but stars have to look seventeen all the time."

Sometimes when she complained about her plight, her mother said furiously, "All you want is sympathy."

"My business *is* sympathy," Judy replied, already conscious of her image.

I know this only from her Hollywood friends, but as a young girl Judy was meek, compliant, and passive in the hands of the studio. She was terrified of Louis B. Mayer's wrath. Then, in spite of the executives, she suddenly realized she was the star who made them a fortune, that they were dependent on her talents for a slice of the studio's big profits. She stopped being the middle-America nice girl, the patsy, and began behaving like a star. It evidently gave her considerable satisfaction, as well as secret amusement. Even when she knew she was being unkind, aggressive, perhaps even cruel, she acted out her pent-up furies.

She was also on a drug schedule. According to a former U.S. commissioner of narcotics, Judy had confided to him that she took pep pills on getting up, minor stimulants during the day, and finally a sleeping pill. The commissioner had helped many movie people who were addicted to drugs, and he recommended that Judy be given a year's complete rest for rehabilitation. Louis B. Mayer flatly rejected his advice. "We have fourteen million dollars tied up in her," he said coldly.

Judy was usually broke. Not that the other young stars on the lot were in better circumstances. Mickey Rooney ended flat broke. Elizabeth Taylor, before she married Mike Todd, was in debt. Miss Taylor never had a chance to get rich until she received a percentage on the film *Cleopatra,* and that was the beginning of her fortune. The Internal Revenue Service was the nightmare of Hollywood. Many who made millions died with empty pockets. That was the beginning of the business managers, who, like agents, took over a player's life.

Even after Ethel married William Gilmore, she did not

loosen her maternal hold over Judy, who was sixteen at the time. She was always in the background, alert to any misdemeanors that might ruin Judy's report card with the studio. The weight problem was a constant cause of arguments. The tendency to put on weight was evidently in Judy's genes, as well as an emotional hazard. There would come a time when she was to eat so compulsively that she put on considerable weight, but under the studio's strict regime, there was little chance of such self-indulgence. She was heir to extra pounds, however, and it didn't take much fat to show up through the camera lens and reduce the studio heads to hysterics. If she partied, she put on weight. If she stayed up late, which she found enjoyable, it was difficult for her to appear on the set the next morning, fresh and dewy-eyed and capable of belting out a song with the Garland élan. She worked long and hard to become a star, and at eighteen she succeeded. Now that the satisfactions of stardom were hers, she didn't know how to exercise them. Although her need for closeness was strong, she seldom was seen with a young man who could be regarded as a serious date. Something in life had already escaped her, and she was to plunge headlong, for the remainder of her life, into an eternal search.

15

Early in March, 1969, I had only to mention that I had to return to New York, and Judy flew into hysterics. New York was a threat to her because of the staggering income tax she still owed. I had incidentally suggested that she appeal to the I.R.S. and see if she could perhaps make a deal with them, but she brushed the notion aside. Now I realize she was too drained to face any such problems.

Our friend and neighbor, Richard Harris, the producer and real-estate tycoon, was interested in one of our projects, a film called *A Day in the Life of Judy Garland.* No film had ever captured the excitement of a Garland audience. And a New York firm made us an irresistible offer: a franchise program to set up approximately five hundred first- and second-run theaters throughout the United States, each theater to seat about 350, the venture to be called Judy Garland Cinema. Judy's role in the company was not exacting. She would make herself available for interviews in New York or California for public-relations promotions on the theaters and for all openings. The company was giving her an offer of cash against a percentage of the venture's profits. Aside from my connection as an executive of the company, Judy would have an income for life. The idea appealed to me enormously. She was tired of having to sing. I knew that if she didn't have to, she would want to sing once in a while. We would be able to live on what I earned, but I was pleased at the thought of providing her with an independent income.

So it was essential for me to fly to New York, where I would set up my part of the minitheater deal. On my return I would present Judy with a contract for the use of her name. I hoped Judy would accompany me, but she refused. She didn't want me to leave her. She screamed and ranted and pulled out all emotional stops. She reminded me of how happy we were in London. I reminded her we wouldn't continue being so happy until I established myself as breadwinner in the family. I didn't intend to live off of her. We parted on a bitter "The hell with you, I hope I never see you again" note.

I missed her and worried about her. And wondered how I could make an overture without losing face. Johnny Ray solved the problem by calling me and putting Judy on the line. When I heard her voice, I realized how much I'd missed her, and there was a break in her voice as she confessed a similar feeling. She was concerned for fear my departure from England would result in another waiting period before we could legally marry. When she was reassured on this point, she settled down in our little house to await my return.

Our reconciliation was beautiful, but there was little time to enjoy it. During my ten-day absence in New York, Judy had managed to sign a contract for a Scandinavian tour with Johnny Ray: four concerts with very little money, no expenses, and too little rest between appearances. Allowing her just one day's pause between concerts seemed to me both thoughtless and dangerous. The only thing I could do was to watch over her and pace her activities. Her rest at the mews cottage had restored some of her strength. Our plan now was to be married and after a brief honeymoon on Majorca continue on to fulfill Judy's Scandinavian obligations.

We were formally married at high noon on March 15, 1969, at the Chelsea Registry Office, and afterward we drove to Marylebone Parish Church for a service of dedication and prayer. In our party were our dear friends Bumbles Dawson and Johnny Ray, who was to be my best man. Judy was in a blue chiffon mini, draped at the neck and sleeves with ostrich feathers, a tiny cap on her head. To hold Judy was like holding a frightened little bird; you felt her bones through the fragile skin and the slight tremor that controlled her. Yet she was radiant. As she faced the spotlight of the press and her fans, she looked poised and confident.

"I feel sixteen again," she said. "I don't look it, but I feel it." And to me she added with a pixie grin, "I can nag now that I'm married."

She had invited her old friends who happened to be in London to the reception at Quaglino's, in the West End. Few turned up, but her fans were there in overwhelming numbers, as well as the press and the photographers. I think Judy was hurt by the indifference of her friends, but she shrugged it off gallantly. There was music and champagne and a magnificent wedding cake that was given to us by Talk of the Town. The cake wasn't taken out of the deep freeze early enough, so we had some difficulty in cutting it, but Judy and I were deliriously happy. We clung to each other and gained reassurance from our closeness. "Finally I am loved," she whispered.

The orchestra played "Over the Rainbow," but Judy didn't feel like singing it. Sitting on the floor of the stage, together we sang "You Made Me Love You." All tragedy and sorrow seemed to be forgotten. Among those present was Patricia Peatfield, the partially paralyzed young woman whose life had been changed when she heard Judy sing "You'll Never Walk Alone." The love of her fans turned the air electric with emotion.

117

"Shall I tell you what it's like being married?" she said to a member of the press. "Suddenly I feel at peace, out of that damned spotlight. That's why I feel so lucky. No more rows, no more scenes at clubs and theaters. I've got the kind of contentment now which passed me by all the time I was in Hollywood."

To a young woman reporter, she added, "I'm going to make this marriage work for both of us—if it's the last thing I ever do in my whole life. There's too much at stake for it to fail. I see it as my very last bid for real peace of mind and contentment. I've suffered too much, and I've been unhappy too long. With Mickey, I feel reborn."

The press was bugging us about the religious ceremony. "What does it matter?" I said in an offhand way. "I'm Catholic, and Judy is Jewish." I said it in fun.

But the next day we got two offers to appear in Tel Aviv.

On the way to the airport, Judy showed me a gift from the Reverend Peter Delaney. It was a facsimile of the entry in the marriage register of a marriage solemnized at the parish church of the parish of St. Marylebone. The principals were Robert Browning and Elizabeth Barrett, and the date was September 12, 1846. I was to find the pamphlet, with a facsimile of one of the *Sonnets from the Portuguese,* among her papers a little more than three months later, when I was looking for something to give me comfort.

16

Judy had a child's wholehearted delight in surprises. Our honeymoon flight was scheduled for a twenty-minute stopover in Paris.

"Let's go out and look around," I suggested.

"But it's such a short stopover," Judy objected. "Where can we go?"

"Don't ask questions, hon."

I had bribed a steward to take off our luggage and hire a car for us. As Judy saw the luggage being stowed away in the cab, she knew what I had done and was enchanted. I asked the driver to go slowly, mindful of Judy's terror of speed in a car, as well as on a plane.

"What about Majorca?" she asked, curling up in the seat and looking up at me.

"Paris is for honeymoons," I replied.

We registered at the Georges V Hotel, freshened up, and then took another cab, asking the driven to take us to the Left Bank. We visited a half-dozen *boîtes*—all dark as caves, with narrow, winding stairs—that were perhaps wine cellars or torture chambers centuries ago. Judy and I must have looked like smugglers in our deep-crowned, wide-brimmed felt hats. After we had a few drinks, toasting ourselves and our future, we were hungry. The driver took us to Raspoutine, and we asked him to wait. Again the steep incline of stairs. Judy clung to me. "Dammit," she said, "nothing's on one level."

All of Paris seemed to be on an Oriental kick. Low couches, thick pillows in Persian colors. "Once you sit down," she said with good-natured grumbling, "you can't budge."

Judy was immediately recognized. Naturally there was much excitement. We managed to order food; it was hours since we'd had a snack on the plane. Before we were served, however, the entertainment began, and we watched politely. "It's like Ed Sullivan's program," Judy murmured, as we listened to the soulful strolling violins, the robust tenor, and the plump soprano. We cringed at the sadistic skill of the knife-thrower.

"I adore those guys," Judy said, laughing. "They come out and take their bows before they've done anything."

The manager appeared before us and asked politely if they might take photographs. Judy nodded graciously, although she was starving. The violins surrounded us with a serenade that was charming but not nourishing. Flashbulbs exploded. "The hell with this," I said, grumbling. "We want to eat."

By now, however, Judy was self-conscious. As the strains of "The Wedding March" quivered in the air, all eyes were on her, and she behaved with extraordinary aplomb, considering that her poor stomach was growling for food. We finally bowed our way out, sprinkled with stardust but still famished.

"Let's try New Jimmy's," I suggested. There we were met by Régine, the fabulous woman who runs the cabaret. She is warm and outgoing, and she and Judy became instant friends. Still hungry but slightly loaded, we decided to try Monsignore's. We didn't think it was really too late for dinner. Nor was the restaurant crowded. Judy decided on veal piccata. The maître d' explained it was an impossible request.

"You have veal, don't you?" I asked.

"Yes, *m'sieur*."

"You have lemon?"

"*Mais, oui*."

"Okay, squeeze it."

In our happy state, this seemed a hilarious conversation. With the veal piccata came the strolling players. Again we were serenaded; again Judy was constrained to control her hunger.

If I give them a tip, I thought, they'll go away. The lead violinist didn't stop bowing his fiddle as he slipped the bills between the strings. Now they played with considerably more zest and animation, like wound-up toys, refusing to budge from our table. Judy said, "You tipped them too much; they think we want more." All the while she was bowing and smiling to everyone in sight. "I'll starve," she murmured in an aside. "In another minute I'll die."

Since she couldn't possibly touch food while she was the center of attention, the best thing to do, I decided, was to take the veal home. I asked for a doggie bag, which upset the management, but they finally agreed to give it to me. When they brought it out on a salver, I took one whiff of it and said, "Please give it to our driver."

They bowed us out, offering Judy a pretty doll as a souvenir, and we drove back to the hotel, passing the Eiffel Tower in the moonlight. At the entrance of the Georges V, I dismissed the driver, tipping him, and we took the elevator to our suite.

"Where's the veal?" Judy asked, with a little tiger growl, preparing to feast.

"You have it," I said.

"I have the doll. Where's the veal?" she repeated.

We'd left the doggie bag in the taxi. But on a honeymoon, who needs food?

17

Judy was ecstatic during our Paris honeymoon. Not even the trouble she was having with a sore foot kept her from total enjoyment. She was often bothered by an old injury to a toenail, the result of an accident from her movie-making days when she danced in so many films. The toe was apt to get infected and become very painful. There was nothing to do but soak it, but she grumbled a little at missing the splendors of Paris.

We left the city with regret to fly to Stockholm for the first concert Judy was to give with Johnny Ray, on March 19, 1969. We made ourselves comfortable on the plane—as comfortable as Judy could be, considering her terror of flying. I loosened my tie and took off my shoes. When the plane landed for a twenty-minute stopover in a small Swedish town, Judy and I remained in our seats.

"Aren't you going out for the interview?" a stewardess inquired.

"What interview?" I asked. "Nobody told me about an interview."

Just then the press came swarming aboard, at least a dozen

men, some armed with cameras. They informed us the meeting
had been arranged by the promoter, so we agreed to it. Judy
was frightfully upset; she wasn't prepared for their appearance, and she wanted time to get herself together. (Even under
ordinary circumstances, Judy needed considerable time before
an interview, and when I grew impatient, she would say, "If
you give me two hours, Mickey, I'll be ready." And she kept
her word.)

Now she didn't even have five minutes. When I showed
some anger at the intrusion, she tugged at my sleeve. "Please
don't get too angry with them, Mickey. They'll take it out on
me."

With a few minutes' grace, we went out, and Judy gave the
interview. I noticed that a sound recording was being done
and also a film, but I thought this was part of the press cover-
age. Although some passengers deplaned here, we saw that all
seats were again occupied. The press had bought tickets for
the empty places and proceeded to watch our every move. Judy
was growing more nervous. I finally made a deal with them; a
couple of the photographers would be allowed to photograph
Judy if the rest left her alone.

In the Stockholm airport we went directly to the V.I.P.
lounge and found more members of the press and a motion-
picture cameraman waiting for us. We finally drove into
Stockholm. The city was crowded with sports spectators, here
to watch the hockey teams—the Russians were playing against
the Czechs. We registered at the Apolonia Hotel and were
given a suite with an adjoining room to be used as a dressing
room. We were lucky to have Bridget Johansson in charge of
Judy's wardrobe. Bridget had been divorced recently from Inge-
mar Johansson, the former heavyweight champion of the world.
She was of tremendous help and even took care of my clothes.

We arrived in the evening. The first of the four concerts was
scheduled for the following night. In the morning I awakened
early and went out for some sightseeing while Judy rested. In
the afternoon we drove to the concert hall for rehearsal. This

was the first rehearsal with the orchestra that would accompany Judy throughout the tour. The players were all Swedish, with the exception of our conductor and Johnny Ray's drummer, who arrived from England. The rehearsal was typical stop and go, as is always the case with a new orchestra. Meanwhile Glynn Jones and I went over the lighting with the electrician and found it a bit frustrating. He didn't speak English, and Glynn and I were unfamiliar with Swedish, so all cues were called out in English and picked up by a Swedish interpreter, who then directed them to the lighting man. That fraction-of-a-second delay in translation can create a dreadful problem.

The wire for Judy's microphone was lost in transport, so another microphone had to be substituted. Judy had liked her own mike because of its small size. It came originally from Tom Jones's television show at the London Palladium, when Judy had replaced Lena Horne, who was ill and couldn't perform. Judy had told me that night in London how much she loved the mike.

Being a dutiful husband, eager to please his wife, I had gone to the audio engineer after the television show and asked where I could get a similar mike for Judy. "Would you give me the name and the model so I can buy one in London?"

The engineer seemed amused. He told me there were only two mikes of that kind in England, and they were used on the *Tom Jones Show*—as if I didn't know. (The microphone, incidentally, was a Senshauser from Germany.) So I asked him for permission to take one to Judy's dressing room to make sure it was the one she wanted, and he agreed.

Judy was delighted. "Oh, yeah. It's great—so nice and small."

Whereupon I said to her, "What d'you mean—you're not giving it back to me?"

Judy stared at me, puzzled.

"Do I have to cue you?" I asked.

Her big eyes reflected a gleam of mischief, like that of a kid filching apples from a neighbor's tree. I then reported to the engineer that Judy wanted that particular mike. The fellow was quite put out, as though the mike were one of a set of his favorite cufflinks. Glynn Jones, who was standing by, nearly broke up laughing, so I said smoothly that Glynn would take care of the situation, which silenced him. But Glynn did. I paid for the mike in the end and tried to persuade the engineer to sell me the wire for the mike with its adapters, but he wouldn't. Judy had the mike she wanted, however.

Rehearsals finished, we returned to the Apolonia Hotel to prepare for the concert in the usual flurry of excitement and confusion. Judy was tired but stimulated. Johnny Ray would perform for the first half of the concert; then after intermission Judy would come on stage. She dressed at the hotel, and we drove to the theater. The stage door was mobbed. The pavements were icy, a hazard under ordinary conditions, but with people pushing and shoving and with flashbulbs blinding us, it was nearly impossible to get up the three or four steps to the building. We finally made it, breathless and disheveled. A dressing room was set up just off the stage, where we dropped our coats. Judy gave a final touch to her hair and dress, and it was overture time. She gripped my hand and whispered her regular litany: "Make me laugh—"

And then she strode out on stage, jaunty, smiling, poised, totally in control. I never got accustomed to the difference in the Judy waiting in the wings and the Judy Garland making her entrance. You wouldn't believe it was the same person.

While she was singing, I doubled around back into the lighting booth for a few minutes, then to the rear of the concert hall, listening for the sound, then into the audio booth, where to my surprise recording equipment was grinding away. Without introducing myself, I asked the engineer for a headset and asked also which one of the controls was for echo. He explained that he didn't have the authority to change the echo level from the advance settings.

"I have the authority," I said grimly and opened it up completely in order to ruin the recording. He was obviously not making a recording for himself, since the equipment was of studio caliber—which meant that somebody in charge was making a professional recording without our consent.

The performance over, Judy was inundated with fans congratulating her. The Swedish entrepreneur had arranged a big party without asking Judy if she'd like to have one. The concert had drained her, and she was eager to get back to relax at the hotel. "Just the two of us," she whispered to me.

Judy's condition worried me. I suggested that the Swedish entrepreneur and his party go ahead without us. We wanted to go back to the hotel to freshen up. While I may have given the impression that we would return, I never actually said we would. Judy was simply too exhausted to join the party.

One of the conditions in the contract which had caused me concern was the lack of rest for Judy between each concert. One day's respite was not enough. Apparently they didn't take into account that we'd be obliged to use that day of rest for traveling. Judy was showing worrisome signs of fatigue. There was a sunken look to her dark, beautiful eyes—always a barometer of how she felt—and she kept saying, "If I could only sleep. . . ."

Then on the off night she swallowed too many barbiturates in a frantic attempt to get some rest. We couldn't revive her. I was beside myself with fright. One of the Swedish men with us was a physician. He agreed that Judy needed an injection of a stimulant immediately, but he was afraid to administer it. He suggested I crush up some amphetamines with water and inject her with the syringe he would give me. I threw him out. Such a procedure might have killed her.

I was frantically slapping her cheeks, trying to wake her up. Then I remembered what my mother did with aspirin when I was a small boy. I crushed some ups with a spoon and mixed the powder with orange juice. I picked Judy up from the bed and held her on my lap, where she cuddled like a babe in arms. All the while I was talking to her: "Wake up, Judy. You're going to be okay, hon. . . ." while I spoon-fed her.

She finally opened her eyes, and a faint smile touched her wan face. She nestled closer in my arms. "Mickey, I'm sorry."

You couldn't stay mad at her. "Hon, it's okay."

She recovered in time and was ready and able to go on, but the officials canceled the concert. They tied up the ten-thousand-dollar advance that had been put in escrow for her.

The last two concerts went off as scheduled and were triumphs for her, with standing ovations from her Scandinavian fans. The promoter, Arne Stivell, and I had a few words —very few, since my Swedish was on a par with his English. We decided that the way to recoup his loss was to film the concerts as part of an overall film based on my original concept of a day in the life of Judy Garland.

Judy was delighted, since I was to produce the film with my new Swedish partner. The idea was one I'd discussed with her while we were still living at the Ritz. She had once remarked that most people don't realize the vast amount of time and energy expended in presenting a concert.

"You're right," I had replied. "Why don't we show them?" I had suggested that we shoot in sixteen-millimeter black-and-white film to achieve a newsreel effect, with the mobility of a hand-held camera, while Judy went through impromptu situations during the day. Then we'd film the concert itself in color. We followed this plan, and achieved some remarkable segments. We never dreamed, of course, that it would be the last record of Judy Garland performing.

It was a short ride to Malmö, Sweden, by prop plane. The hotel was perfect; our suite had an adjoining wardrobe room and a fine view of the water. We were an hour by boat from Denmark.

"Hon, would you like to go out to dinner?" I asked.

"Yes, of course. Where?"

"To Denmark, naturally."

The suggestion fascinated her, for she had a great love of water. Leif Matheson and the camera crew then made arrangements for us to board a ship for the brief trip to Copenhagen. We were guests of the captain in his quarters. Captain Christiansen was a warm and jovial man who reminded us of Victor Borge. He allowed us to stay on the bridge with him at one point. "I'm going to retire," he told us with a chuckle, "buy a small boat, and charter it to rich Americans."

"Why wait?" I asked. "Let's take this one and head south."

His wife was delighted to meet Judy and made a move to sit down beside her, but Captain Christiansen stopped her. "Up, up," he said. "I am the captain of this ship. I'll sit next to the lady."

Our visit to Copenhagen had not been announced by the press, so we had a relatively quiet and relaxing evening. We ate and window-shopped and enjoyed being by ourselves. Judy looked more rested and was in better spirits.

We returned to Malmö by hydrofoil, which was a great mistake; the trip was noisy, bumpy, and wet, and all the good Judy had gained from our spontaneous jaunt was undone.

The following day, Sunday, was Judy's next concert, at the King Kroner Club in Malmö. Problems began to pile up. Whoever measured the stage must have used a fractured ruler. It had to be extended to accommodate the large orchestra. Even at that, there was little room left for Judy and Johnny to move around during their performance. It was almost impossible to tone down the brass section to the necessary degree. The dressing rooms were perched at the top of stairs that lurched like a ladder. The bottom step was missing as you exited from the stage. Johnny forgot about it after his performance. I damned near broke my neck helping Judy offstage; as she handed me a bouquet of roses with unwrapped stems, thorns bit into my hand like twenty vaccination shots.

Here too while Judy was on stage, I ran up to the balcony to check on the sound, lighting, and camera crew. I discovered the recording equipment was monaural and promptly blew my stack. Recording under studio conditions is difficult enough. Recording a live performance on location presents incredible odds, but you record in stereo, usually eight-track, and do your mixing (that is, blend the instruments by section, along with the voice on a separate channel) afterward. This idiot was mixing live!

Another party after Judy's performance. It was held in the penthouse, and we were informed who the guests were to be. On our way out we stepped into the gambling casino for a short while. A woman guest was pocketing an ashtray as a souvenir. I asked the manager, who was watching her, if we might also have a souvenir. He was very gracious, thinking, no doubt, that I too had my eye on an ashtray. Instead I went directly to a big potted plant, which I picked up and handed to Johnny Ray, who looked like he was in a skit from Olsen and Johnson's *Hellzapoppin*. I also grabbed the casino sign with its brass base. I thanked the manager with quite a flourish, and fortunately my antics amused him. Since we were uncertain of our welcome at customs, I removed the sign from its base, wrapped it up as a picture, and passed the stand off as a microphone stand. The inspector looked at it strangely, but we were out of customs before he could object.

Later the brass sign, like our rubber plant, Herman, added to the mod atmosphere of our mews house. When we were expecting guests, we put it outside the front door. It was astonishing how many strangers came up and rang our bell, honestly believing the cottage was a casino. This always puzzled us because everything on that sign was in Swedish except for the four oversized playing cards in its center. "Sorry," I would say to innocent strangers. "Members only."

Radio Denmark was eager to carry an interview in depth with Judy and toward that goal arranged for her to be questioned by Hans Vangkilde the day following the Copenhagen concert, which was the last time Judy was to appear on stage.

It contains remarks that were familiar to me, since Judy had reiterated them, and they were memorable for their poignancy.

"It's lonely and cold on top. . . . You're surrounded by people who are not truthful and who are using you. And if you're unaware, as I am, and if you're a woman, it could get pretty rough sometimes. . . . You don't always keep on the top. No one does. My career, my life, has been like a roller coaster. I've either been an enormous success or just a down-and-out failure, which is silly. Because everybody always asks me, How does it feel to make a comeback? I don't know where I've been. I haven't been away. I've been working all the time. . . .

"I've worked very hard, you know, and you plant—I've been lucky enough, I guess—to plant a star. If you've done that, then people want either to get into the act or else they want to rob you emotionally or financially, whatever—as they've done me. Then they walk away, and my God, it's lonely.

"Show business has become much rougher, the people—since I was a little girl first entertaining, not the people on the stage, not the entertainers, but the people who you are surrounded by, the agents, the press. It's gotten rude!

"I don't mind people coming up on the street who recognize me. I don't mind that, not if they're nice. I like to meet people, and it's fun to walk down the streets of a foreign country and have people come up and say hello. I like foreign countries. I like to shop and look in windows and collect porcelains. . . .

"In my private time, I make hats. I made this one I'm wearing. Well, I guess you'd just say it's a black broad-brimmed hat with a silver lining. . . . I designed the dress I wore on the stage in the concert last night here in Copenhagen. That was really the first I ever had time to execute and design. . . .

"I've been in show business too long, and I didn't have any fun in my life until I met Mickey Deans. I really haven't had a rich life until now, but it's been an interesting life. I like to sing now because I know I don't have to, because I'm happily married to a man who is about to give me the protection and help I need, and I can just do a concert now and then, when I feel like it. And at night when I've done a concert, I don't have to be alone in a hotel room. Now I can go home with my husband, and that's much nicer."

I treasure the tape of that interview for the optimism and health in Judy's outlook. This was a recording of a woman contemplating a new life.

We made progress on the film of a day with Judy. We were both photographed on the street, shopping at the hotel, and finally they filmed Judy and Johnny at their concert. It was agreed that I would have the American rights and the Swedish managers the rights to sell in Europe. But suddenly our Swedish friends disappeared with my production and refused our telephone calls and telegrams. I was finally obliged to fly to Sweden with our English attorneys and prevent them from selling or showing the film on the basis of the Swedish patent laws. Shortly afterward we went to the courts in London to prevent other distribution.

Judy was totally intrigued by my efforts for her. She would tell her friends, "My husband fights for me. My husband stopped the bad people from doing evil things to me. My husband takes care of me." I believe this unpleasant episode finally cemented Judy's complete trust in me.

Judy did not adjust well to the weather in Copenhagen. Winter left the populace exhausted, and although the snows had melted, there was not yet, late in March, a sign of spring. Night came much too early, and you needed aquavit to keep the blood moving in your veins. Judy, with her sensitivity to color and light, seemed to take on the melancholy of the city. Even the charm of our suite at the King Frederick Hotel failed to brighten her spirits. Yet we soon learned that the people of Copenhagen are a wonderfully patient lot, looking beyond the melancholy winter to a splendid spring.

Hans Jorgen Erickson, the hotel manager, had stood waiting at the doors for us as we arrived that first day in the chauffeured car. It was still raining heavily; the sky was munitions gray. But here was this distinguished Dane, holding a bright spring bouquet in the shape of a rainbow. He presented it to Judy as she entered the lobby, and she read what he'd written on the card: "To the only performer who can carry us all over the rainbow. Judy, we love you." The vision of this spare, impeccable Dane, graying blond hair above his open, fine-boned face with its deep-blue eyes, bending down to her with that exquisite bouquet was almost too much for Judy. I could see she was on the verge of tears. She accepted the flowers with some embarrassment and murmured an almost inaudible, "Thank you. . . . "

Mr. Telle Saaek, the reception manager, stood behind the dark-mahogany desk, waiting to greet us. Erickson had assigned him the task of looking after Judy's needs while she was a guest there. The lobby, although elegant, with paneled walls, antique furnishings, and portraits of the Danish monarchs, was small and narrow, with only a series of glass windows dividing it from the exclusive lobby restaurant. At the moment, this small area was packed with newsmen and newswomen and photographers, altogether about forty-five of them. Telle Saaek told me later he couldn't help noticing how like a small broken bird Judy looked as Erickson and I guided her to the elevator, after promising the news people that Judy would greet them shortly in our suite.

Meanwhile Johnny Ray arrived. Before going up to his suite (a smaller one on the same floor), he gallantly lifted a vase of flowers from the lobby and carried it upstairs to Judy.

We found rooms 511 and 512 charming, recently decorated with antique furniture and exquisite porcelains. The suite was tucked under the cozy eaves, where the rooms slanted and conformed to the architecture. The bedroom was paneled in warm wood, the bed itself a marvelous outsized four-poster. The bathroom was fully tiled, the dressing room completely mirrored. There was another bathroom off the living room which connected to the bedroom of 510. Since Judy was traveling with a great quantity of baggage and a large wardrobe, we decided she should have 510 as well. To cheer her up I had repeated what Erickson had told me—that this suite had housed many of the great performers, among them Sammy Davis, Jr., and Marlene Dietrich.

"The press is waiting," I said to Judy, who was cuddled up in an armchair. "Shall I call and say you're expecting them?"

"In a minute," she said vaguely. "Oh, Mickey, what shall I wear?"

In less than a half hour, I sent a call down for the press to join us in the suite, and I also ordered drinks and food. The news-media people were pleasantly surprised. They evidently had thought Judy might not agree to meet them. Well, for three hours of waiting, I kept them well fed and their glasses constantly replenished. Most of the time, I was behind the bedroom door, cajoling Judy to pull herself together, helping her dress and apply her makeup. From time to time I'd come out into the other room to assure them Judy would join them as soon as possible. She'd taken many ups, but they weren't doing anything for her.

"Judy, you've got to come out," I pleaded. "It's important for the concert. If you keep up this delaying tactic, they'll start comparing you with Marilyn Monroe."

Judy finally made her appearance, wearing a glittering black jumpsuit and holding a glass of vodka and pineapple juice in her hand. She looked fresh but delicate as she sat down on the couch, flanked by Johnny Ray on her left and me on her right. But her ready wit kept the members of the press amused. It was a bravura performance, considering her great fatigue.

The newspapers were kind to her, but there was a reference to her fragile appearance and mention of the canceled performance in Sweden and speculation as to whether she was strong enough to carry out her commitment to appear at Falkoner Centret Theater on the twenty-second. Mr. Blicher-

Hansen, general manager of the theater, was concerned, as eleven hundred seats had been sold for a record 125 kroner (about $18) each. This was a price that only one other artist, Maria Callas, had been able to command, although most of the great contemporary artists had performed at the theater in its ten-year history. Blicher-Hansen was also deeply concerned about Judy herself.

No more than I was. There was no sense in coaxing her to eat when she could scarcely swallow and her digestion was bad. When I was obliged to attend a business meeting the next morning, I asked Telle Saaek to stay with her. She was obviously in better spirits and even eager to venture out. Bundled in her fur coat and her big hat, she went down the street, escorted by the hotel manager, and visited a porcelain shop, where a large, beautiful plate attracted her attention. "I'll buy it for our house," she said, and had it wrapped and charged to her hotel bill. Then she and Telle left. Everyone connected with the project had doubts that Judy could give a concert, but they didn't know Judy as I did; the scheduled performance was the lifeline she desperately needed.

As the concert was arranged, Johnny Ray filled the first half. Judy was to appear after intermission, first to sing a duet with Johnny, "Am I Blue," and then continue alone for the last half of the program, which would last about sixty minutes. She was wearing a red chiffon dress with ostrich feathers edging its hemline. It was perhaps a poor choice, considering how thin she was, but there was something valiant in its bright color, like a red badge of courage. She was only ten minutes behind schedule, but perhaps the audience was worried about her, for their greetings were composed of emotions—love, shock, compassion, empathy—that do not normally greet the entrance of an artist. Judy stood beside Johnny as though holding him for support, and together they sang "Am I Blue." Usually when she strode on stage, it was the radiant Judy, the performer, but tonight she seemed to be feeling her way. The audience, sensing it, responded warmly. "We love you, Judy," they shouted, imbuing her with their confidence in her.

A stool was placed center stage, and Johnny walked off, leaving her alone, sitting there, the spotlight shining on her. Suddenly, in some magical way, she was the Judy the world knew. She was superb for the span of the performance as she summoned from the deepest and most remote parts of her being the energy, control, and concentration. "I may never go home," she called to them as their applause warmed and strengthened her. Those of us backstage listened with awe. People were crying as she perched at the edge of the stage, her great lonely eyes seeing all, loving all. If at times she had wavered or forgotten the lyrics, her love for her audience, giving all she had to them, more than reimbursed them for the lapses. They gave her a standing ovation; they shouted and wept and could not get enough of her. It was not only charisma or the Judy legend: This was the magic that the great movers of mass audiences have. You had to see it to believe it. Finally Blicher-Hansen came on stage and presented her with a huge bouquet of flowers in the shape and colors of a rainbow. He walked off, leaving her, small, fragile, yet so alive, like a flame, alone on the stage.

"Goodnight," she screamed, throwing kisses to her fans. "I love you very much."

And then she was gone.

Except for one paper, the reviews were good, among her best. The *Politek* wrote: "When Judy sang 'Over the Rainbow,' it was as if she sang it for the first time in her life, innocent and sweet. It was so beautiful we cried. Everybody in the theater stood up and cheered." There was no doubt that the concert had been a success.

Once it was over, however, Judy seemed to fall apart. She had gone beyond the point of no return; as far as energy was concerned, hers was totally depleted. She was out of Ritalin and very anxious; she had exceeded her dose that day and prematurely exhausted her supply.

"Mickey, I must have some," she insisted. It was now late at night, and I had no idea how to procure them for her. I spoke to a couple of bellhops and finally one agreed to take me to a hippy discotheque. The bellboy made a connection, and I paid a hundred dollars for a hundred pills. On my return to the hotel I found Judy still up and irritated. But I told her I had got them and that they were there if she needed them, and after fussing awhile, she dozed off without taking them. The sleeping pills, without the countereffect of the ups, finally did their job. In the cold, bleak dawn I turned off the lamplight and sat there at her bedside, looking down at her, so delicate and worn, and wondered where to turn for help in restoring her waning health.

Johnny Ray left that morning, as did Arne Stivell, although the film unit remained behind. We were not in the best of spirits. One cruel review and unkind satirical drawing of Judy from the dissenting newspaper had upset her. She fretted, unable to control her feelings. What upset me the most was that her health seemed to be deteriorating; it was not as good as it had been a few weeks ago. Even I, who was with her nearly every minute, was aware of the fact that rest and sleep were not the restoratives she usually banked on.

We left Copenhagen the following afternoon. Judy had a personal good-bye for everyone: Telle Saaek, Hans Jorgen Erickson, the staff, and the telephone operators. She was warm and charming. She wore one of her mod hats, and she held a vodka and pineapple juice in her hand. The city was cold and gray, but as I helped her into the limousine, she carried brightness with her.

18

Once a bad contract has been signed and sealed, there seems to be no way to make it right, particularly if the opponents are of different cultures and there is a language barrier. No matter how much we talked and arbitrated and came to agreements, there were still tag ends of the Scandinavian tour that came to plague us.

One of the Swedish entrepreneurs evidently had talked to the Swedish newspaper *Ekstrabladet*, which ran a story to the effect that the film *A Day in the Life of Judy Garland* would show her nude. This was totally untrue, but a denial never has the impact of the original statement. I would now be obliged to fly to London the following Wednesday, when the London court would make the decision on the ultimate fate of the film. We decided to spend a long weekend in Spain, a rest from the unbelievable cops-and-robbers experience in Sweden.

In the sun Torremolinos, on the Costa del Sol, is the blue of the ocean, the glitter of the sands, the red of clay-tiled roofs. Once a simple village, it is now a compound of modern hotels and an encroaching horde of artists, expatriates, and tourists. You have to look to find a Spaniard.

When we arrived, the sun had disappeared behind a dark, threatening cloud. Our hotel was pleasant enough, and flowers were waiting in our room. Unfortunately, a suite wasn't available, but the room faced the sea, with a door open to a small balcony. In the dark, pinpricks of light along the jagged coastline made it seem bright and festive. The weather was cold and threatening, though, and Judy took to her bed, completely exhausted. During the night she went to the bathroom and slipped, bruising herself lightly. I teased her, calling her Miss Chiquita Banana because she bruised so easily. "In a week, if you eat properly, you won't bruise," I said.

In the morning, while she was resting in bed, I decided to go downstairs to the lobby for newspapers. When I returned, she was locked in the bathroom. She responded with a drowsy, "Yes," but it was impossible to rouse her. I became frightened and broke down the door—to find her asleep on the floor. I picked her up and carried her back to her bed. The next morning we moved into an available suite. Judy thought she'd had a heart attack and recalled with wry humor the harrowing time in Hong Kong when it was feared she'd had a coronary. She was in the hospital at the time, and one of the nuns decided she was dead. When she came to, Judy had quipped, "Thank goodness. I thought someone had sent me to the wrong heaven!" The Chinese nun had thought this funny, and they had laughed together.

The local doctor was concerned about Judy. He changed her pills from Ritalin to a considerably milder medication, Longacton, and suggested that she be moved to the hospital. But I felt that I could help Judy more in the hotel, where she was protected from the press and bad publicity, which would worry her. So I stayed with her, making a joke of everything to keep her spirits up. I thought she was responding, but she fell again in the bathroom. She had been sick to her stomach as well, and I cleaned her up and carried her to the bed. She was conscious, but she seemed unable to hold herself up.

"Don't be angry," she whispered.

I held her on my lap and in my arms and tried to feed her

some cold grapefruit juice, which she loved when her mouth was parched. I held her and rocked her like a small child, and she turned to me and smiled, the most innocent goddamned loving smile, and I started crying.

She said, "I promise I'll be good," and I just held her and kissed her and rocked her back and forth. She was so frightened. She didn't want the doctor to come. She was terrified that she was going mad. I promised to keep the doctor away. By the time the maids came in, I made sure she was clean, her hair brushed back, and she was dressed in a pretty nightgown.

After a few days she seemed considerably improved. She was in good spirits, eating, and determined to get well. Her sense of humor returned, which made her as always a delightful companion. I had released the chauffeured car and rented a Fiat, and I took Judy for a ride along the coast. It seemed therapeutic.

But that night a change came over her. At first I thought she was talking in her sleep. Then I realized it wasn't me she was talking to but people who weren't around. She was ordering them to go away. For the first time since we were married, I felt sheer panic. My only thought was to get Judy back to London. Somehow I managed to get a plane reservation and got through to Matthew West, our public-relations man in London, asking him to arrange for a car to meet us at Heathrow Airport and to have the mews cottage ready for us.

I dressed, bundled Judy up, and guided her through the lobby and into the car without attracting attention. The press had mercifully deserted their post.

It was late at night and the air chill and damp, even with the car windows shut. Judy wasn't aware of what was happening. I held her close and prayed.

The plane was a B.E.A. Caravelle, with seats facing backward. I led Judy to a seat isolated from curious eyes, although to my discomfiture, another traveler soon chose to sit across the aisle from us. Judy was still irrational but fortunately her voice was low, the words slurred. I pretended to understand what she was saying and made what I hoped were appropriate replies. Still, the stewardesses and passengers nearby couldn't help but notice the behavior of the little lady who was rolling and unrolling an imaginary ball of yarn, who picked imaginary lint from my clothing, and who continued a conversation with a number of people visible only to herself. Fortunately, nobody appeared to recognize her.

I'd alerted Matthew West to have the car at Heathrow, but our flight landed at Gatwick Airport. It was three in the morning, and I had only a handful of Spanish coins and two five-hundred-dollar travelers' checks that were too large to cash at that hour. I sat Judy down beside the luggage in order to keep an eye on her while I tried to get a bill changed. I was finally successful and hired a car and driver. It was a tortuous drive home through a thick, moonless night. The driver was driving by instinct, guiding himself by the reflections alongside the road.

At one point Judy became disturbed again. She began screaming: "Watch out—children in the road—" He swerved and nearly crashed into the guideposts. As soon as we reached home, I rang up Dr. John Traherne, who came over immediately.

He wasn't sure what was wrong, but he feared possible brain damage. He warned me quietly to be prepared for the possibility that she might not fully recover. He gave Judy tranquilizers and left, promising to return the next day.

It was a long, dark night, but in the morning Judy woke up bright and alert, with no recollection of what had happened to her in the preceding twenty-four hours. After he examined her again, the doctor suggested that what Judy had suffered was the trauma of drug withdrawal—the abrupt discontinuance of Ritalin and the change to Longacton, which was milder. We hired a nurse to stay with Judy.

Meanwhile my lawyer, George Eldridge, and I went to court to keep the film *A Day in the Life of Judy Garland* in London. We claimed that we owned the world royalties and my "partners" only 50 percent of the Swedish royalties. The court felt that our case was with my "partners" in Sweden and not with the laboratory in London which had processed the film.

So the film was back in the hands of the Swedish entrepreneurs, who booked a return flight to Sweden. Our lawyer felt the only recourse was to discover a loophole in the Swedish laws which would enable us to upset the English order and have the film returned to us. It was urgent for us to fly to Sweden immediately, to be on the same flight as my Swedish "partners." We left Judy in the care of the nurse. I was deeply distressed about embarking on that flight, but it was vitally important to save the film. I dreaded to think what those people might do to exploit it.

There was no end to our James Bond experiences. As we boarded the plane, we saw a coffin being loaded in the baggage section. "You know who's in that coffin, George?" I whispered. "Probably Arne Stivell, hanging on to the film and gloating, 'Mickey can't find us here.'"

In Sweden we had a difficult time locating a Swedish lawyer who knew theatrical and contractual law. Without a lawyer possessing a Swedish degree, George Eldridge couldn't go into court. Finally George did find an attorney who had studied in the United States, and between them they unearthed a copyright law that made it a criminal offense to show any of the disputed film footage in Sweden.

I returned to London, tired but elated. Judy was considerably improved. I learned, however, that her representative in France had taken the initiative and arranged to book her in Paris the following month. Our solicitors accompanied me to his office. I was told Judy had agreed to do this concert. It wouldn't do to tell him Judy was in no condition to perform, so I deliberately made exorbitant demands—the right to film the concert, all television and motion-picture rights, the musicians to be paid by the organization and for overtime as well, and a suite at the Georges V.

"No deal," he snapped, which was exactly what I wanted.

Judy was making progress, but she found the weather depressing. Our friends Matthew West and Brian Southcombe, who were also our press representatives, had a cottage in Hazelmare, an hour's ride from Waterloo. They invited us out for the weekend, and Judy was delighted. Judy was very fond of Brian and Matthew; they are intelligent, cultivated, and soft-spoken. She adored trains with the passion of affectionate memory. The happiest part of her childhood was spent on trains, traveling from one town to another for vaudeville engagements. The glimpses of unshaded windows, houses where families lived together, people pausing by the tracks while the gates were down, children waving, warmed her heart and triggered her imagination. "I used to make up stories about the people we saw," she confided to me. "I think sometimes I envied those kids."

We occupied a compartment on the train which was totally private and accessible only from the outside of the car. Judy fretted for fear a strange passenger might join us, since the compartment was large enough for six. She suggested that Matthew use her lipstick to scrawl, "Chicken-pox victims," on the glass doors. Fortunately, no one intruded, and she spent the hour's journey sitting close to the double glass panes, looking out at the flying landscape. She seemed relaxed and content.

The cottage in Hazelmare had privacy, being set back from two other cottages on a thickly wooded lane. It was fair-sized, two stories high, with a marvelous big country kitchen that had its own huge hearth. Judy's upstairs bedroom overlooked the garden. Here we sat and talked about her health. Without frightening her, I suggested that although she was emotionally connected to pills, the time had come to make a clean break. With the help of us all and her own will to get well, she would make it. She tried so hard that weekend, sitting in the sun, resting, eating tiny amounts, and sleeping a good deal. It was the sleep that was important. I remember a doctor saying to Judy once that our health is based on the amount and the kind of sleep we get.

She was making such favorable progress that when Monday morning arrived and I had to return to London, she agreed to remain at the cottage for the week. Brian and Matthew would be with her, and I would join them every evening. We had received news from our London lawyers which lifted our spirits. Our Swedish attorney, Anders Saxon, was preparing a memorandum setting out the Swedish law that related to the copyright of the film. It was all in our favor. Things were looking up. If only Judy's health would improve.

The sun warmed the earth, and spring gave a sampling of its bounty. Judy ventured into the garden and watched Matthew dig in the rich, damp soil. The air was fragrant with growing plants. She talked idly of our stay in Paris and how we had watched the dawn from the steps of Sacre Coeur and wandered through the Tuileries, like so many lovers before us. She showed a great interest in the plants Matthew was cultivating and asked what species they were. She was her most gentle and endearing. On a gallant impulse Matthew denuded the garden. She returned to the house, her arms filled with blossoms, her spirits responding to their color and fragrance. Matthew continued to work in the flower beds, and when he returned finally to the kitchen, he found Judy sitting there, grinning and enormously pleased with herself. She had spent three hours reorganizing the kitchen; all china, utensils, and silver were in neat little groupings according to size and contents, the flatware lined up separately in its narrow stalls. He was delighted, since it was a chore neither he nor Brian relished. From then on Judy spent much of her time in the kitchen, often on cooler days reading before the cheery fire. Sometimes she lingered in her bedroom, listening to the radio, singing to herself, making notes for lyrics, or reading. She preferred biographies to fiction, and that week she was devouring *Citizen Hearst*. She had had no political affiliations since her brief campaigning for John F. Kennedy, but she was a liberal and a passionate defender of the individual's rights.

This was again a new side of Judy. She seemed at peace with herself, and the tranquility of her mood was reflected in her physical well-being. She was recuperating, yet I had the uneasy feeling she'd not reached the plateau of strength that had been hers before the Scandinavian trip. This was difficult to recognize because I was with her all the time, and when she felt good, there was a surge of the old vitality, which disarmed me. In my heart, though, I feared that her vital forces were draining away.

She was troubled by my absence in the city, but she no longer panicked. She showed concern if I happened to be late, however. "You don't think he's been in an accident?" she would ask.

"I'll ring up the office," Matthew would answer, and usually he found that Brian and I were about to leave for the station.

"I know he'll never leave me," she said once, "but things could happen like they did with my father."

She was often in the garden, waiting for me. After a cheerful dinner we sat watching old movies on television. She turned off the sound and ad-libbed her own commentary throughout the film. She made up her own story and added dialogue for the characters and situations. No matter what sort of film it was, Western, drama, love story, Judy's unique interpretation always turned it into an outrageous comedy. When the week was up, she was ready to return to our mews cottage. She was bright and cheerful. She curled up in the front seat of the car, her lap filled with fresh-cut flowers; she was twisting her wedding band, as she often did when she was happy. She reached out and touched the ring finger of my left hand, which was on the steering wheel. Originally she had refused, with that unpredictable streak, a double-ring ceremony, but after the church ceremony, she had changed her mind. This decision, I've always suspected, was due to the interest she thought I was paying a young lady. So we had a double-ring ceremony, and my circlet was probably the widest band in existence.

"I want everybody to know we're married," she declared.

"Mickey, you won't take it off when I'm not around, will you?"

I gave her my word.

One evening, however, as we were on our way to a masquerade party (Judy as a clown, I as an American Indian), I realized I'd left my ring in the soap dish in the bathroom. While I was debating whether to mention this oversight to Judy, she turned to me, visibly distressed, and said, "Mickey, I feel perfectly awful, but I left my wedding band on the dressing table at home."

It was the first and only time this ever happened.

19

F̶ew people in the theater hold possessions dear. Judy, for instance, had lived in big houses filled with fine vintage furnishings. Her first husband, David Rose, had had a definitive
collection of miniature trains. Her second husband, Vincente
Minnelli, a man of impeccable taste, had had a collection of rare
porcelains. Yet except for her clothes and her press books,
Judy claimed no sense of ownership. She treasured a photograph of herself and John F. Kennedy, a color shot in an or-
nate silver frame, a box with a snipping of my hair, and the
framework of our wedding cake. She had several pairs of ear-
rings which she prized, and when she misplaced one earring
shortly after our return to the mews cottage, she muttered,
"That's my mother—"

"What'd you mean, hon?" I asked.

I discovered that whenever something went wrong, Judy
would say, "That's my mother," as though her mother could
still, from the grave, exert an unhappy influence on Judy's existence. In the years I knew Judy, she often mentioned her
mother in great bitterness, but this was, of course, during the

time she was suffering greatly and it was impossible for her to find any redeeming virtues in her mother. "She was really the Wicked Witch of the West," she would repeat, and then after an outburst she would admit, somewhat shamefaced, "I never really hated her."

"I know," I said, "but whom else can you blame?"

Sometimes it's easier to deal with hatred than love. Sometimes love is the problem that can drive you up the wall or onto the couch. Judy could talk about her anger at her mother, but she couldn't deal with the intense love for her father.

In spite of her anger, Judy longed for her mother's love and for her mother's approval. One Christmas she had a batch of her poems bound and presented the volume to her mother as a gift. It was not a present that Mrs. Garland could understand, but she did thank Judy nicely. Whenever Judy was crushed by her sense of aloneness, she withdrew into herself and wrote poetry that was touchingly indicative of her isolation and yearning. The poems seem to have been lost.

Ethel had married William Gilmore, a pleasant man, but Judy found it difficult to accept a stranger in her father's shoes. Her relationship with her mother was unpredictable, at times affable, at times bitter. Ethel had been handling Judy's money, and not too successfully, until Judy was married. Yet she and her new husband, William Gilmore, were evidently in favor of Judy's romance with David Rose, since they accompanied the young couple to Las Vegas for what was practically an elopement. It was Ethel also who set up the management of Judy's home with David. Later, during Judy's second marriage—to Vincente Minnelli, the gifted director—Judy asked her mother to take charge of the nursery and the baby, Liza, while she reported back to work at the studio. An agent who handled her then recalls that there was no sign of disharmony between Ethel and Judy, that in those days the young Minnellis appeared to be an ecstatically happy family and there was no indication whatsoever of mother-in-law trouble. It is possible that during Judy's sessions in analysis the hidden anger against her mother was first ventilated. Perhaps before, Judy had always stifled her hostility, refusing to face it. That she had just grounds for her anger, judging by Ethel's extravagance and lack of financial good sense, is obvious. But misunderstandings didn't come out into the open until much later, after Judy separated from Vincente Minnelli. She was living in the Beverly Hills Hotel, aware for the first time in her life of having to pay bills herself. Ethel asked Judy to buy her a new car, and Judy, strapped for money, offered to pay for a secondhand car, an offer that evidently offended her mother. Ethel once sued her daughter for support, which was certainly the cream of the jest, considering the way she'd squandered Judy's earnings. Yet her effect on Judy was painful and permanent, and Judy suffered a breakdown after her mother's death. Too many emotions had been suppressed, and when a sense of guilt brought them to the surface, they were more than Judy could take.

All the men in her life were no doubt the elusive image of the Good Mother who would accept her, warts and all, who would love and cherish her. A friend of Judy's, a thoughtful, scholarly man who knew her well, once said sadly, "No matter how much love she gets, it isn't enough for her. Her needs are voracious. She is rather like Marilyn Monroe; she swallows her men."

Now I began to understand in context her often-puzzling behavior, when she would switch abruptly from a charming woman to a willful, contrary child who would goad me beyond measure. And all the while those dark waif's eyes were watching slyly: Will you love me, no matter how badly I behave? Will you, will you . . . ?

Sometimes Judy would suddenly react to others as her mother had to her, leading them on to expect something warm and kind—and then suddenly pulling the rug from under them. But I must say, those moments were rare. Mostly she seemed to treat people close to her as she longed to be treated in return.

Judy and her children: Liza, the daughter of Judy and Vincente Minnelli, inheriting her dark, striking appearance, her immense unchanneled talent from both parents, her high-key, nervous manner from Judy, her unbelievable capacity for good feelings and love for the world from her own miraculous little being. Lorna and Joey, children of Judy and Sid Luft, her third husband. Lorna, all little girl's curves and feminine vivacity. And Joey—Joey, thin, sensitive, introverted; Joey, Judy's image in male form, those enormous eyes with their whites and luminous quality, the great compressed feeling within the young boy's framework. How passionately Judy loved them, and how devotedly they loved her! The response between her and her young ones was something rare and beautiful. At a time when the generation gap is so painful in many Establishment families, Judy and her children glowed. When they were together, there was not a more joyous group in the world.

Now that we were back at the mews cottage, Judy spoke more freely about the children. It was June, and she had not seen Lorna and Joey since the preceding October. Sometimes she tried to rationalize by suggesting that the separation gave them an opportunity to gain their own strengths, but in her heart she didn't believe it. She had a deep hunger to be with the children, but she was almost fearful of making the first move toward them. My own feeling was that the two younger children, Lorna and Joey, should be spending more time with their mother, and our plans were hopefully to make arrangements for them to be with us in London for the summer. Meanwhile every so often I would put in a trans-Atlantic call from another room, and when the call came through and they were all on the wire together, nobody questioned who had initiated the move. They were so happy to be talking to each other. Judy plied them with endless questions about their lives. She worried less about Liza, now grown up, happily married to Peter Allen, and busy with her own career. She was enormously proud of Liza's success. At the same time, with

149

typical Judy ambivalence, she wished Liza still needed her. Trans-Atlantic calls to the United States were as casual as calls next door. Although Judy hadn't met my parents, I introduced them to her over the telephone, and after that, my wife and my mother held endless conversations and became telephone buddies.

Among Judy's personal treasures was a red leather-bound notebook that Roddy McDowall had given her years ago for the sole purpose of blowing off steam. It was called *Ye Olde Bitch Book* and had a thick sheaf of blank pages. She had been advised to write down whatever annoyed her and then tear up the page. It was good therapy, but in the past weeks Judy had made less and less use of it. She was developing a serenity of spirit which was heartening to see. She was no longer shy about expressing her sentiments. She could be as gloriously sentimental as a teen-ager. One day, having had no time to go to the barber's, I snipped off the ends of my hair. Later I discovered Judy had bought a beautiful jade box for the locks, adding a card with the date.

We decided to buy the mews cottage. Each day, the house became more and more our own. The safe in the living-room wall had been hidden behind a painting. We removed the painting and framed the safe. We bought furniture, most of it unfinished, and we sanded, painted, and finished the pieces. Judy had never before had an experience like this. At first her interest span was brief, but after a while she was able to sustain her efforts, and she helped in the slow finishing process that resulted in accomplishment only after many hours of boring labor. She so enjoyed all this; she was so proud of our efforts.

The skylight in our dining room was its only source of light. We bought yards of gold satin from a nearby shop and proceeded to make a tent of the room. We spent hours at the task, Judy holding the fabric while I was high on a stepladder, stapling material to the ceiling and walls, laughing as we banged our fingers, growing tired and impatient, resting and beginning over again.

She was earnest about her wifely responsibilities and made a valiant effort to cook dinner for us. I would look in at the kitchen every so often, remembering what Liza had once told me about Judy's culinary efforts. Sometimes when she and the children were together, Judy would decide to cook a dinner or bake a cake. Liza or Lorna would come into the kitchen and find a cyclone, pots and pans everywhere, burners going, batter ready—and Judy sound asleep, curled up on the floor.

During these days Judy, although improving, needed to be watched constantly. She had a tendency to fall down and hurt herself which came, although I didn't realize it, from a lack of coordination. Her vision wasn't good, either, although she refused to admit it. I was watchful without making her aware of it, remembering that Delores Cole had told me that when Judy was still working on the ill-fated *Valley of the Dolls,* she complained once of not being able to see.

We tried to coax her appetite with some of the good beef and fish London is famous for, but nothing satisfied her more than a bowlful of mashed potatoes laced with rich chicken gravy. If she was hungry, she'd gobble it up the first thing in the morning. It was filling and comforting and was perhaps some sort of symbol of security. She was voluble in her love for London and vociferous in her dislike of Hollywood. California was to her a miserable state of mind, what with its crass flesh-peddling, its exploitation, and its commercialism. There were too many painful memories of the film capital. She loved the privacy London afforded her. She felt safe here from the harassment to which the Internal Revenue Service subjected her in the States.

Most of our friends in London were from the entertainment field, but gradually we began to know our neighbors, who were mostly married couples and not associated with the theater. As Judy's strength increased, we went for long walks again, pacing ourselves so she wouldn't become fatigued. Her color improved, and she was eating more. Often when she couldn't sleep, we ventured out in the streets in the early dawn. It was a marvelous time to enjoy the sights, the churches and palaces and stately houses. Sometimes we got lost and stumbled on a network of crooked lanes whose ancient atmosphere would quiet our laughter and fill us with an awesome sense of personal discovery. This was the kind of life that was new to Judy —free of pressures, threats, schedules. We were both going through a transitional stage, growing, reaching out to each other in new understanding.

A friend of mine, when he heard of our marriage, sent me an excerpt from Erik Erikson: "Love . . . is a mutuality of devotion forever subduing the antagonisms inherent in divided function."

We were beginning to be hip to Dr. Erikson.

*Here and on the following four pages
are scenes from some of the Garland films.*

She made several films with
Mickey Rooney in the late 1930's
and early 1940's. This photograph
is from *Strike Up the Band*.
(Photo courtesy of the Museum
of Modern Art Stills Archive)

Judy was fourteen when she
made *Every Sunday* in 1936.
Here she is seen with another
M.G.M. star, Deanna Durbin.
(Photo courtesy of United Press
International)

The Wizard of Oz was perhaps Judy's most popular film. In the picture at the top she is with costars Jack Haley, Ray Bolger, and Bert Lahr. Margaret Hamilton (left) as the Wicked Witch of the West and Billie Burke (below) as the Good Witch cast their spells on Judy. (Photos courtesy of United Press International)

Scenes from the 1944 film *Meet Me in St. Louis* (above) and the 1948 release *Easter Parade* (below) (Photos courtesy of the Museum of Modern Art Stills Archive)

Judy and Van Johnson (above)
in the M.G.M. hit *In the Good
Old Summertime* and a scene
(left) from *A Star Is Born*
(Photos courtesy of The
Bettmann Archive, Inc., and the
Museum of Modern Art Stills
Archive)

Judgment at Nuremberg, above, was probably Miss Garland's finest dramatic performance. Below she is seen in her last cinematic performance, *I Could Go On Singing*, a 1962 United Artists release. (Photos courtesy of Springer/Bettmann Film Archive and the Museum of Modern Art Stills Archive)

of Judy Garland

(Photos from Steve Young and Mickey Deans)

The face, the voice, and the style and determination were always projected to the audiences she loved. Critic Rex Reed summed up her appeal when he introduced her last recording by saying, "She asked for more sympathy than we could afford to give her, and sometimes she got on our nerves, but then she'd step out on the stage.... She always paid her dues by making her audiences smile and cry and — I hate to say it — get involved." (Photos courtesy of Springer/Bettmann Film Archive)

20

That gentle, tranquil, all-too-brief period in the mews cottage. Judy often looked through her old press books, the written and pictorial history of her life. Even when memories stung, her wit did not desert her. When I tried to console her with the suggestion "What the hell, hon, nobody has twenty-twenty foresight," she retorted, "Yeah, but did I need to wear blinders?"

The truth, too painful for her, was also likely to hurt the man in love with her. For Judy had been in love often; it was part of her desperate search for reality. It is impossible to view her fantastically successful peak years at M.G.M. without considering the effects of her first and second marriages and also the fact that she now had an agent, or a series of agents, who were considerably different from her original manager, Mama Ethel.

Hollywood agents, like the original Hollywood producers, are a strange breed; smooth-talking, unctuous, in their dark suits, white shirts, and dark ties they often reminded their clients of embalmers. The profession itself appears to have been initiated as an offshoot of the hegemony that was in power. It seemed that heads of major studios had relatives—the population explosion was a ghetto way of life—and what do you do with nephews, cousins, distant relatives, who make claims on you?

Agents operated in a strange position that never seemed to affect their sense of barter or loyalty; the art of the double cross was perfected with a kind of "Would I lie to you, Louie?" deadpan sincerity. Yet even the callous emotions of these flesh-peddlers were touched by Judy's personality, as well as by the fact that she represented to them a fantastic source of income (10 percent of her earnings). She was in turn warm, friendly, hostile, difficult, loving, and unpredictable. She was very fond of Keith Brown, who was then with the Bert Allenberg agency. Keith took care of her radio bookings, and he recalls that she was absolutely magnetic. By the early forties she was no longer the plump, precocious child from whom the studio could hide her fantastic success. She was gloriously aware of her place in the M.G.M. hierarchy, and she enjoyed her position and its fruits. (Later, however, when she was cast adrift from the studio moorings, she was to recall bitterly only its threatening and domineering attitude, but at the height of her popularity she relished outwardly the satisfactions of her position.)

"And there were times," another agent friend of hers told me wryly, "when she let you know it." Judy could pull rank on you if she so chose.

Her first husband, David Rose, and her second, Vincente Minnelli, were outstanding men who gave much to her.

"The trouble with Judy," a friend who knew her during her first marriage told me, "was that she had no adolescence. She went from child to woman." The missing link nearly destroyed her.

There were few early teen-age crushes because Judy did not feel capable of coping with a boy-girl relationship. She was inwardly too shy. Besides, the studio was not merely a duenna but more like a Calvinist parent.

The adoring world thought it would be natural for Judy and Mickey Rooney to pair off in life, as they did so exuberantly on screen. Yet although Judy showed her affection for Mickey Rooney, it remained a friendly, utterly wholesome relationship. Mickey was brash, volatile, mischievous, enormously talented, and the most generous of friends. His weakness for tall, willowy beauties may have been the reason for his platonic feelings for Judy, which didn't help her ego, but he was curiously gallant where her feelings were concerned and always maintained that his affection for her kept him from involving her in his hectic, irresponsible life-style. Certainly their feelings for each other were deeper and more durable than most Hollywood relationships, and I still remember the warmth and admiration in Judy's voice whenever she spoke of him.

One of her first romances was with Tyrone Power, the handsome idol of the war years. "We were very much in love and going to be married," she told me. "But during World War Two someone convinced me I had fallen in love not with Tyrone but his picture on the cover of *Photoplay*."

It's not really out of context that movie stars—not the starlets who use the casting couch as a means of upward mobility but the authentically talented young actresses—often lead lonely private lives. Judy suffered through this period. Sometimes, she said wryly, she felt like a wallflower at the studio parties, where the middle-aged star-maker executives mingled with the eager young buds—until, of course, the moment when Judy was asked to sing. During that period she went out with a number of young men, but seldom did she date a man more than once. She had the usual run of crushes, but her first serious love after Tyrone Power was for David Rose.

David was an accomplished and successful musician. An Englishman who had studied music in the United States, he was at that time conducting a radio program starring Tony

Martin. He was an attractive man with the innate kindness Judy so desperately needed. They first met during a Bob Hope radio show, on which Judy was making a guest appearance. Their courtship, between Judy's working days and David's evening shows, stretched out for two years. More than a love of music brought them together. In the last year of her life, I never heard Judy express anything but admiration for David Rose.

When they announced their plans to marry, the studio brass went into violent action, not with guerrilla warfare but with blunt, outright edicts. Her fans would be disillusioned. After all, they thought of her as little Dorothy or as Judy, the girl-next-door companion of Andy Hardy. Marriage would destroy her image. But for once, her mother stood up for Judy. Ethel and her new husband William encouraged the young couple to elope, even flying to Las Vegas with them for the ceremony on June 10, 1941. Judy at nineteen was curiously unprepared for the role of wife, just as she was unprepared for any role but that of a triple-threat singer, dancer, and potentially first-rate actress.

You'd think that a girl of such extraordinary caliber should have been spared the everyday problems that beset a young matron. Judy, with all the good intentions in the world, had no time for the demands of a husband and a home, not at the rate the studio was using her. David had lived previously in a small, attractive house in the San Fernando Valley. Aside from his music he was greatly interested in miniature railroads and had a large authentic collection. A quiet, self-contained man, he didn't give a damn about the Hollywood brand of society, but Judy did; during that period she truly enjoyed an active social life. Friends who lived through that marriage with the Roses suggested it resembled that of Marilyn Monroe and Joe Di-Maggio. Judy persuaded David to give up the place in the valley. They moved into a big Hollywood-style mansion, the former home of the late Jean Harlow. Judy wanted to assume the role of a young Hollywood hostess; she longed to be the chatelaine of a well-run menage. But she was completely ignorant of the way to run a house, to plan menus, to arrange for dinner parties. Ethel took over, easing the way so Judy could devote all her time to her work. A series of couples wandered in and out of the big house. Hollywood servants are a notorious breed, pampered and coddled because their busy employers haven't the time to check on them and must therefore rely on their ministrations as an act of faith and need. As a result servants are the most status-ridden snobs of the Hollywood hierarchy, and although they are hired to run a menage properly, they are mostly ambivalent in their reactions to their luminary employers: You need me, you can't manage without me, therefore I am better than you. You may be a movie star, but you can't order a meal, you can't market, you can't function as a human being without me.

The couples Ethel engaged came and went. They had only cool amusement and indifference for the young bride, who knew nothing about running a house and was too honest to pretend knowledge. Judy turned to them for help and got instead a contemptuous reaction. Sensitive to any suggestion of being considered inadequate, she suffered cruelly. She could touch the hearts of the world with her voice, but her servants judged her by her inability to create a dinner menu with vintage wines which would give her guests pleasure. Judy was sometimes too rushed to get home for dinner even when guests were expected.

David was forbearing, aware of the strain she was under, but life was no longer as ordered and tranquil for him as it had been in his bachelor days. Judy, loving him, wanting desperately to keep him happy, did her girlish best. She even showed a loyal interest in his hobby of miniature railroads and added a new depot to his collection.

In this tenuous marriage it was the studio that turned out to be the Wicked Witch of the West. The top brass were against the marriage from the beginning, primarily because they were convinced Judy's fans would not accept her as a young matron.

When their little gold mine showed another obstinate streak and willfully eloped, the studio executives contributed enthusiastically to the destruction of the marriage. David Rose was eminently suitable to be Judy's mate. He had taste and humor, but he was totally unable to cope with the studio's sly, insidious forms of blackmail, which included threats to his own career. If Judy expected her David to fight the studio Goliath, she was sadly disillusioned. No one man could single-handedly take on Louis B. Mayer and his servile henchmen.

Judy expected in marriage a miracle man to save her. What she got was a charming, cultivated man, a fine musician who had no taste or talent for Louis Mayer's hysterics and devious ways. It is a testament both to David and Judy that their marriage managed to survive for eighteen months. Their separation was more in resignation than in the storms that accompany most breakups. How could any relationship survive the demands of stardom and Louis B. Mayer's disapproval?

Sometimes Judy was on stage twelve hours or more a day when a movie was actually being filmed. Even before production began, there were a multitude of demands on her time. Costume-fittings, sessions with the studio photographers for new still pictures, time spent with the publicity men who made demands, arranging for magazine photographers, interviewers, appearances to extoll the forthcoming film—voices screaming at her, a thousand demands for her attention: Judy, you've got to do this for the press. Judy, you can't gain another pound; the costumes won't fit. Miss Garland, your housekeeper telephoned—there's a crisis—

One small girl, looking far too thin, having the shakes from the ups and the lack of sleep, sometimes so jittery that she lost her breakfast, and all these demands on her, everybody wanting something. The fact that these demands were ostensibly for her good and were part of the stardom syndrome didn't make it any easier on her nervous system. She was already trapped by her talent and her great hungers into the life-style that would finally destroy her.

The sad thing is that she never got a sense of peacefulness until those last days in our mews cottage. A friend of hers told me later, "Part of Judy always belonged to the peaceful Kansas farm in *The Wizard of Oz*. I can see her rocking on the porch or in the parlor, with Toto at her feet."

How long Judy could have accepted that kind of mid-America life is questionable. The point is that she never got it. And when she reached the depths of exhaustion, when this kind of rest was the therapy she needed, she was far too spent to be restored by its benefits.

As an M.G.M. star she could accept with the objective eye of a professional her fine work on film, but her inadequacies as David's wife tormented her. And to top it all, she was dieting again. She was on a perennial regime of black coffee, cigarettes, and the abominable chicken soup that Louis B. Mayer insisted on feeding her. Little was known about proper nutrition then, and several stars actually starved themselves into ill health and death. So Judy's marriage and her first real hope of identity perished in the tragic glitter of stardom. The parting between her and David Rose was friendly, in sorrow rather than bitterness, and perhaps less the result of conflicting careers than the studio's determination to punish her for defying its expectations.

Meanwhile the studio kept her on a treadmill. In 1941 there was *Babes on Broadway*, using a timeworn plot—ambitious kids trying to make it big on Broadway—as a showcase for the studio's junior talent. Here Judy not only sang well but showed considerable unexpected talent as a mimic. (Perhaps her remarkable vitality and freshness stemmed from her recent marriage; the studio had deliberately put her back to work directly after her elopement with David Rose.)

A year later Arthur Freed and Busby Berkeley produced another likeable musical, titled *For Me and My Gal*. Arthur Freed, a distinguished songwriter whose hits included "Singing in the Rain" and "I Cried for You," produced fourteen of Judy's films at M.G.M. He was an early and loyal admirer who first announced that the big-eyed, stocky little girl had what her sisters lacked. These Metro musicals weren't much on plot or originality, but they were enormously satisfying bonbons. This time Judy had a new leading man, Gene Kelly, who'd made a great success on Broadway in *Pal Joey.* And George Murphy, much later to become senator from California, played the role of the boy who didn't get the girl, the nice guy who finished last. Senator Murphy remembers Judy sitting on a piano, imitating the late great singer Helen Morgan, while listeners were speechless with awe.

Judy was worried about *For Me and My Gal.* Since Gene Kelly was a professional dancer, she was apprehensive about their dance sequences together for fear he might find her inadequate. When Judy grew too thin, as she did in this movie, her weight barely touching ninety-eight pounds, the healthy vitality of the mid-American girl burned away, leaving her frail, her facial bones too prominent but with a kind of unique beauty.

Time magazine commented on her growing "dramatic sensitiveness, discipline, and talent." Now the good years of success were ahead, and all signs were go. Judy was a hot property, and the studio knew just how to turn out the musicals that displayed her at her best. In 1943 there was *Presenting Lily Mars,* based on a book by the fine interpreter of America, Booth Tarkington. It was a story of the rags-to-riches career of a small-town stagestruck girl, and after it was finished, Joe Pasternak, the producer, complimented Judy on being a quick study with lines and lyrics. The film was extravagantly mounted, but *The New York Times* suggested that M.G.M. should allow Judy to grow up and stay that way.

Exhibitors were screaming, Give us Judy! Give us Judy and Mickey! And the studio obliged. Judy and Mickey in *Girl Crazy.* Judy singing those memorable George Gershwin songs: "I Got Rhythm," "Embraceable You," "But Not for Me," "Bidin' My Time." Squeeze in at least one more gold nugget in 1943: *Thousands Cheer,* with Mickey Rooney. And the kids

(Give us Judy and Mickey!) in a series of guest appearances
that had the fans standing on their ears. "Let's go, kid," said
Mickey, grabbing her hand as they rushed out of the wings
onto the stage, young, bubbling with high spirits, the epitome
of healthy, exuberant young America.

Nobody mentioned the pep pills. Or the sleeping pills. Or
the fact that between pictures Judy would go on an eating
binge, gorging herself on the goodies the studio denied her.
There may have been a double reason for this carbohydrate
bender. She may have been suffering from low blood-sugar and
needed the quick energizer to pick her up from the momentary weakness. Or perhaps it was rebellion against Mr. Mayer's
despised chicken soup. Or even part of her deep antagonism
toward her mother and her great unrequited love for her
father. There were so many confusing, perplexing strands in
the pattern of her character that even those close to her were
baffled. Her sudden fluctuations in weight, however, were not
entirely the result of overeating. No one really knows what effect the ups have on the metabolic system, and Judy was beginning to suffer with retention of fluid. Still, before a picture
started, she could go on a starvation diet and lose the weight
quickly. No one seemed the least worried that this constant
gaining and losing might play havoc with her glands. There
were some rumors in rumor-happy Hollywood that Judy was
hooked on drugs, but loyal friends vigorously denied it. Addiction meant hard drugs, which Judy never touched. Who ever
dreamed you could become addicted to dexedrine? And nobody under the influence of hard drugs could turn out the
fantastic number of films Judy did. Not only for production values but for quality have these films of the forties become clas-
sics.

In 1944 there was the big one: *Meet Me in St. Louis*, on a
par with *The Wizard of Oz* and listed by *Variety* as one of the
All-Time Box-Office Champions. This was not only a milestone in her career but also a turning point in her private life
again.

Meet Me in St. Louis brought her and Vincente Minnelli together. Minnelli, a dark, striking, attractive man, a former stage designer, was a man of impeccable taste and artistic dedication. Unlike many of Hollywood's early directors, he was never superficial. He was tireless in his efforts to understand the characters of his film and to bring out the best in his actors. He and Judy had in common an enormous respect for their work, but their approaches were diametrically opposite. Minnelli rehearsed endlessly; his need for perfection knew no bounds. Judy, a perfectionist by instinct, rehearsed, did one take, and that was it. At first his exacting approach to directing had irritated her.

The film itself was set at the turn of the century and was full of wholesome sentiment, rich with nostalgia. Whether Judy originally balked at the assignment because of Minnelli's reputation as being a somewhat difficult and overly demanding director was never clear to anyone close to her. It took considerable persuasion on Arthur Freed's part to overcome her original objections, and fortunately she respected Freed, who from the beginning had shown such faith in her future. It was in this film that the world first heard Judy sing "The Boy Next Door," "Have Yourself a Merry Little Christmas," and, of course, "The Trolley Song."

Although Minnelli was given credit for the superb production of *Meet Me in St. Louis*, Judy showed little interest in him until the following year, when she did a straight drama, titled *The Clock*, again produced by Arthur Freed. Earlier in Judy's career, *Time*, not usually given to bouquets, had suggested, "If she were not so profitably good at her own game, she could obviously be a dramatic cinema actress with profit to all." She was at the peak of her fame, and the studio was paying her five thousand dollars a week.

The Clock, in 1945, gave her the first opportunity to exercise her talents as an actress. The story concerned a brief wartime love affair, tense, poignant, and touchingly dramatic. Robert Walker, Judy's leading man, was an unusually sensitive actor. Fred Zinnemann was directing, but he was taken off the production because, according to rumor, he and Judy didn't get along well. Vincente Minnelli was put on to finish the project. Now the timing seemed to be fortuitous. The growing love between Judy and Minnelli was as tender and poignant as the film they had just completed. Judy was always at her radiant and glowing best when she was working with a man she loved.

Minnelli, himself immensely creative and sensitive, appreciated Judy's many facets. He took an interest in everything she did. An erudite young man, he influenced her tastes. He persuaded the studio to let her act. *Time* gives Vincente credit for bringing "the budding talents of Judy Garland into unmistakable bloom."

They were married June 15, 1945, a week after her divorce from David Rose became final. The studio was delighted with Judy's choice of a new husband. Louis B. Mayer gave the union his unrestricted blessings, foreseeing, no doubt, a whole string of gilt-edged successes. Judy and Vincente lived, as befitted their roles, at the crest of a hill with the dream factory spread below them, and if any young couple had the right to believe in life, liberty, and the pursuit of happiness, it was the Minnellis.

21

Whenever Judy had a good thing going for her, it was almost as if she had an equal need to destroy it. Was this the result of the massive doses of amphetamines and barbiturates or
of the early pressures that now couldn't be contained under
the demands of work and wifehood? Yet she never lost her
great enthusiasm, and she and Vincente had a marvelous relationship where talent was concerned. Being such a creative
man, he helped to shape her talent. He had a definite function
in her life.

"Judy was a highly personable girl with a rich, funny wit,"
an old friend of hers told me recently, "but she was very ma-
nipulative. Whenever she answered the telephone, her voice
would change, assuming different roles, so that the caller was
convinced it wasn't Judy at all."

During this period the studio stars were all good friends,
and there was considerable socializing among them. Minnelli
was more socially inclined than David Rose had been, but he
was also disciplined. He was responsible for the whole picture

that was being shot, so he was not one to close the nightclub or the party. But if Judy was having a good time, she'd refuse to leave. She could stay up all night, being stimulated by the amphetamines, and her behavior would grow increasingly erratic. It was a great pity because she was at the peak of a career that gave her independence and adulation, and the fact that she couldn't enjoy it all was surely the result of accumulated fears. But then, how do you get a girl in Judy's position to deal with reality? At times she was extremely rational and logical, but often she was bombed out of her mind. By now those close to her realized the damage the pills were doing to her. They tried to cut them off, only to discover the servants were sneaking them in.

Yet in spite of the problems of two personalities, two careers, it is possible that Minnelli, with his rare character and dedication, might have succeeded finally in helping Judy explore and discover the truth about herself. But the attachment for amphetamines together with the influence of the star syndrome were taking her farther away from what help he, with a kind of loving shyness, extended to her.

At first the high spots in the marriage were predominant. When their first and only child, Liza, was born, they were ecstatically happy. Ethel was overseeing the nursery of her grandchild at Judy's request. All was in harmony between mother and daughter. One of Judy's agents, Keith Brown, doesn't ever remember hearing Judy say an unkind word about her mother.

Liza's birth was difficult for Judy, involving a cesarean section. Judy's health wasn't good; large weight losses and gains and the toxic results of the pills had left her weak. It took her longer to recuperate than was anticipated. The studio was growing impatient. Judy had expressed a wish to retire. Perhaps the image of an idyllic home life, off pills, being a wife to Vincente and mother to little Liza, had more appeal than the trappings of stardom. Perhaps some deep instinct for self-preservation was warning her: This is your chance for the rainbow, Judy—don't blow it.

A good marriage, but Judy was suffering. Quarrels with Vincente. When she walked out on him and the baby, she was psychically walking out on all that was good and healthy in her life. But he persuaded her to come home, and she did. Her attitude must have puzzled Vincente: She had so much going for her; why then the unpredictable behavior? It was hard for a disciplined man to grasp her inner problems.

The studio meanwhile had pictures lined up for her. Despite her growing rebellion, the top brass knew that when you had Garland in a picture, she'd come through in all departments. She sang as only Garland could, she could act up a storm, she danced well, she could turn on the charm.

22

Look through her scrapbooks, and you see only success. Judy triumphs. 1946, you remember, is the year Liza was born. March 12, 1946.

It was a good year for M.G.M. and Judy Garland, now a superstar. *The Harvey Girls*, another lavish Technicolor production, is also listed by *Variety* as one of the All-Time Box-Office Champions. The story, trivial again, was based on Fred Harvey's waitresses traveling to the untamed West, but it had Judy's marvelous hit song "On the Atchison, Topeka, and the Santa Fe." Ray Bolger was in the film with her, and a handsome young actor, John Hodiak, was her lead.

Released also that year: *Ziegfeld Follies of 1946*, produced by Arthur Freed, directed by Minnelli, had a parade of M.G.M. stars, with the studio's imprint of lush settings as well as talent. Fred Astaire, Fanny Brice, Lucille Ball, William Powell, Gene Kelly, Red Skelton, and of course, Judy.

It was a year of triple hits: *Till the Clouds Roll By*, the biography of Jerome Kern, with Judy singing "Look for the Silver Lining" and "Who?" while Lena Horne chanted another

Kern classic, "Why Was I Born?" and Dinah Shore sang "They Didn't Believe Me."

In 1948 Judy starred in *The Pirate*, a musical based on the S. N. Behrman play, written originally for the great stage stars Alfred Lunt and Lynn Fontanne. She was visibly ill in this picture, her nervous gestures and trembling hands betraying her taut nerves. But when she sang the Cole Porter song "Be a Clown," you forgot everything but Judy out there, performing. In the same year Arthur Freed produced *Easter Parade*, with music and lyrics by Irving Berlin. Again, it was an M.G.M. natural, with Judy in a familiar role, that of the small-time dancer who finally makes it big, and opposite her was Fred Astaire. *Easter Parade* is still seen on television and is another of *Variety*'s All-Time Box-Office Champions. Everyone loved the film, including most critics. Kate Cameron, of the New York *Daily News*, while giving it three and a half stars, suggested, "Judy, wan and frail, needs a little more flesh on her bones to give her more verve and bring her up to her old standard as an entertainer."

Later that year she appeared in another musical, *Words and Music*, a romanticized biography of two highly gifted musicians, Richard Rodgers and Lorenz Hart. Mickey Rooney played the role of Hart, the ill-fated lyricist who was a victim of drugs. Judy sang two memorable songs that were to become part of her repertoire: "Johnny One Note" and "I Wish I Were in Love Again."

Time called her "the triple-threat girl."

23

The contemporary star speaks casually of "my analyst." Almost all the young talent today is in analysis or has been analyzed. Sessions at Esalen, group therapy, group encounters, are discussed with almost embarrassing candor. "But when I went into analysis back in 1942," Judy told me, "you'd have thought I was committing the Original Sin."

She was going through a period of great emotional and physical stress, and at the suggestion of a dear friend she consulted Dr. Karl Menninger. The Menninger Foundation, in Topeka, Kansas, has pioneered in many methods of restoring nervous and confused people to a vital balance and an ability to return to a normal way of life. Dr. Menninger sent her to see Dr. Ernst Simmel, a distinguished psychologist who was a refugee from Nazi Germany. Her mother, ever alert to any move that might lessen her influence on Judy and might anger the studio, heard that she was in analysis and relayed the news to Louis B. Mayer. Mayer didn't see the danger signs in Judy which were portents of an emotional breakdown. He only saw that Judy might be lost to M.G.M. and that the psychiatrist might lessen Mayer's influence on her. This he wouldn't tolerate, and Judy finally gave in to his demands. The old fear of the male authority figure was still strong. She gave up analysis—for a year.

In the interim nothing improved for her. She was working hard, and when she worked, she was on Ritalin and barbiturates. She swung to extremes in temperament; she was either in a manic mood or deeply depressed. A man who was deeply in love with her at the time and concerned about her welfare said that she loved intrigue whirling around her, she wanted excitement and loud music and the unfettered bustle of night life. "And," he added sadly, "she goes for what she wants."

Later on, Judy sensed that she must go back into analysis because it was probably the only door marked "Hope" for her. "I got up at six, went to my analyst's for an hour, used up a box of Kleenex, and got to the studio set by eight," she told me in a rare moment of confession. "And by the time you've finished with your fifty-minute session, dredging up the past, you're not much good for anything else for the rest of the day. I worked until six, saw the analyst for another fifty minutes, and then drove home."

Home to the elegant house Minnelli had decorated with superb taste and where little Frances Gumm felt ill at ease and out of place. Minnelli, a thoughtful, introverted man, found it increasingly difficult to understand her erratic behavior. For him the studio was the Establishment, and Judy, a generation before today's rebellious youth, was suddenly very anti-Establishment. To Minnelli she was a girl who had the world before her, who was admired and worshiped, and who risked it all with her baffling behavior. No doubt he was a demanding husband, as well as an exacting director, but he was utterly devoted to what was in her best interest. They stayed together, patching up their marriage mostly for Liza's sake and sometimes enjoying periods of happiness.

A friend who knew Judy then said she behaved schizophrenically, but a psychiatrist might not have branded her as such—because there was always a foreign agent behind it. People habituated to amphetamines often develop symptoms of paranoid schizophrenia.

"Why am I like this?" Judy once asked a friend despairingly. "I don't want to be." There was a new problem. If some of her problems were ironed out in analysis, new ones appeared. And now Judy became chronically late.

Hollywood is compulsively time-conscious. Minutes stack up in dollar signs; the adding machine runs relentlessly, chalking up overtime for unions, for the staff, for everybody involved in the making of a film. And Judy, who since her vaudeville days had been taught to respect promptness, was suddenly acting like a primadonna, not out of ego but from deep-rooted pain.

The set was ready, the staff was ready, all was in waiting. Thousands of dollars were involved in each take. Where is Judy? You feel the tension. Was this Judy, the good little trouper? A new Judy, shut in her dressing room. If she didn't feel like learning her lines, she made an excuse not to. She missed early appointments. She was suddenly costing the studio thousands of dollars, all unnecessary cost. The more directors and producers tried to talk to her—and this included Minnelli—the more suspicious she became. She felt they were all just pacifying her so that she would continue to produce. She felt like a money-making machine. Nobody really cared about her.

It is only fair to look at both sides of the coin. Judy was late, and they called it temperament. They saw it for everything but what it really was—a warning of a physical and emotional breakdown. Not that the studio brass could be entirely blamed for their apprehension. They were businessmen, and there were millions of dollars tied up in Judy. Once, she had three pictures on Broadway, and the studio was worried for fear some scandal or adverse publicity about her would kill the films. In the late forties the American public expected their film idols to be above scandal.

And the lateness of their star. At M.G.M. they couldn't balance the budget any longer. Her time lag was now costing them as much as 20 percent of the picture's cost. When she tossed away her inner time clock, Judy took another step closer to her break with the studio—the only authority figure still able to control her.

Analysis didn't help. As a matter of fact, she felt worse, which often happens in analysis when the patient is touching on forgotten memories that bring up moments of terror. She decided to quit, although the analyst warned her grimly against her suicidal impulses.

Her marriage was breaking up. "I can't hold a man. I can't live a civilized life. I am nothing but a pair of lungs and a voice box." This was not self-pity but her objective evaluation of herself.

Once, during our long evenings at the mews cottage, she said simply, "Mickey, if I represent people's dreams, I represent a lot more than I can really handle, a lot more than I really am." She was so tired of being Judy, the living legend, and she was trying so valiantly in the last weeks of her life to be just herself.

The last years of the forties had been a treadmill for her. In 1948 she was scheduled to go to work on a new film, *The Barkleys of Broadway*, to be directed by Minnelli, but meanwhile she was ordered back for retakes on a prior film. The pressures built up. She took to missing complete days, and finally Louis B. Mayer, goaded by her behavior, summarily fired her.

To have the umbilical cord severed was a shock. Judy came to her senses, rigid with terror. But the studio, deciding to punish her thoroughly, gave her role to Ginger Rogers, who turned in a superb performance.

Judy was now in emotional exile. The press had reported only her tardiness and temperament, never mentioning the complete exhaustion. It was impossible for anyone who'd seen Judy in her successful films to picture her so physically and emotionally depleted that she could scarcely get out of bed.

After proper punishment, the studio finally chose to forgive her. She was ordered to report back to work on the film *Annie Get Your Gun*. The part of Annie Oakley, which Ethel Merman had played so brilliantly on Broadway in the stage production of the Irving Berlin musical, was a plum. But again there was the absenteeism, the mounting costs as a result of Judy's behavior. This time she was replaced by Betty Hutton.

The studio nevertheless was loathe to write off its little golden goose, and Judy was finally, like a child, given one more chance. She redeemed herself with charm and grace in *In the Good Old Summertime* in 1949.

The pattern continued, however, and by now she could no longer maintain even the semblance of a good relationship with Minnelli. There is little doubt that her illness cost him much in emotional strain. What is shocking is that everyone was still saying, Yes, she's difficult, she lets you know who she is, but if you coddle and pamper her, you may get a performance out of her—and when she performs, she's the greatest. Nobody thought to say: Look, this young woman is desperately sick and something must be done. . . .

Something finally was. She went to Peter Bent Brigham Hospital in Boston, where her illness was diagnosed simply as overwork and exhaustion. Rest, proper nutrition, the kind of therapy that built up her wavering self-confidence, were the tools that gave her a fresh will to live. When the studio summoned her back to Hollywood for a new musical, she felt an emotional obligation to Louis B. Mayer, who had personally lent her the money for her hospital bills. Once again, though, the old sadistic pressures were applied. She was immediately put on another stringent reducing diet. She was badgered and scolded. All the old insecurities returned. She wanted to work, yet something inside of her stopped her. Still, there was enough renewed vigor to get her through the picture. *Summer Stock* was proof again that Judy was never defeated. "The great song and dance actress makes this movie a personal triumph," *Life* commented. The film was highly profitable for the company, and Judy was then cast in *Royal Wedding* opposite the man she idolized, Fred Astaire. But it was the same story over again. She was promised a vacation that never materialized. She was back on black coffee, cigarettes, sleepless nights, and ups. The press turned against her, and it was more than she could take. She tried to commit suicide with the jagged edges of a drinking glass. It was a cry for help, but they still weren't listening, and now it was too late. Judy was fired for good. And as usual, she was broke.

Again Louis B. Mayer showed a streak of generosity toward her. He wrote her a check to tide her over. But Judy was finished at the lot that had been home for her from her beginning adolescence until the present, when she was twenty-eight. The press was now with her. Her old friends on the lot never forgot her.

Joe Pasternak has often said that although Judy was getting difficult to work with, there was only one Judy. "I don't think any actress was as loved by the American public as Judy," he maintained.

She certainly wasn't feeling loved in those days. She fled from marriage and the beautiful home at the crest of a winding road, a home where among Minnelli's treasures she had always felt herself an intruder. With Liza she rented a spacious suite at the Beverly Hills Hotel and hid from the world. Judy's bills had always been taken care of by the studio or her husband. Her income was astronomical, but so were her expenses, particularly her medical bills. Her daily analysis sessions came to fifty dollars each, and this treatment went on for years. When she went to a sanatorium, the bills ran to three hundred dollars a day. There was a lien by the Internal Revenue Service for taxes that she owed for the years when her mother hadn't paid them. Yet now, starting out on her own, she felt a momentary surge of exultation: I am free. I can eat. I have so much to live for. Soon it was evident to her that she was embarking on a new life-style. She *was* independent. But broke. And this was a helpless situation for her. She had Liza, she was deliriously happy with the leisure to be a mother, but the hotel unfortunately was politely reminding her about her bills. Impulsively she packed her bags, flew to New York, and checked into the St. Regis. She felt like a dropout and enjoyed every minute of it.

And then she met Sid Luft.

24

Because of Judy's two children by Sid Luft, Lorna and Joey, it was inevitable that I would at some time meet their father. The prospect worried Judy greatly. She was terrified, she confessed, of Sid's charm and persuasion. He was so smooth and convincing that she feared he would turn me against her.

"Oh, for God's sake!" I exclaimed. "You're not alone anymore." But it was just further proof of how vulnerable she actually was.

As a matter of fact, I had heard that Sid was a genius as an organizer and promoter, and he had a way of giving you his undivided attention which was supremely comforting. He was big and trustworthy-looking, and Judy, who had always been envious of the role David Selznick played in Jennifer Jones's life, decided that Sid could play a similar role in hers.

Judy had friends who had always been tender and kind to her. Frank Sinatra, for instance, showed the durable traits of a true friend. When she was in the hospital in Boston, seeking to regain her strength, flowers arrived daily from Sinatra. He even flew in a planeload of friends from Hollywood to cheer her up. And among the staff at the studio she was deeply loved for her many acts of kindness, which she executed with a kind of shy generosity. (If you needed a loan, you could turn to Judy, and she was always embarrassed when you returned the money.) But she felt she never had anyone to lean on.

Then she met Michael S. Luft, who was known as Sid, a former pilot and more recently a theatrical producer and an agent. The timing was right, each seemed to fill a need for the other, and within a short time Sid became her manager. Judy always functioned best when she was working with a man whom she could love, so all circumstances seemed fortuitous. Sid gave her waning confidence a booster shot. More important, he enforced discipline upon her. Judy lost weight. Out of the rolypoly little woman emerged the ravishing Judy of her most successful M.G.M. films. Some of the great achievements of Judy's career came about during her turbulent ten-year alliance with Sid Luft.

It was Luft who decided she should make the best of her break with M.G.M. and return to vaudeville. Judy knew live audiences; she responded to them. It was inevitable that those who adored her on screen would pay well to see her live. Here was the adored Dorothy of *The Wizard of Oz* in person.

Sid, a superb manager, arranged for her appearance at the London Palladium, which guaranteed her twenty thousand dollars a week. He counted on the English fans' love for Judy and felt it would be both appropriate and felicitous for her to make her concert debut in England. Judy agreed with him, but her sense of fear was growing with each day's preparation. "I feel like the Cowardly Lion," she grumbled to herself. As her initial enthusiasm waned, friends in Hollywood like Fannie Brice (whose tragic personal life Barbra Streisand was to interpret a decade later in *Funny Girl*) coached her with pep talks.

Finally it was opening night at the Palladium, and Judy came out on the big stage and started to sing, feeling her way, seeking to establish a rapport with her audience. The moments immediately before the performance were an exercise in agony. Will they like me? Will I bomb? Once Judy was on stage, the trembling, the sweat, the sickness to her stomach, were forgotten. It seemed to be going well. Then she turned too suddenly on stage. She slipped and fell. With the bright, spontaneous rejoinder that was to become part of her concert technique, she said ruefully, "That was the worst exit ever. . . ."

The English, who revere good sportsmanship, responded with cheers and a standing ovation. From then on to the end of the performance it was Judy at her best, her voice and expressions poised and professional. In her final number she wore the tramp suit she made famous in *Easter Parade*, her cheeks smudged, a tooth blacked out, the gallant, zany little tramp singing "Over the Rainbow." It was too much. The audience exploded. The Judy cult planted its first magical seeds.

Sid was evidently satisfied; his faith in Judy was paying off, and this, he assured her exuberantly, was only the beginning. This was no comeback; it was Judy as she'd never performed before. She responded to her English audiences by singing as though her voice would wipe out the pain and the hurt and would promise a new beginning. Unlike Edith Piaf, Judy could sing of sorrow, of abandonment, of partings, without the pessimism and resignation of the French sparrow. There was always the optimistic yearning in Judy's voice, the true believer's faith that somehow the world would fall lovingly into proper perspective. Now Judy blossomed. After a few more equally brilliant appearances in England, she allowed Sid to persuade her that the next inevitable step was the Palace, in New York.

How many times in the M.G.M. fantasies Judy had portrayed the young vaudevillian who dreamed of "playing the Palace"! Sadly enough, there had been no vaudeville at the Palace for nearly two decades. And now Judy was to bring back the "two-a-day" vaudeville-type show, at $4.80 for a top seat. Sid astutely arranged for a first-rate variety show. There were Smith and Dale, a team of comedians with whom the American public was long familiar, Max Bygraves, an English comedian, and Judy's Eight Boyfriends, a group of personable young men who framed Judy's act. Adding to Judy's confidence was the fact that Charles Walters was in charge of the production. Walters had directed *Easter Parade*, as well as other of Judy's M.G.M. successes.

Opening night was October 16, 1951, and in honor of Judy's return to her first love the audience that came to pay her homage was composed of society and professional friends, as well as her fans. The incandescence that is the gift of a precious few shone with rare brilliance that evening. Judy's performance that night at the Palace has remained an unforgettable experience.

Abel Green, of *Variety*, spoke for the world when he mentioned Judy's "simon-pure stellar quality." She was placed on a pedestal with the great American personalities Fannie Brice, Sophie Tucker—and the greatest heart-wrencher of them all, Al Jolson. Judy single-handedly was restoring vaudeville to its former glory. After four months of sellout houses she could still have continued her record run, which no one had ever equaled, but it was decided that she would appear in Los Angeles, at the Philharmonic Auditorium. Now Hollywood welcomed her not as the little black sheep but as a great star in a fresh medium. The auditorium was sold out for a four-week run. Judy's talent was idolized. It was not sentiment alone because a star whose luster had waned was suddenly recharged with luminous brilliance. It was the sheer indescribable magnetism that Judy exerted in person on an audience. She was on the crest again, and this time she was independent; there were no strict, insensitive studio mentors to detract from her glory.

Of course, there was still her mother. Ethel was suing Judy for support, which seemed an ironic note, considering Ethel's lack of good judgment in handling Judy's finances. There were rumors that Ethel didn't approve of Sid as a potential son-in-law. His former wife, Lynn Bari, had gone to court asking that payments for support for their son be raised. According to Miss Bari, Judy had earned about three quarters of a million dollars in 1951, and as her manager, Luft no doubt received a handsome cut. Naturally, this information didn't sit well with the columnists and reporters, who had heard the story of Ethel's financial plight. Ethel withdrew her suit, but Lynn Bari did not, and the court ruled that Luft had to pay double the previous amount for the support of their child.

Even her great new success as a live entertainer did not smooth away the trouble spots in Judy's life. She was, however, inordinately grateful to Sid, who had done such a great job in making her comeback possible. She was grateful, and she was in love, and on June 11, 1952, she and Sid were married in Los Angeles. Her first three marriages all took place in the month of June.

Judy was at her peak as a performer again, although there were persistent rumors and concerns about her health. The tragedy that rocked her emotional balance, however, happened in 1953, when her mother, who was working for the Douglas Aircraft Company, was found dead of a heart attack on the company's parking lot. It was another trauma for Judy, a severe one. Misunderstandings between mothers and daughters are common events, but when the daughter is a film celebrity and the feuds are played out in an arena with spotlights glaring, the whole world listens in on what should remain a family secret. Everyone was watching for Judy's reaction. The news itself had come while Judy was rehearsing for a charity benefit. The shock nearly toppled her. Perhaps she felt, like many of us do, that her mother was indestructible. Although she saw little of Ethel, the mere knowledge that her mother was alive was a reassuring measure that the world went around on its axis. And now, suddenly, finis. Anger is perhaps the other side of love; with death, anger seems superfluous, and love, now lost, takes its own unique toll.

Judy withdrew from the world into her own dark arena, where pain couldn't be blocked out. She fought her private demons for two long years.

Sometimes you wonder, How did it all begin? That was Judy, ruminating out loud, talking to me about the sore spots, the abrasions, the wounds still bleeding under the rough scars. The little threads that look so innocent and meaningless begin to weave a subtle rope that eventually strangles you.

From "fun" to "funny farm" is a short leap, really, and anybody is vulnerable during the slippery climb to the peak—particularly a young girl who is sensitive to criticism, who has dreams she cannot understand, and who writes poetry she is too shy to share. The teens are difficult years for everybody; even the twenties, when the character takes shape, are tough years. Add to this the stimulants that take you out of your mind. Up you go—whee! But down you come, and God, the blues, the downs. You sit there, and there is nothing behind the big mournful eyes because you're deep in your own world, down, so down. When you are lost in an endless black tunnel and you know there's no rainbow left for you, the funny farm isn't so bad. You scream at first. Why not? How can they humiliate you? Don't they know who you are? Those screams they try to silence, with injections, with a tub of warm water, even with a straitjacket, don't they know those are gut-level screams, coming from so deep inside you that you didn't know those depths existed?

They said of Judy that she wore her heartbreaks like campaign medals. Which they were. And all the time something inside her crying silently: Help me, somebody. I am contributing to my death, and I don't know how to stop myself.

She came out in the sunlight again. She knew that the only way to escape the pain of being is to retreat from life, and this she never did for long. All that was healthy in her cried out for a chance to work again. She had an idea for a film, a remake of an old one, deeply moving and sentimental, called *A Star Is Born*, which in 1937 had brought tremendous acclaim to Janet Gaynor and Fredric March. It was a story that touched the heart, having a kind of universality that would move fans of all ages. It involved a young, immensely talented actress whose career was rising and an aging matinee idol on the way down. Eager to use all her talents, Judy wanted to film it as a musical. Her instincts were sound. Sid persuaded Warner Brothers to underwrite the project. Knowing Judy's reputation, the Warners shrewdly arranged that the Lufts would not share in the movie's take until after all expenses were recouped. The film was budgeted at $2,500,000. It came in after a ten-month filming at a cost of over $6,000,000. It was a mess in the making, but it turned out to be a glorious success for Judy, the director, George Cukor, James Mason, and the entire production. The score was by Harold Arlen and Ira Gershwin and included the memorable song that became part of Judy's repertoire, "The Man That Got Away." There was also the spectacular sequence "Born in a Trunk," created by Leonard Gershe, which traces the humble, dedicated strivings of a vaudeville singer preparing for her great moment. The ravages of Judy's illness, the disquieting expressions of her inner panic, did not keep her from giving full expression to all her talent.

Of *A Star Is Born*, released in October, 1954, Bosley Crowther, of *The New York Times*, said: "Cukor gets performances from Miss Garland and Mr. Mason that make the heart flutter and bleed. Miss Garland is excellent in all things but most winningly perhaps in the song 'Here's What I'm Here For,' wherein she dances, sings, and pantomimes the universal endeavors of the lady to capture the man. . . . It's something to see, this *A Star Is Born*." The film was both a financial and an artistic success, and Judy's interpretation of Esther Blodgett is considered her finest performance.

So Judy was riding high again. Her difficult behavior during the filming of the movie was forgiven. She was nominated for an Oscar. During the final part of filming of *A Star Is Born* she was again pregnant. (She already had had a child by Sid, a girl, Lorna, born the first year of their marriage.) The night the Oscars were to be awarded, Judy was in the maternity ward of the Cedars of Lebanon Hospital, in Los Angeles, having been delivered of a baby boy. She was exhausted, the delivery having left her weakened, and she was apprehensive about the child. The doctors expressed their concern about him; his chances for survival, they warned her, were slim.

While she was in a fog of exhaustion and anxiety, she realized there was considerable activity in her sickroom which had nothing to do with the nursing care for a recent mother. Men from the television studios were bedecking the room with cables and wires, adding a microphone, which they hid under Judy's sheet. The idea was that if Judy won the Oscar, she could have a two-way conversation with Bob Hope, the perennial master of ceremonies. Very dramatic. Very much in keeping with the Hollywood of 1955.

When the man from Price Waterhouse handed over the sealed envelope and the winner was announced over television ("Best Actress: Miss Grace Kelly"), the men in Judy's room did a fast cleanup job. Everything was dismantled, and they disappeared, disgruntled, bored, carrying their equipment with them. Judy and Sid were left alone. It couldn't have been a happy occasion.

But for Judy there was a fresh satisfaction. She and Sid had a home now in Holmby Hills, she had a family—Liza, Lorna, and baby Joey—and she resolved to make a nest for them and give them generously of the love and support she'd felt missing in her own childhood. Again, however, her dreams gave way to disillusionment. The marriage did not come up to her expectations. Sid, superb coordinator that he was, was in the "Judy Garland business," which she had originally encouraged but which now meant to her an exploitative situation, reminding her unpleasantly of her days at the studio. They lost the unity of purpose which first brought them together. Still, Sid could exert enough discipline to keep Judy singing. He introduced her to a nightclub audience for the first time in July, 1956, at the New Frontier Hotel, in Las Vegas. Somehow Judy managed to perform superbly; the Las Vegas audience responded to her as they might have to Al Jolson, and Judy, in a winning streak, broke all box-office records.

And so it went in the following years. Judy made her television debut in September, 1955, on the *Ford Star Jubilee* series. Jack O'Brien, the reviewer for the New York *Journal-American*, a man who pulled no punches, saluted her as "the greatest natural talent in show business." She returned to the Palace in New York with somewhat fewer accolades for her second appearance there, although the plaque in her dressing room noted proudly: "THIS WAS THE DRESSING ROOM OF JUDY GAR-LAND, WHO SET THE ALL-TIME LONG-RUN RECORD, OCTOBER 16TH, 1951, TO FEBRUARY 24TH, 1952. RKO PALACE THEATRE."

During the next decade Judy's career swung again, from high to low, from peak to valley, and all that time she was em-battled in quarrels and reconciliations with Sid Luft. In the decade of their marriage Judy separated from Sid four times, and yet she always changed her mind and returned to him. There were explosions, quarrels over the custody of Lorna and Joey, whom both parents loved dearly. Meanwhile Judy's health was deteriorating again. She was having a problem with fluid retention, and as a result her body was bloated out of shape, her face puffed out, her ankles thick and swollen. She was sick and in pain, and yet she performed. As she was singing before a noisy, drunken crowd at the Flamingo Hotel, in Las Vegas, on New Year's Day, 1958, she was treated rudely by some of her audience, who jibed at her overweight, always a sensitive subject with her. And if this weren't enough humil-iation, her appearance at the Metropolitan Opera in the early spring of that year compounded her sense of inadequacy. It was evidently Sid's idea to arrange for her appearance at the Metropolitan, and it was a good idea. But Judy was suffering from exhaustion. At 160 pounds she was shockingly over-weight. The first half of her program at the Metropolitan was a sad caricature of the real Judy Garland. She was badly dressed in red velvet, and her voice was not at its best. It was surely during this time that her audience began to feel compas-sion and pity for her, as well as admiration for her courage and a sense of identity with her anguish. It would seem as though this were actually the end of Judy Garland. And then, with the mercurial change so characteristic of her, she came out for the second half of the program in her tuxedo, with her legs in long black stockings, and she proceeded to dazzle her audience with a display of the Garland talent at its peak. The audience found it a moving, almost unbelievable experience. Many wept. This was the kind of mass catharsis that was to become a part of the

Garland charisma. And there was also a strange, morbid feeling with it, the kind of mass sadism that is seen at the Indianapolis auto races, where the spectators come to watch racing fools court disaster.

It was a dreadful year for her. She wanted only to be at home with her children, but she needed money, she always needed money, and so she was signed up to appear at Brooklyn's Town and Country nightclub. Ben Maksik, owner of the club, had misgivings. He thought Judy was very sick and shouldn't really be working at all. But the Garland magic triumphed over the Garland problems, at least for eleven days out of a three-and-a-half–week contract. She had found it necessary to ask Maksik for a fifteen-thousand-dollar advance in order to pay off the musicians after she quit the show at the Flamingo Hotel in Las Vegas. And now, everywhere, palms were stretched out.

Judy said, "Give my money to me, not to my husband."

Her husband said, "Give the money to me. I manage her affairs."

Her agency said, "Give it to us."

And the New York State income-tax department was after her for back taxes.

Judy was again separated from Luft at this time, and she and the children were living in a rented house in Brooklyn. She was daily getting deeper in debt for all sorts of professional and private expenses. Her maid quit. Maksik, trying to smooth over the rough spots, gave a party for Joey on his third birthday. Judy never appeared, and she called in later that she was indisposed because of an attack of laryngitis. She did show up that evening, however, an hour late for the show. She went on at ten o'clock and sang two songs, one of which was "Life Is Just a Bowl of Cherries."

"I'm sorry," she told the audience. "I have terrible laryngitis. I wish I could go on, but I can't. But it doesn't matter anyhow because I've just been fired."

Afterward there were reports of loud words from her dressing room, where she seemed to be arguing with some of her colleagues. She had recently argued with any number of people connected with her performances. How much of her temper was due to physical sickness—she was dizzy and nauseous most of the time and had a horror of throwing up in public—and how much to a fear that her voice was betraying her cannot be surmised.

Ben Maksik said bitterly, "We were lucky to get even one night from her. Every night it was a mess. We waited an hour or so for her to go on. Then we would put up a sign saying, 'NO SECOND SHOW.' People would say, 'Ben, what is this?' I would just run in my office and hide." He said that Judy had quit, although she claimed to have been fired.

That's the kind of year it was. All valleys, dark and threatening, and Judy, who wanted to do so much for her children, who had longed to be with them, was suddenly desperately sick again. Diagnostic tests showed that she was suffering from a severe case of hepatitis. To those who knew her and appreciated what she had endured in recent years, it was a miracle that she survived. The doctors warned Sid that she would probably remain a semi-invalid, a state that Judy, with her biting humor, decided wouldn't be half bad. As a matter of fact, she liked the prospect of never making another appearance. Evidently, performing in public was increasingly more painful for her. She languished happily in the hospital for five months and recuperated at home with her children around her for another four months. As she grew stronger, she made a valiant gesture to help John F. Kennedy in his campaign for the presidency. It was the second time that she showed an interest in public affairs. Earlier she had been among the most passionate defenders of "The Hollywood Ten," a group of writers who were waging a private war against the inquisition of Senator Joseph McCarthy. To Judy, John F. Kennedy was a knight in shining armor; he encouraged memories of her girlish dreams. As a matter of fact, they became good friends, and when Kennedy was in the White House, she often called him for short chats.

Once she felt stronger, Judy couldn't languish. She took a plane to London, even then her favorite city in all the world, and the fact that she was willing to fly showed encouraging signs of mental and emotional stability. For years she'd had a phobia about flying. Shortly afterward she was joined by Sid and the children. She found that she wanted to sing again. "Whenever we needed money for the rent, I performed," she was to say later. But it seems reasonable that after a long rest the old habits, instilled deep as Pavlovian training, would assert themselves. Judy was going to sing.

So she was back at the Palladium. As usual, she was ambivalent about the engagement. She loved to be working, but she hated to be exploited. Yet it pleased her mightily to prove the doctors wrong. She *could* work again. She usually carried a tall glass with her, taking an occasional sip, but it was more fruit juice than vodka. She made a terrific impression at the Palladium. She sang thirty of her favorite songs, and again it was Judy at the peak, Judy singing with that crescendo of great power, with skill camouflaging the occasional tonal weaknesses, but with all the delicate shading that broke your heart. Her audience was enraptured. She went on tour in the English provinces and gave two thrilling performances in Paris.

And once more Judy was at a crossroads in her life. She was no longer in love with Sid Luft, and yet she still respected his advice in business. At that time in New York, however, a bright, innovative young agent, Freddie Fields, left the giant Music Corporation of America to try his fortunes on his own. He had much going for him; wit, knowledge, respect for talent. He gambled on a hunch that Judy's golden days were still ahead of her. Judy liked him and was willing to entrust the future to him.

Fields did well by her. He was the Pygmalion she so desperately needed at this crucial period. He had faith in Judy, and he communicated this faith to producers. Judy had been waging a bitter war with C.B.S. for three years; she had initiated a suit against the network for allegedly having broken a contract with her. Fields cleared up the feud and sold her to the network for a television spectacular. He signed Judy for a small but vital role in Stanley Kramer's *Judgment at Nuremberg*, which was to bring her second Oscar nomination, this time as Best Supporting Actress. And then, no doubt, trusting in Judy's returning health and glowing happiness, he booked her for a series of one-night concerts. Judy traveled. Judy sang better than she had in years. Judy lived through the loneliness of empty hotel rooms to survive and prove that she was indeed, as one critic was to call her, "a Lady Lazarus."

Then Fields and his partner, David Begelman, decided that another New York appearance was inevitable. They took a chance and booked Judy into Carnegie Hall on April 23, 1961. It was a pleasant time in her life. Her weight was down, her spirits up. Freddie Fields and David Begelman, as her agent-managers, backed her with all their considerable resources. And on April 23, 1961, Judy created history at Carnegie Hall. As she had at the Palace. As she had a dozen times in her fantastic career. There was no way to evaluate Judy's capacity for a comeback. It is virtually unknown in theatrical history. Just when people wrote her off, she bounced back, fresh, spirited, projecting that amazing sound, that sense of communication, that "X" factor that defied analysis. The critics who branded her Lady Lazarus (so often doomed, so many suicide tries, so many neurotic quarrels) stood up and cheered the new Judy Garland at Carnegie Hall.

A recording of that session remains. The conductor was Mort Lindsay, a fine musician and a dear friend of Judy's. The superbly trained musicians in his thirty-nine-piece orchestra responded to his great musicianship and Judy's extraordinary vitality and voice. There were over three thousand people in the audience, many of them famous, most of them Garland fans. But this night it didn't matter what your station was. Henry Fonda, Carol Channing, Julie Andrews, Richard Burton, composers, songwriters, fans from New York, from the suburbs, from distant cities, all gathered here, half anxious, breathless, waiting for the resurrection of Judy Garland.

How big a part courage plays in talent no one can ever judge. And no one has ever given Judy credit for her immense reservoir of sheer beautiful courage. People in the entertainment field called her the Iron Butterfly, but few have ever mentioned the fact that it takes plain guts to get up before an audience and begin all over again, knowing that although some have come to admire, others are just waiting for you to fall on your face again.

Judy herself shrugged it off. "If you're Garland," she said, "what else can you do but sing?"

When she sang at Carnegie Hall that night, what could you do but listen? This was Judy, alone on the stage, framed by Mort Lindsay and his orchestra, Judy singing "When You're Smiling." And proving as the program went on that her gift for music was an open door to love. Her audience was enthralled, aware of the fact that this was not merely a concert by a great singer but a glimpse of sheer perfection. No one could ever dismiss Judy as a pop singer, a movie star, a consummate vaudevillian. The skill of the true artist was there, concentrating the hunger, loneliness, and sorrow, the frustration and beauty of life, into a few simple lines of music. Tears ready to be shed glimmered in your eyes, and you felt that prickle of recognition in your skin. You wanted to share, to reach out and touch your neighbor; there was a simplicity and purity in the air that sophisticated Manhattan had seldom experienced.

The familiar Judy favorites. The first section included "When You're Smiling," "Almost Like Being in Love," "This Can't Be Love," "Do It Again," "You Go to My Head," "Alone Together." Between numbers she chanted, "One, two, three. . . ." As the concert went on, the emotions of the audience seemed to fuse into one great wave of feeling. Tears were near the surface; Leonard Bernstein was unashamedly weeping. She continued through her repertoire, all the loved songs: "The Man That Got Away," "Come Rain or Come Shine," "A Foggy Day," "Stormy Weather," "You Made Me Love You," and they couldn't get enough of her.

"I'll sing them all, and we'll stay all night. I don't ever want to go home."

Nor did her audience.

"Aren't you tired?" she asked.

"No, no," they chanted, mesmerized.

"We'll do one more," she said, and with remarkable energy, she gave them her gay, irrepressible "Chicago." It was finished, but it was not enough for them.

Variety reported:

New York's Carnegie Hall was supercharged on both sides of the footlights Sunday evening. Pandemonium broke loose, and a standing ovation stalled the songfest for several moments.

After her twenty-sixth number of the evening, she halted the tumultuous applause demanding still another encore. . . . Few singers can get as much out of a song as Miss Garland. . . . The tones are clear, the phrasing is meaningful, and the vocal passion is catching. In fact, the audience couldn't resist anything she did. . . . The aisles were jammed during the encore. . . . She followed with additional numbers, "After You've Gone" and "Chicago," which brought her songbag for the evening up to twenty-six numbers.

Hedda Hopper reported with remarkable accuracy, "Judy Garland took a jam-packed crowd in Carnegie Hall in her arms, and they hugged her back—never saw the like in my life. We laughed, cried, and split our gloves applauding."

And charging toward the stage in a loving mass was the audience, absolutely overcome in their need to touch her. "Judy," they screamed, "Judy, Judy. . . ."

"Goodnight. I love you very much. . . . Goodnight. God bless."

She was at the peak again, and she went on tour, giving concerts in sixteen major cities with fabulous results. If the nights in strange hotel rooms in strange towns were lonely, she didn't complain. She was caught in the glittering web of success again. The ups did more than keep her body charged. She was gay, happy, loved, and under these circumstances, she had incredible energy. *Judy at Carnegie* won a Grammy Award, and the two-record long-playing album had a fantastic sale.

She filmed her role in Stanley Kramer's film *Judgment at Nuremberg.* She performed in nightclubs and on television. Then Stanley Kramer asked her to appear in a new film, called

A Child Is Waiting, which was the story of a music teacher who comes to a school for mentally retarded children.

Judy had a special feeling of tenderness for these children. She had first known them at the Peter Bent Brigham Hospital when she was under the care of Dr. George W. Thorne. She was beginning to feel better, when she asked permission to visit the ward of these wounded children. Most of them were very outgoing and greeted her joyfully, but one little girl was completely withdrawn. On her Judy showered love. The child was mute, retreating into her own world. Judy would come and sit with her every day, but the child never said a word. Judy visited the children daily for ten weeks. They grew to love her, and by giving to them, she experienced the healing that her spirit so desperately needed. When it was time for her to leave the hospital, the children kissed her good-bye and gave her little bouquets of fresh flowers. When she reached her dark-haired, silent little friend, Judy leaned down to kiss her. "I have to leave, hon."

The small girl looked up at her, still mute. Then she leaned forward on her knees. "Judy," she cried, stricken, "don't leave, Judy. . . ."

Judy picked her up and rocked her, and then the words spilled out, nearly choking the little girl, but it was a catharsis, perhaps for them both. Remembering these children, flawed but so lovable, Judy agreed to play in the film. The critics appreciated her fine work.

But now, the cycle repeated itself; once more she was sliding downhill. The demands on her made it impossible for her to sustain that force of vital energy. In July, 1961, she suffered through a serious kidney ailment that left her weak and debilitated. (There had been warnings that the massive doses of amphetamines might trigger kidney attacks.) Acute laryngitis plagued her. Her tendency to stagger and fall resulted in several serious injuries. The news media implied that Judy was either drunk or high on drugs. Neither was true. Her tendency to stagger was a family trait that she had inherited. She was unable to digest solid food, and this new malady was to torment her for the rest of her life. She had to be coaxed (which irritated her) to take even a few mouthfuls of food. No more food binges.

She agreed to meet Sid for purely business reasons. The meeting, which included her agents and business associates as well as Sid, must have disturbed her greatly, for the following day she and the two Luft children took off unexpectedly for England. The reason for the flight, she explained to the press, was that her husband threatened to have her declared an unfit mother. The words "unfit mother" burned in her tired brain. They reminded her of the horrors of her own childhood. She was in her way a completely devoted and loving mother. You needed only to see her with the children to appreciate the warm bond that held them together. She and Sid tried a reconciliation, but it didn't last more than a month. The last film she did in London, *I Could Go On Singing*, did not especially satisfy her. Her life was at a standstill.

The unspeakable horrors of her loneliness were tormenting her again. She got in the habit of telephoning friends at late hours and then talking nervously, compulsively. Even those who loved her found it difficult to be tolerant. Judy always believed her sense of isolation was unique. What she didn't realize was that most artists bear the scars of loneliness. It is part of the creative syndrome. Her fear of being alone verged on hysteria at times. She was never sure that the ones who left would return again. (After discovering this side of her character, I could understand why she would become so disturbed about my coming home late from an appointment.)

During a depressed period she used her ups and barbiturates with abandon. She was in a depressed period because there was no love in her life. Friends have since told me that Judy was always at her best, as a woman and a performer, when love walked in. She always needed a man in her life, but for Judy, the sexual side was less overwhelming than the voracious craving for love. She often said a woman was incomplete when she was not in love. And with a wicked grin, she added that she expected to try marriage again even when she was an old lady.

Whenever, during a concert tour, she met a rich and influential man, she would say, "Gee, why doesn't he marry me, and I'll stay home and cook." She spoke in jest, but there was always an undertone of deep inner wishfulness.

Once again Freddie Fields and David Begelman came to her rescue. Although a recent television special had turned out to be a disappointment (an hour special with her friends Frank Sinatra and Dean Martin), C.B.S. signed Judy in 1963 for a weekly television series. Thirty-two shows, taped. Nobody believed she could stand the strain of a weekly TV show—except those who'd seen her perform miracles before.

Judy never spoke about her television series. I had heard her on talk shows, where she was always a welcome guest, with her enchanting slight stutter, her humor sharp and devastating, her talent for a riposte equal to the quick wit of a Jack Paar or a Johnny Carson. Earlier in her career, when she got back her radio rights from M.G.M., there was talk of her doing a weekly radio stint, but those advisers who knew her well decided she wasn't up to it. She already had a low tolerance for long hours of rehearsal.

An old friend of hers recalls that in the M.G.M. era, whenever she went to a recording studio to cut a record, she would take the entire day off from production but promised to show up on the set the following morning. So the movie staff would be summoned, and they would wait for hours. Judy would eventually ring up and say she was too tired to come to work. Perhaps she spoke the truth, but the studio decided she was throwing her weight around at a fantastic cost to the production in progress. And now, more than a decade later, what with her illnesses and bouts of exhaustion, there was a strong probability that she had even less energy to cope with the draining demands of a new medium. But C.B.S. needed a showcase to break *Bonanza*'s hold on the Sunday-night television-viewing audience.

Much has been written about Judy's hoped-for but ill-fated television series, and all of it has been to her disadvantage. She came out sounding like a boss-lady bitch, unpredictable, callous, demanding, and totally unprofessional. The facts were condemning on a surface level. The deeper truths, which those around her seemed incapable of seeing, were much more revealing. Judy Garland, the precious million-dollar commodity, was again a very sick woman. She was surrounded by timid yes-men who were dedicated to making her happy and who felt the best way to achieve their goal was to listen to her jokes, to trade witticisms with her, to be indulgent with her whims, and to spend half the night staying up with her, not to allay her fears but to help her pass the hours until dawn, when she could finally sleep.

Judy was not strong enough to embark on this project, but those who manipulated her destiny were either unconcerned with her health or took for granted that a superstar with her unpredictable moods was still professional enough to turn out an exacting weekly television series, a task that has left strong performers in shambles. It evidently never occurred to anyone to ask, Is Judy well enough to do this? Will she hold up under the grind of daily rehearsals, a weekly taping, and then, with perhaps one day of rest, the whole routine played all over again?

They were working under wish fulfillment instead of reality. In their favor it was said that Judy's moods swung up and down so much in the span of a week that just when you thought she was finished and gave up on her, she'd marshal her energies and deliver a superb performance. The fact that she'd collapse afterward seemed to affect nobody. The staff saw only the performance. Isn't she great! Judy the superstar, she did it again.

The television series. Judy Garland on TV. The final field to conquer. It came about, evidently, after Judy appeared on the *Tonight* show with Johnny Carson and was so amusing, in such good voice, and altogether so fetching that the C.B.S. top brass were open to persuasion when her agents broached the idea of a TV series.

Like all stories about Judy, rumors flew, gossip was bandied about, and the truth was hidden in a veil of speculation. Her tardiness was almost habitual; she was often indisposed, which was considered a euphemism for nerves, temperament, intoxication, or drugs. With this reputation, how could C.B.S. hazard the projection of a weekly television series, which would require Judy to work consecutively, as she had worked during her M.G.M. tenure? It was evident to those who knew her well that Judy was still subconsciously in fierce rebellion against the regimentation of her M.G.M. days, and it was a kind of psychic rebellion which often completely immobilized her. A performance that had seemed simple to her in her youth was now monumentally difficult. Yet so great was her aura that C.B.S. was willing to gamble something near a million dollars on her reputation, popularity, and unflagging talent. The fact that Judy was not a well woman didn't intrude on negotiations. She was a star, and all luminaries are considered temperamental and difficult. What C.B.S. planned to do was to surround her with pleasant professional people who would dedicate themselves to making her happy and making the series palatable for her. There was a great deal riding on the project. James Aubrey, then head of C.B.S., was counting on Judy to perform a miracle.

The whole company executed a number of charming ploys to keep Judy happy. The short walk from the stage to Judy's dressing trailer was painted to resemble the Yellow Brick Road in *The Wizard of Oz*. Stage 43 in C.B.S. Television City was made smaller to insure a more intimate effect, and the whole staff, including producer George Schlatter, was involved in a gigantic effort to make Judy feel at home, at ease, relaxed, and happy.

Although she was tense, nervous, and apprehensive about the series, she was able in the first few tapings to produce some of the old Garland magic. In her first taped show Mickey Rooney was her guest, and the combination wiped out the intervening years. They were the bright, uninhibited, immensely talented kids, singing, acting, clowning together, as they had in the flossy M.G.M. musicals. The pure professionalism of the duo, their unbelievable love for and loyalty to each other, was so extraordinary that the tough, cynical staff was touched. It was an auspicious beginning for the *Judy Garland Show*. Judy was at her professional best, and it was rumored that C.B.S. was riding a winner.

Yet the series did not run according to schedule and hopes. Some problems and setbacks are natural in taping a series with a great star. Although much has to be decided before rehearsals—songs for the star, her guests, their duets together, scripts, costumes, sets—the staff was unduly sensitive to the whims of their star, perhaps too aware, too eager to coddle her, to make her happy, to make the series a "fun" happening.

Everybody was walking scared. Judy owned a piece of the million-dollar project, so the staff was accountable not only to C.B.S. and the power structure of the production but also to the "boss lady." They were all just as scared as Judy was and far less sensitive. The success of the first show lulled them briefly. Everyone was sympathetic when Judy decided not to tape a show one week. She was having trouble with her husband, Sid Luft, she said, and her nerves were shot. The staff was disappointed at the news, even though it meant time off. They were still keyed up with the success of the first show and eager to produce another winner.

The first thirteen weeks were an exercise in patience, frustration, and anxiety for the staff, but nobody suffered more from her actions than Judy herself. "Call me unpredictable," she had sung on the first show. She was not actually unpredictable; she was plain scared. She was deeply worried, sensing the top brass were not exactly ecstatic about the show. She was anxious because the production was costing considerably more than its original allotment, and much of the unnecessary expense was her fault because she was paralyzed by indecision. She stalled to avoid a confrontation, to avoid facing the basic truths from which she shied away to save her sanity.

She often couldn't sleep, of course; not even the barbiturates relaxed her. And when the night loomed like the music in Musorgski's *Night on Bald Mountain*, her fear and insecurity surfaced, and she appealed to her staff to reassure her. The men took turns spending from midnight to dawn at Judy's house, talking to her, listening to her, soothing her. The Dawn Patrol became Hollywood gossip. And C.B.S., evidently disappointed with results and ratings, summarily fired George Schlatter, the ebullient but careworn producer of the *Judy Garland Show*, as well as most of the staff.

Now C.B.S. brought in Norman Jewison as director for the next eight shows, and he, quiet and confident, anticipated no problems with Judy. At first he had none. When the chemistry was right between Judy and her guests, she discarded her apprehension and the basic Garland talent shone through, bright and clear. Donald O'Connor, as guest for one segment, brought out the best in Judy, who had known him since they were both in vaudeville and had great respect for his talents. The next day a telegram was delivered to Judy: "CONGRATULATIONS ON A WONDERFUL SHOW LAST NIGHT. KNOW IT WILL BE A BIG HIT IN THE COMING SEASON. JOHN F. KENNEDY."

As the tapings went on, Jewison found that his original confidence had been considerably overinflated. A few of the shows were first-rate, especially when Judy had a guest that put her on her mettle—Barbra Streisand, for instance—but the series was beginning to show premature age. When she was good, Judy was very good indeed, but when her interest lagged, as it often did, gloom settled over her like a heavy cloud, and there were bad vibrations all around. Judy was obviously depressed and convinced the series was going down the drain. Five months elapsed, with a change of staff, before the first thirteen shows were finally taped. Now a new group took over. In spite of a series of setbacks that were partially the result of her nerves, Judy turned in a warm and highly successful Christmas segment, taped with her children. Without consulting the studio brass, she sang as a memorial for the late John Kennedy "Battle Hymn of the Republic." All that she felt for the martyred President, together with the sorrow and anguish in her own heart, came through, and as she stood alone on the runway, singing, "Mine eyes have seen the glory of the coming of the Lord . . ." it was a performance unequaled in the memory of many who heard it. The tears gushed forth without embarrassment from both staff and audience. It was the touch of genius that set Judy apart from the mere performers, and the audience, feeling the magic, responded with a spontaneous standing ovation. This was Judy, the legend, whose like had not yet been seen, the Judy who, in spite of her unconscious fears that had sabotaged the show and run up monumental overtime pay for the stagehands, technicians, and cameramen, still delivered a performance that couldn't be surpassed.

She was, however, again in a serious depression, living on Ritalin and barbiturates. It was decided to take a week's break from taping. Judy flew to New York, where she met Bobby Cole.

Jilly's was one of the fun spots that amused Judy, and during her New York stay a friend brought her there to see Frankie Randall. Bill Colleran, the gentle man who was now Judy's producer, accompanied them. The bar is constructed around the piano, and the "in" customers at Jilly's usually came to sit there and listen to the pianists. Bobby Cole was at the piano, and since he was singing Cy Coleman songs, Judy, being a great Cy Coleman fan, listened intently. Bobby sang "You Fascinate Me So," which happened to be a favorite of hers.

"Why don't you sing Coleman?" Bobby Cole asked her.

"Gee, I'd love to do some of those tunes," she said. "Not necessarily on my TV show. . . ."

Bobby Cole was not experienced in dealing with a superstar. He realized only later that when you have a million-dollar industry going and the customers love it as it is, you don't make changes. If Judy was to break in a new song for her repertoire, much thought and planning would have to be involved. You'd have to decide where to insert the song, in what spot in the act, for this decision is important and critical. Whenever you want to put a new number in the act, it means new arrangements for a thirty-piece orchestra.

Bobby was not aware of the problems involved in putting together a Judy Garland television show. As a matter of fact, he was not particularly a Garland fan, but shortly before meeting her at Jilly's, he had heard a tape of her Carnegie Hall concert. It happened on New Year's Eve in 1964. Delores, his wife, was in the hospital, and Bobby had to borrow a car to drive home that night to Long Island. Usually he took his car out of the street garage and parked it at the curb so that at four in the morning, after his final set, he could dash out to the car and quickly head home to Long Island. This night, however, he had come into the city by train, as the parkways were coated with ice. He drove home cautiously in the borrowed car, listening all the while to a tape of Judy singing at Carnegie Hall. He was so impressed that when he reached home, he stayed in the car, listening to the tape again.

It was fortuitous that a week later Judy went to Jilly's. Bobby walked over to her, bowed, and said, "Dynamite." They discussed her Carnegie Hall concert, and Judy was pleased with his praise, which was the cool, objective praise of a seasoned performer.

Bobby Cole considers himself basically an orchestrator. Among musicians he is regarded with respect. He is something of an iconoclast. Whatever he does has never been what anyone else does. He was, of course, flattered at Judy's interest, particularly since he knew that the *Judy Garland Show* had the finest musicians working. When she asked him what he thought of her orchestra, he said frankly that the only thing he didn't like was that on the album it sounded like a "pit" band. He was not making a pitch. It was a musical rapping feast. But he did suggest that perhaps she didn't need all those musicians; it might be possible for her to cut down to a small band. Bobby himself had the ability to listen to any arrangement and copy it or cut it down.

At no time did she say, "Listen, I dig you. I want you to come out to the Coast and take over." He would have refused, because musicians just don't do those things. It was in his nature, of course, to reach out, to stretch for new ideas; still, he thought their talks were nothing more than an exercise in musical ideas until Judy's producer, Bill Colleran, dropped in one evening to Jilly's.

"Listen, Bobby," Colleran said. "We want you to come to Hollywood." He did not suggest specifically that Bobby would work on the show, but he did want to pick Bobby's brain for any new ideas that would be of value to Judy. Colleran was rather evasive about Bobby's role in the series; he just said, "If you come up with any ideas, tell me."

"But what am I supposed to do?" Bobby asked. "What's my job?"

"Well, you can help Judy. She needs new material. I will pay you a thousand dollars a week."

"Look," Bobby said, "I don't want to just go out there and hang around. If I can't perform a musical function. . . ."

But the Coles were swept up in Judy's impulsive plans. Judy got on the telephone with Bobby's wife, Delores, bubbling with enthusiasm. "When Bobby gets settled, you and the children come out there, and we'll have a wonderful time," she promised.

Only when Bobby arrived on the Coast did he realize Judy and Mel Torme were embroiled in a hassle that he could be drawn into. From what Bobby gathered, Mel was performing his duties as his contract called for, but there seemed to be a current of unpleasantness. Bobby felt that none of this concerned him, however. "At this time," Bobby Cole told me later, "I was not out there to replace Mel but to work with Judy on new material and new songs, and if she decided to use them on the show, beautiful."

As was often the case with Judy, gossip spread. Judy was at her happiest and performed superbly when there was a man in her life, and gossip decided Bobby Cole was the new love. As a matter of fact, someone on the staff reported a hysterical long-distance call from Bobby's wife, weeping, begging them to send her husband back, as she was pregnant.

"Nothing could be farther from the truth," Bobby told me emphatically. "Delores was not pregnant. Closer friends than Judy and Delores couldn't be found. Delores was with her all during Judy's concert tour after the TV series and even for the brief time Judy was working on *Valley of the Dolls*."

One evening Judy rang Bobby at his apartment. "Bobby, Mel isn't going to do any more arrangements. I have Vic Damone coming on the show. I want you to write a special for the two of us."

"Wait a minute, Judy. . . . I can't do that," Bobby objected, feeling uneasy. "It would be in poor taste. It would put me in a bad light."

Judy could be stormy and childlike. "You know something" —her voice sounded injured—"I am paying you a thousand dollars a week, and here I am in real trouble and you won't even help me. D'you think that's fair? Now I have to go out and get somebody else to do it while I'm paying you all this good money. . . ."

Bobby was now acutely uncomfortable. He felt awkward, and yet he knew he had to give in. So reluctantly he set to work on an arrangement for *Kismet*.

"I worked on the seldom-sung songs of *Kismet*," he confessed, "and it was pages and pages long. Vic Damone took one look at it and disappeared. I know now that I overwrote. After three tapings it came off, but it was a costly success."

Bobby said he would never have dared to offer advice and ideas if he'd had any idea of the superstructure of Hollywood and the television business. He thought originally that all he had to do was to make a suggestion to Judy, and if she liked it, she would so tell her producers, and it would be done. Not true.

"To deal with Judy, you had to deal in services, in working toward making her look good, not in wanting the limelight yourself. Which could have been one of the reasons for the falling-out between her and Torme. When you worked with Judy, you had to be completely committed to her," Bobby said.

"That didn't mean ass-kissing either," one of her friends said. "Judy didn't like that. She shrank from aggressive people too; they seemed to bring out the worst in her."

Whether it was inherent in her nature and intensified by the amphetamines or whether it was the result of exposure to abrasive people, Judy was hypersensitive. She could pick up bad vibes from five hundred yards away. One of the reasons she was so devoted to Delores Cole was that Delores was honest, straightforward, and unassuming. She didn't send off any bad vibes. Judy didn't like people with hang-ups. She had enough of her own. She was drawn to people with genuine feelings.

Delores remembers how considerate Judy could be. Whenever they were trapped in a crowd—and crowds seemed to gather wherever Judy was—she would make certain that Delores or anyone who was with her wasn't pushed aside. Later, when Judy again played the Palace, there was always a group of fans waiting at the stage door, and she would look over her shoulder to make sure Delores was with her. "Wait a minute— waaaitt a minute!" she'd command in her inimitable way, and sometimes she'd even go back into the crowd to rescue Delores. She was fantastically concerned about those close to her. She was very tender with children. When the youngest Cole boy was tired and weeping after a day's outing, Judy took him into her dressing room and let him help her apply her makeup. One of the reasons children adored her, her own included, was her talent for reaching them at their level.

The Coles discovered that when she was a mother, Judy was a supermother. While they were taping the TV series, she decided one day that they must take all the kids to spend the day at Pacific Ocean Park. She managed it superbly, although it was obviously a tremendous effort for her. Peter Lawford was with them, and Lorna and Joey with their nanny. They all had hot dogs, popcorn, sideshows—the whole bit.

"She wound up with miles of people following her," Bobby recalled, "but she was having a great time with the kids. Then she noticed one of the amusements, a kind of giant barrel. Nothing would do but we must try it. Well, we all climbed in and held hands while the huge barrel started whirling—I guess the whole idea was centrifugal force. We were all doing fine, laughing and shouting. . . .

"Peter and I were each holding Judy by the hand," Bobby added, "when suddenly we realized she was beginning to slide down. Now how could we ever explain to C.B.S. if their million-dollar property sank and fell out of sight at the bottom of a barrel in Pacific Ocean Park?"

The sun was hiding behind the horizon, and they were all feeling the delicious exhaustion brought on by fresh air and amusement-park goodies. Judy, however, was still charged up. "Now we're all going down to see the octopus," she decided.

They vetoed. And she listened.

When Bobby first arrived in Hollywood, Judy wanted to show him how healthy she was. "I'll pick you up at your apartment," she said, "and we'll meet Peter Lawford and all go out to dinner."

Bobby was waiting outside his place on Wilshire Boulevard when Judy drove up, almost lost behind the wheel of a big Lincoln. She was beaming.

"I jumped into the front seat," Bobby recalled, "and Judy was busily making plans. 'We'll have fettucini,' she said."

It was midnight, and the roads were deserted. Although Judy was driving very well, Bobby suddenly had the feeling that she should no more be driving the Lincoln than he should be piloting a 747. All of a sudden they swerved from the highway and took a sharp right turn into the Veterans' Base Complex, where they found themselves in a maze.

"Wait a minute, Judy. Stop!" Bobby said as they were driving around garbage cans. "Why did we come here? Why did you do this?"

"Well," she said reasonably, "didn't you see that car?"

"What car?"

Now that she mentioned it, he had noticed the faint headlights of a car far back in the distance. She had immediately scooted off the road, although there was no possible danger. This was the kind of fear which attacked her. She was convinced the car was going to ram her.

When Bobby told her secretary, Karl Brent, about the incident, Karl said, astonished: "You mean she actually drove it?"

Judy was usually so terrified in an auto or plane that she would sit, huddled up, her knees held against her chest, but she had summoned all her resources to show her guest that she was quite normal. It made him understand, also, why she needed constant assurance in her TV show.

"Of course Judy was illogical," said a friend who was close to her during that period. "Of course she was completely irrational. Anyone else taking twenty-five amphetamines a day would be irrational too."

Bobby recalled that many mornings Delores would fill part of the pep capsule with sugar. "Better that she should get diabetes," he said with bleak humor, "than get high on all those amphetamines."

When she wasn't singing well, her extraordinary sense of showmanship carried her through. Before each taping, though, she was nearly rigid with fright. Bobby Cole would lead her up the Yellow Brick Road to her dressing trailer, which C.B.S. had arranged at considerable expense for her comfort. There was a small tent outside where she could make changes.

"I need a Ritalin," she would say. "I need a Ritalin. I've got to have another Ritalin."

Bobby turned to Karl. "She won't go on until she has another Ritalin."

"I can't give her another one," Karl said. "This makes forty."

"But she won't go on. . . ." Bobby repeated. "She won't come out of that tent."

Judy was a rattling bunch of nerves, waiting for the amphetamine. But Karl would be watching the monitor, or sometimes he'd disappear purposely. If he was watching the monitor, he'd say, "Hold it; just shut up. . . ."

"But I promised her—she's waiting for it——"

"Hold it, dammit!"

The music started, and Judy stepped out of the tent. The change in her was unbelievable. No longer was she pale, tense, sick. She was transformed into the radiant superstar. The minute the announcer mentioned her name, the change came over her. Only those close to her were aware of this phenomenon, and they knew she could go on without that last Ritalin.

Toward the end of the next series, Judy was saturated with amphetamines and sleeping pills. One evening when Bobby was working with her at her house, she got sleepy and went to bed. He waited in the living room for a while to make sure she was all right. Suddenly he tensed, hearing a sound in the bedroom. She had awakened and was about to take three more sleeping pills after the three she had already swallowed. She had to be watched constantly, and later on, when Bobby was her conductor on a concert tour, Delores was always with her.

The insomnia was growing worse as the fears compounded. Judy, with her built-in sensitivity, knew all was not well with the television series. She had counted so much on its success to replenish her bank account, to restore her place as a superperformer, to give her the inner sense of dignity and respect she so desperately needed. Whether she faced the cold facts—that much of the foundering was due to her behavior—will never be known. Daily she grew more apprehensive. She often stayed awake for three and four days running until finally she collapsed into a state of exhaustion that was called sleep. Some nights, when the amphetamines charged her up and her brain reeled from paranoiac visions and she dreaded being alone, she called on the staff of the show to come to the house and bail her out of the dark pit of terror. A series of the men drove to Judy's house to participate in the Dawn Patrol. They spent hours listening to her, trying to bolster her up. What no one seemed aware of was that she was desperately ill and unable to carry on.

"Judy was not the kind of a person with whom you could come on straight ahead," a friend said. "Not a woman so filled with ups and downers. You had to know how to handle her."

"She was a public person," another suggested. "You couldn't take this little creature who would reduce an audience of fifty thousand people to frenzy and tears—and expect her to behave like a normal person afterwards. You had to have an inner clock to understand Judy. If someone upset her during the day, a hundred people might suffer for it. And what really upset her was not what she would rant about."

It was insupportable toward the end. The fact that she showed up at all was a daily miracle. Once when Bobby Cole called for her to fetch her to the studio, she decided to stop in her garden to pick flowers.

Bobby finally lost his patience. "You want to pick flowers— that's great—but the car's waiting, the staff's waiting. If you're in no hurry, I'll just go and take a shower while you're out there picking daisies."

You had to play by Judy's rules when she was upset, though. Those close to her grew adept at spotting trouble in the wings. Suppose a woman happened to catch her going into the studio and clucked over her with syrupy sympathy: "Judy, how are you?" She'd answer, "I'm fine, how are you? I've been fine for years," but she'd be boiling.

While she was preparing for a taping, they learned to hold back with any joke or story until the hairdresser had finished with her. Sometimes the poor fellow had to squat on the bed to comb her hair. If her gown wasn't ready, it was safe to tell a joke then because she wouldn't be diverted from what she had to do. It was a battle of wits between Judy, who lagged and vacillated, and the staff, which was obliged to get her ready on time. As a result, everyone close to Judy had to be sensitive, like finely tuned machines. "You had to have eyes in the back of your head," Bobby said. "To understand Judy when she was performing was a science in itself."

A psychiatrically oriented observer suggested: "When you're dealing with a star whom you're asking to earn thirty thousand dollars in a night, you're dealing with effect, when actually the cause should have been taken into account."

They watched over her not only because as Judy, the superstar, she was entitled to it but also because after the momentarily difficult tantrums Judy, the human being, was so utterly endearing. One of the nicest things about Judy—which was unfairly criticized—was her need to touch and be touched. It was not only a seeking for reassurance from another human being, but it was also her means of communicating. "Sometimes you'd get so mad at her you'd want to kill her," a friend said, "and suddenly she'd hold out her hand to you, and she'd be so sweet. What could you do?"

The unspoken rule was that you didn't start her on an anecdote while she was trying to eat. Some idiot, wanting to court attention, might say, "Hey, Judy, what about that time in Philadelphia? . . ." Judy would forget about food and exclaim, "Let me tell you what happened . . . " and that meant she wouldn't be eating for the next twenty-four hours. Or some clod who happened to be in the party would turn to her, his mouth full of food, and say, "Hey, Judy, you're not eating. It's not good for you, not eating." That would tick her off. That was the end of the evening.

She couldn't bear vulgarity. "Some klutz would barge in with a friend and bellow, 'Judy, I'd like you to meet a fan of yours, Rosie—Rosie, meet Judy.' That sort of vulgar familiarity would drive her crazy," an interviewer reported. Judy wanted Rosie to like her—she wanted everybody to like her—but at the same time she wanted Rosie out of there.

Another type that drove her wild was the middle-aged middle-class woman (sometimes a sponsor's wife) who sailed in, bedecked with jewels and furs, saying loftily, "My dear, you were just wonderful." Judy would snort, and her snort would become a Bronx cheer. This lady, whose husband had made it big, would trigger a furious reaction in Judy. You had to be careful to screen out people of that caliber. Otherwise, before you knew it, there'd be no television show.

You had to play by Judy's rules. It behooved the staff to keep klutzes out of her way.

The taping of her final television show was an ordeal that no one likes to remember. The technical staff had been working all morning, and at six in the evening all was ready for Judy to do her "Where Is the Clown?" number. After a harrowing series of attempts and frustrations the clown number was taped (although never used). Judy was in the striking white costume for her closing speech, which was given to the music of "Born in a Trunk." She spoke of her gratitude to the viewers and implied that she found concerts preferable to the television medium because there she could rely more on her instincts and call on her experience.

Who was to blame for the failure of the show? Was it possible that had the series been extended, it might have taken fire? According to the Nielsens, the series was catching on in popularity, but the front office had decided against it. It was too costly, too enervating.

Judy, completely shattered, disappeared, checking into a sanatorium for a rest cure. One of the most exciting, exhausting, and terrifying series of all time was put away in the archives of television history.

After a brief rest cure in Boston, Judy returned to New York. The first people she called were Bobby and Delores Cole. As always after an enforced rest, she looked well and seemed cheerful, except for money matters. Twentieth Century Fox, in what seemed to be a stroke of shrewd publicity, offered her a role in the film version of *Valley of the Dolls*. The Jacqueline Susann novel was not only a best seller but also the talk of Hollywood and the gossip columnists, since one of the characters, Neely, was evidently patterned on Judy. She wasn't cast as Neely, though, but as Helen, an older, harder, sex-hungry Broadway star. Judy had qualms about accepting the assignment; she felt that her fans would be outraged to see her in such an unfavorable role, but she was desperate for money. She asked Delores Cole to accompany her to the Coast, as she needed a companion.

Twentieth Century advanced her five thousand dollars for her work in *Valley of the Dolls*. She handed the check to Delores. "Run down to the bank and cash it right away," she said.

Delores told me later, "She was happy that day; the pressure was temporarily off, and she worked well."

Once the production started, she grew anxious and fell back into the old dangerous pattern recalled from her M.G.M. days: ups and downers. She began giving the crew a hard time. Sometimes she'd keep them waiting two hours or more, which was costly to the production. Tempers grew heated. After all, Judy was no longer one of the top stars of M.G.M., and even Marilyn Monroe at her peak had been punished for tardiness on the set. Still, the only time Judy was actually absent was when she had the flu and was confined to her bed for four days. Otherwise, she appeared on the set every day.

Evidently, however, her disposition was causing uneasiness; there were rumors that she was being difficult. One day two men from the front office came into her dressing room for a talk. They were disturbed about her tardiness, but they assured her they were willing to give her another try. Later her agent telephoned and said he would straighten it out. Judy trembled and paced and waited, wanting to throw up the job and yet knowing how desperately she needed the money. What had happened to her that people could treat her with such a lack of respect? Respect was something that meant more to her than money and fame and power.

Hollywood had treated her badly, and she detested Hollywood. Yet she never kept a blacklist of those who injured her, although about five years before her death she mentioned in an article some of the injustices and cruelties foisted upon her. She had bounced back from every misfortune. She retrieved every blunder . . . well, nearly every blunder. But now it seemed that she had reached a dead end. She felt like a lonely traveler at a deserted railroad station after the last train has gone.

Delores had spent six weeks with her, but she had to return to Bobby and her children on Long Island. She telephoned the studio and suggested they hire a nurse to stay with Judy and see that she got to the studio on time. Delores flew home, confident that Judy would be taken care of. She was shocked to read Judy had been fired.

Earlier in 1965—that appalling year—Judy wasn't well enough to tour, and her money was again running out. The house that she'd bought after *A Star Is Born* and the furniture that Warner's had given her after the film was completed still gave her some security, but Hollywood had nothing to offer her. Nevertheless, to her astonishment she was invited to sing at the 1965 Academy Awards. She was astonished at the bid, knowing that the Hollywood hierarchy had a horror of dealing with failures. In the 1960's she had twice been nominated for Academy Awards, but the happy days when she and Sid were members of the Holmby Hills Rat Pack—an exclusive group of stars that were prematurely anti-Establishment—were gone. The members of this group, with Humphrey Bogart as the leader, were all immensely talented, and all had a great contempt for squares, for anything pretentious, and for anyone pompous. Judy was a vice-president of the Rat Pack, and her bright, caustic wit contributed much to the gaiety of their meetings. They were the irrepressible dead-end kids who took pleasure in deflating Hollywood, and Judy had spent many happy evenings with Bogart and his wife, Lauren Bacall, Frank Sinatra, Peter Lawford, and the rest of their cronies.

Now, as she waited in the wings before her number at the Academy Awards, the brightness that was Judy Garland was dim. Among the television staff, those who knew her were not dismayed, however. She may have flirted with physical suicide but never with professional obliteration. She stood in the wings, thin, almost gaunt, shaking so badly that it looked like another total collapse. Once her name was announced, though, she walked out with that unique pigeon-toed stride, using the microphone chord like a whip, looking collected, and smiling —the performer. The audience of super-egos stared at her uncertainly, wondering if there was anything left of the youthful Judy, whom her grandmother had named Little Miss Leather-lungs. She was not in good voice, but she was Judy Garland, and she won them over. Soon they were applauding—as much for her courage as because they were afraid of their own futures. If it could happen to Judy. . . .

Judy's impulsive gestures, born out of her deep unabated need, often had a way of betraying her. Mark Herron came into her life at a moment when she had an even greater than usual need for kindness and affection. The failure of the television series left a deep hurt, compounded by the breakup of her friendship with Glenn Ford. Failure was a condition Judy seemed to accept more readily than her many brilliant successes. Mark was among the people who used to come by her California house shortly before the television series was banished from the air. He was an affable young man, quiet and unobtrusive, and she found his presence comforting, since he often remained behind after the others departed and listened sympathetically to her problems.

Fields and Begelman arranged for her Australian tour in 1964, but this time they did not accompany her, which was a tragic mistake. She had an entourage, but among them no intimate friend to sustain her. Mark Herron seemed the logical choice as a traveling companion. The Melbourne concert was a catastrophe, but she redeemed herself in Sydney. The physical strain depleted her, however. She was plagued by laryngitis and chest colds, which were to be expected, since amphetamines have a tendency to weaken the body's recuperative powers. She left Australia ill and depressed. Mark accompanied her to Hong Kong, and it was here that she collapsed of what she later called a heart attack. It may actually have been a breakdown as a result of the massive doses of amphetamines, which have a tendency to speed up the heartbeat.

Judy as always made news. In photographs taken of her in Hong Kong, Mark was in the background but always present. Her friends were aware of her interest in him, but they didn't take it seriously when she announced she had married Mark in June, 1964, aboard the Norwegian cargo ship *Bodo*, three

miles off Hong Kong. She had been separated from Sid Luft
for two years but was not, as far as her friends knew, legally
divorced from him. Then Mark Herron announced she had ob-
tained a Mexican divorce and was therefore free to marry again.
Actually, her divorce from Luft was not legally final until November, 1965. So she married Mark again on November 14,
1965, in Las Vegas, but the marriage petered out shortly. And
while she was involved in the filming of *Valley of the Dolls*, she
was obliged to appear in court for hearings on her divorce from
Herron, which certainly added to the strain.

The misadventures of the year told cruelly on her. She was
sick again. For a long time. "Sometimes I feel like I'm living in
a blizzard—an absolute blizzard," she said mournfully.

In midsummer, 1967, Sid Luft entered her life again. She
needed a shoulder to lean on, and he offered his. She remembered the early days of their marriage and so trusted him
again. He wanted to form a company called Group V to act as
her agent and manager and to help her build up trust funds
for the children and a base of financial security for herself and
him. She agreed.

In August, 1967, Sid booked her into the New York Palace
again for a four-week run. Joey and Lorna came to New York
with her. Judy was completely strung out. She was swallowing
handfuls of the fifteen-milligram Dexamil capsules every day.
She dreaded the Palace appearance, knowing it would be com-
pared to her first concert there, which was still spoken of with
reverence and awe. The fantastic amount of ups she was taking
had a deadly effect on her. Although Lorna and Joey were in
the same hotel, she wouldn't see them. She was even terrified
to step out of her bedroom to speak to a friend. Rather than
allow her children to see her in such a state, she would forego
the pleasure of being with them. It was her strange way of protecting herself and them.

"Can I see Mama now?" Joey would beg Delores Cole.
Bobby, who was conducting Judy's orchestra, would reply,
"All right." Then he'd ring up her room and say, "Judy, get
yourself ready. We're bringing the children." She longed to see

her children, so she'd make a tremendous effort to function normally.

"Yet there were times," Bobby Cole told me, "when this was the greatest family I've ever seen in my life." Although Sid and Judy were now divorced, she still listened to him when it came to her profession. "After a performance," Bobby continued, "we'd sit in the Palace until all hours of the morning, and we'd laugh and tell funny stories, and Judy seemed so happy—"

She was always happy when the performance was behind her, when she could relax with Liza, Lorna, and Joey. Sid was always around. When the chemistry was good, it was perfect; when it was bad, it was a disaster.

Sid seemed to know how to manage Judy. After the performance he would say, "Now, Judy, are you going out with Delores and Bobby?" And to the Coles he would suggest, "Don't keep her out too late."

When he was around, he rationed her ups. Sometimes Judy would be chasing Sid around backstage and begging, "Aw, Sid, give me just one more."

"No more, Judy," he would say. And he wouldn't give in.

Group V arranged for Judy's last concert tour—Westbury Music Fair, on Long Island; Springfield, Massachusetts; Camden, New Jersey; the Palace in New York City; and from there the major cities. But by midsummer of 1968 Sid Luft had allegedly turned over her contract for a loan. Judy's home and possessions in California were no longer hers.

She was living alone and was completely broke. Finally, with that extraordinary surge of strength that always came to her last-minute rescue, she decided to make a fresh start once more. She would embark on a European tour, beginning in London, the city she so dearly loved. She would thus free herself, she thought optimistically, of the entanglements of Group V.

But first she needed to regain her strength. Whenever she was so physically depleted, she turned to her old cherished friends, the medical staff of the Peter Bent Brigham Hospital in Boston.

They had helped her so many times in her hectic life. She was nearly penniless, but good friends, among them Kay Thompson, helped with her expenses. By the time she returned to New York in the autumn of 1968 we began to see each other often, not only at Arthur but also away from the club. And it was decided that I would fly to London with her when she began her engagement at Talk of the Town and there we would be married.

25

Where did all the money go?

Ten million dollars. That's what Judy earned during her career, and now she was broke. First, her mother frittered away her earnings. Then she was in the hands of various agents and of Sid, all of whom took a percentage of her salary off the top. She paid all hotel expenses for herself and those traveling with her. There were press agents' salaries and lawyers' fees and medical expenses and liquor bills for guests and entertainment fees. No matter how much she earned, and it was often thirty thousand dollars a week, her managers evidently did not warn her to put aside money for her taxes. So the Internal Revenue Service was after her.

Now, however, in the spring of 1969, it looked as though Judy could earn a bundle without having to work too hard for the rest of her life. Plans for the minitheaters were developing, and I was due in New York to finalize them. This time Judy chose to go with me so she could sign contracts and be helpful to me. She felt the investors would be reassured if they saw her happy and in good spirits. And well. We flew to New York and stayed at a friend's apartment for the duration of our three-week visit. While I attended business meetings during the day, she usually remained at home, resting.

Coming back to New York brought to her mind nostalgic memories. Here all of her memorable M.G.M. films had opened, and crowds had gathered to acclaim her. She mentioned the satisfaction it had given her to work with Fred Astaire and how in *Easter Parade*, a favorite of hers, she had worked fantastically hard to match Astaire's sense of perfection. And *A Star is Born*, still her favorite of all her films. And the Palace. She had brought vaudeville back to the Palace, which in 1932 had turned into a straight movie house.

And the less happy memories: rooms in strange hotels, enclosing space, empty space, and the loneliness while in a crowd, surrounded by the people of her entourage, not really people but robots in dark suits and white shirts, each protecting his share of the pie. Life had too many ghosts for her.

Still, she bore up valiantly. She was on tranquilizers during this trip rather than ups and downers. She was trying so hard to cut down, and she was doing it. We were reaching each other with love, patience, and understanding. Dr. John Traherne, her London physician, now believed Judy could be cured of her addiction, because she wanted to be cured.

Motivation meant so much. When we were in Spain, Judy was not yet sufficiently motivated. The Spanish doctor had put her on Longacton, one of the very old tranquilizers. He had said to me in Judy's presence, "She doesn't need those stronger pills. See how bright and alert she is?"

Whereupon Judy said, "I took a couple of Ritalin before you came in." She was so much like a precocious kid that we had to laugh.

Whenever we did go out in New York that last time in May, Judy was right in fashion with her mod clothes. Yet I believe that in her mind she still saw herself in checked gingham and Mary Jane slippers. She looked very "in," however, with her boots, her brief skirts, her big floppy hats, and the huge dark glasses that kept slipping down off the bridge of her small nose.

One day Bob Jorgen took her to Revelation, where she added extravagantly to her new wardrobe. Then he guided her into a florist's shop to buy her flowers. The florist refused to take any money. "You've brought too much happiness to the world," he said quietly. Judy was touched, so deeply that she couldn't count on her usual repartee. She wrote the lyrics of a song, "Words from a Flower Vendor," and hoped I would set them to music.

Bob was with us nearly every night except when we were out on business. By now Judy decided Bob was her best friend, as he was mine. He took her to Maxwell's Plum for lunch one day, and an old friend of mine came over to speak to him. Judy moved closer to Bob for protection, and he realized then that unless they happened to be her audience, she was afraid of people she didn't know.

One night we drove out to New Jersey and stopped by the various nightclubs where I had gotten my start. At one spot I played a bit of "Over the Rainbow," and tears came into her eyes. She was always building me up, never allowing a touch of "Mr. Garland," always saying, "Mickey did this for me. Mickey did that for me." She added, "I have someone to take care of me."

Judy had never met my parents, although I had introduced her and my mother by trans-Atlantic telephone. Now they were to meet. My mother wanted to make a big family dinner, but I said no. Nothing bores me as much as family dinners. I get impatient and itchy.

One night when Judy and I were at the apartment with Bob, I said, "Come on, we're going over to Jersey." This gave Judy about twenty minutes to get ready. I then called my parents and told them to expect us in about an hour. Judy wanted to go to the hairdresser, but I said, "No formality." Bob was in jeans and a sweat shirt, and he too came as he was. We drove out to Jersey in Bob's car. Judy was trembling. She gripped our hands—and she had a powerful grip. Once in my parents' house, though, she gradually relaxed.

My mother was in her element. She is at her best when she is mothering, and Judy, so frail and tiny, came in for her share. "Do you have a doctor over there? How is the heating? Do you get enough sunshine?" my mother asked her.

My parents brought out pictures of me as a kid, fortunately none of them on a bearskin rug. They beamed at Judy as they told her boring anecdotes about my childhood, but Judy wasn't bored. The feeling of family was strong in her, and she soon realized that my mother had symbolically put her arms around her. "If you'd only come out here for a few weeks, I'd make you well," my mother said.

My mother's complete acceptance of my wife was terribly touching, particularly since I remembered her reluctance when I first told her of our plans for marriage. "Mickey, are you sure?" Mother had asked. "She's a divorced woman." Now it was just the other way around; Mother was saying, "Mickey, are you taking care of Judy?"

As we were driving home over the George Washington Bridge, Judy said to Bob, "You know, they really loved me. And you know, Bobby, if anything ever happened to Mickey, I could really go there and live. They'd really want me."

Toward the end of our New York stay, she said mournfully, "Oh, I'm going to be forty-seven." Her birthday was the following month, on the tenth of June. "In three years I'll be fifty."

"Oh, for Pete's sake," I told her, "time doesn't matter."

I didn't have the heart to tell her immediately that her reputation for tardiness and no-show was causing problems in my negotiations with the businessmen who were planning to build the Judy Garland Cinemas. Suppose she didn't show up for the opening of a theater, or suppose she was drunk. What would they say in Wichita or Kansas City? I felt the men were making a mistake, but they terminated negotiations. I did not hide the truth from her or lie to her. She faced it. She was hurt, but she still walked tall.

What she wanted to do was to catch the first plane back to

London. Within two hours she had packed for both of us, had dressed, and was ready to leave for the airport. I'd never seen her move so fast.

Bob saw us off. "Mickey, take good care of Judy," he said. "I want to take good care of Mickey," she told him.

She didn't see her children on that last trip to the United States. She wanted to quite desperately, yet fear restrained her. She did see Peter Allen, Liza's husband, who was also her friend. After her ill-fated Australian tour Judy had discovered two talented young Australian brothers, Chris and Peter Allen, performing in a Tokyo nightclub. She was impressed with them and used them in her own concerts later, in Miami, Toronto, and Las Vegas. She then played matchmaker between Liza and Peter. The couple was married on March 3, 1967. They were rather opposites. Liza, like Judy, is warm—she likes to touch—whereas Peter has an English kind of reserve.

"In Liza I see the happiness I never had," Judy said. "I want her to have it all. But without the heartache."

Liza was the child of a movie star. Children of movie stars don't realize that nobody else lives like their families, with a couple of Rolls-Royces and a wine cellar. If you were Judy's daughter, you took that life-style for granted, even when there was no money.

Judy often said, "I share my problems with my children, so they know what the score is all the time. I tell them I'm short of money, and they understand. They want to help. They have seen me go through absolute hell. They've gone through it with me, which has made us laugh and love a little harder."

They certainly laughed a lot. Judy and Kay Thompson were dear friends, and when Kay's inimitable *Eloise* was published she sent Judy a copy. The book has to do with the antics of a precocious little demon who lives at the staid Plaza Hotel in New York City. Judy read the story to Lorna and Joey, who were inspired to follow Eloise's antics. "And don't you think they got bags and filled them with water and sent them down the mail chutes?" Judy told me. "Just like Eloise."

Liza was a born mimic. No guest at the Minnelli home was safe from her, even when she was a toddler. She had an uncanny sense of caricature, as well as a voice and Judy's mannerisms. Judy never exploited her children, but Liza was so obviously gifted that she appeared on stage during Judy's first engagement at the Palace. She danced while Judy sang "Swanee," and the number was a show-stopper. In the beginning Judy was against Liza's becoming a performer, but later she was inordinately proud of her firstborn's talents. "I'm your best example of what not to do," she often told Liza.

Liza made her screen debut as Judy's daughter in *In the Good Old Summertime*. At fourteen she served her apprenticeship in summer stock, in which at fifteen she played, and very creditably, the title role in *The Diary of Anne Frank*.

"Liza has more love to give than anyone I know. Everything Liza says comes out appropriate and lovely," Judy had told me proudly.

During our stay in New York I met a young man who'd been among the backers of Liza's first New York play, a revival of *Best Foot Forward*. He told me about an incident on the first night. Liza was enormously excited. Judy had promised to come to the opening night and bring Lorna and Joey with her. A good many critics and Broadway people who wouldn't ordinarily attend an off-Broadway opening were there. Liza had arranged for three seats down front for her family. The house was sold out, and as the curtain rose, all three seats were still empty. At the end of the first act, Liza peered out from behind the curtains. The seats were vacant and remained so for the entire play. Liza could scarcely bear to take the time for the curtain calls. Nor did she hear the lavish praise: "She's unmistakably a Judy."

She rushed directly to the office and telephoned Judy. "Mama, are you all right?"

The young backer, who happened to be in the office, surmised that Liza was terrified that something had happened to Judy. She listened, looking more and more distressed. "But, Mama, I *told* you it was *tonight!* How could you forget?" She seemed to be close to tears. Yet as the conversation continued, he had the feeling that in a subtle way the mother-daughter roles had been exchanged, and Liza was consoling Judy. "Don't feel badly, Mama," Liza said. "You can come tomorrow."

Liza's hurt was eventually salved when Judy arranged for her to appear at the Palladium with her. Live at the London Palladium! This event took place after Judy's breakdown in Hong Kong. (Mark Herron, while he was still her husband, had arranged for the program.)

On stage at the Palladium Judy came on strong with her first number, "The Man That Got Away," and in her voice was the eternal sorrow and longing of the rejected lover: "There is nothing sadder than a one-man woman looking for the man that got away."

And then, after the applause subsided and with the most touching pride and tenderness, Judy said, "Ladies and gentlemen, Miss Liza Minnelli." Liza, although aware of what it meant to be on the stage of the Palladium, singing with Judy, the living legend, wasn't paralyzed by it. She belted out "The Travelin' Life" and "The Gypsy in My Soul" so beautifully that for a moment Judy was startled, perhaps suddenly realizing that her eldest child might soon overtake her. Maternal pride conquered, though, and soon they were singing a duet to the music of "Hello, Dolly!":

"Hello, Liza, oh, hello, Liza. It's so nice to have you here where you belong. . . ."

And Liza: "You're looking swell, Mama. . . ."

A tremendous ovation, of course, and pride flowing so strongly between them, competition forgotten, as they sang "Together." Judy: "Wherever I go, I know she goes. . . . It's me for you, and you for me. . . ."

Liza was such a happy child in those early years of Judy's

marriage to her father. Vincente, with deep paternal affection, took her to the M.G.M. sets, where she could ride on the camera boom. She had dinner with her parents often. Sometimes she slept with them, and in the night they'd reach out and hold hands across her little body. Those early years were solid and gave her much to build on later. There were bad memories too, though, like the time Judy went away (probably for a rest cure) and Vincente and Liza saw her off. Judy was crying so much that Vincente went on the train with her, and their small child was taken home by her nanny. Mostly Liza tries to remember the nice things about everybody, particularly about her mama.

On the plane flying over the Atlantic to London in June, 1969, Judy lay back in her seat, her head to one side, and she said suddenly in a soft, tentative voice, "I suppose it is too late for me to have another child. . . ." She smiled wryly, aware that it was only a fantasy, that in this area there was no longer hope of a new beginning. But I have wondered since if she had suddenly felt mature enough to be a mother, if the fragments were falling into place and creating a beautiful and complete whole.

I reached out and took her hand. Somehow I was reminded of what had happened after her famous Carnegie Hall concert, when Judy stood on stage alone, her fans demanding more and more. At last she said, "We don't have much more."

In the audience someone cried, "Just stand there, then."

26

Although she was shockingly frail, Judy returned to our mews cottage with renewed spirits. On the plane she had diverted her mind from her usual terror of flying by outlining a new concert. Before we had taken off for New York, I had discussed with Richard Harris, our friend and neighbor, two possibilities for Judy—a concert and a film documentary that was to counteract the Scandinavian film. This was to be a sound, well-thought-out, and carefully planned documentary called *A Day in the Life of Judy Garland*. Judy was enthusiastic about both the film and the concert. I encouraged her because it was important for her to have something to strive for. The rejection of the minitheater entrepreneurs had hurt her deeply.

Bumbles Dawson had opened the house for us, and later Richard Harris stopped by. We talked for a while, then Judy excused herself and went up to bed.

"Is she all right?" Harris asked me.

"Tired, that's all," I replied. Later one of our neighbors, Gina Dangerfield, called to ask about Judy. She said she was going to Bromley that evening, as her friends singer Jackie Trent and Jackie's husband, orchestra leader Tony Hatch, were having the grand opening of a new men's apparel shop they owned. She invited us to join the party. Judy decided at first she didn't want to attend, but I was afraid she was entering a deep depression and thought it might do her good to go out. By the time Miss Dangerfield and Richard Harris arrived to pick us up at nine in the evening, Judy was in better spirits. We drove to Bromley, which was only a short ride from our cottage, to find the shop extremely crowded. Judy didn't mind; she was gay and talkative.

It was a pleasant evening, but for the next few days Judy preferred to remain at home. She was reading the biography *Nicholas and Alexandra,* and she brooded over the tragic fate of the Russian royal family. "If the woman who claims to be Anastasia really is the czar's daughter, it must be dreadful for her, trying to prove her identity and nobody believing her," she said.

During this week we discussed the possibility of her turning to the Catholic faith. Liza is a Catholic, and I am too. "I'd really like to," Judy said with a wistful note, "but I don't know if I can cope with all the necessary instruction."

Bumbles Dawson came over one afternoon, and she and Judy had a pleasant visit. Later Bumbles said that Judy had been in a reflective mood but in good spirits. I clutched at every suggestion that she was improving, although my eyes could see the physical deterioration. She was failing.

Before our last trip to New York I'd bought some unfinished furniture, and now I thought it would please Judy if I finished the pieces. I brought home tubes of ready-mixed plaster and showed her how to put the mixture in water and shape it into a molding before it was dry and could be baked in the oven. "Let me try," she said.

I stood back and watched her. She was quite helpless, and I wondered if she had never played with clay as a child. Finally she said, exasperated, "Oh, Mickey, I can't do anything with it!"

"You're doing fine," I said, encouraging her, but the design kept breaking apart. "Keep your hands in the water; just keep kneading it." She finally produced a piece of molding, and I painted it gold.

"I didn't do too badly?" she asked.

"You did it great, hon."

When she went upstairs to bed, I took the bit of molding down to the kitchen and heated it until it was hard. Then I went into her dressing room and borrowed the Tiffany box containing the pearls Tony Bennett had given her for Christmas. I placed the little gold-leaf molding in the box at her bedside.

Friday was the Reverend Peter Delaney's birthday, and he'd invited us, along with other friends, to dinner. Peter had known Judy about nine years, and they were close friends. Judy looked forward to the celebration, but she was concerned because we'd neglected to buy him a gift. "Can't we give him the Royal Copenhagen plate I bought for you?" she suggested. "He always admires it, and I know you don't like it because you use it as an ashtray."

I agreed and added that I would stop by a boutique and buy something amusing for him too. When I left her, she had taken out her red leather-bound *Ye Olde Bitch Book* and was writing in it. As a rule, once she had written down her feelings and had thus relieved her tensions, her anger would be dissipated. She would then tear out the offending page and destroy it. The last page of the book had been left intact, though, and I found it later. She had written Sid's name along with a comment that a friend had sent her a clipping from a New York paper. Sid was having a legal hassle over an unpaid hotel bill for one of her appearances under the auspices of Group V. She wasn't concerned about Sid, but she wrote "Joey and Lorna," underlining their names. It worried her that the children might again be exposed to unpleasant publicity.

We didn't stay long at Peter's dinner party, although Judy appeared to be enjoying herself. She had a difficult time getting to sleep that night, even with barbiturates. She was very restless and still awake when the postman came at eight in the morning. She went down to collect the mail but didn't bother to read it. I was asleep upstairs, so she wrote me a note, leaving it on the television set:

Dearest, yours and my mail arrived, so I've put yours in the second drawer right of desk.

Mine is in the second drawer left of desk. I'll have something to eat now—then sleep.

I love you, Mickey.

> Forever,
> Judy

On Saturday, June 21, we spent a quiet day at home. We listened to our favorite records, I played the piano for Judy, and we taped some of her favorite numbers. I still have the tapes, and I can feel, when I listen to them, the intensity of Judy listening as I played them for her. Her voice comes though clearly, "Great—groovy—brilliant, darling. . . ."

I was suffering from a sore throat that day, and Dr. Traherne had sent over some penicillin tablets for me. Judy and I had planned to go to the theater, but I was so uncomfortable that we decided not to.

Later in the day Philip Roberge, who has a theatrical agency, dropped by. By then Judy felt a little ill too, and Philip offered graciously to fix us all some dinner. Judy had eaten earlier, so she excused herself and went upstairs to bed.

Philip broiled hamburgers, and we ate as we watched the television documentary "The Royal Family." He left before midnight, and I went to our bedroom. Judy was still awake.

"Hon, I don't know if I should sleep in the same bed with you," I said. "I've got a mean sore throat."

She didn't say anything, but with a rueful smile, she pointed to her own.

"You too! Now we'll both have the flu."

She laughed rather painfully. I slid into bed and held her close and kissed her on the cheek. She curled up with her legs against my back. I fell into a deep sleep and was awakened hours later by the shrill insistence of the telephone.

It was Charlie Cochran calling from California. We talked for a few minutes, and then Charlie said he'd like to speak to Judy too. Her side of the bed was empty. I called out to her, but there was no answer. I knocked on the door of the bathroom. Silence.

"Judy—*Judy*—"

The door was locked; she always locked it.

Aware that her reaction was sometimes unpredictable, I said, "Hon, are you mad about something?"

No answer.

"*Judy*—"

I went back to the telephone. "Charlie, Judy will call you later," I said hurriedly. Then I flew back to the bathroom.

"Judy, are you all right?" I shouted, thinking she had probably fallen asleep. But there was also a sense of foreboding. I climbed out of the window of the dressing room, walked over the roof, and peered through the window of the bathroom. I saw Judy sitting on the john and thought at first she was asleep, for her arms were on her lap, and her head was resting on her arms.

Oh, thank God, she's all right, I thought. She hadn't fallen or hit her head, as she'd done so many times before. From this side of the glass pane she looked peaceful. I pried the window open and removed our bottles and toothbrushes from the sill. As the light came into the room I noticed that her skin was discolored, with both a red and a bluish tinge, and that her face was dreadfully distorted.

"Judy . . ." I said. I managed to get my foot over the windowsill. "Hon . . ." I went over and picked her up. Blood came from her nose and mouth, and the air escaping from her mouth sounded like a low moan.

"Oh, my God, no! Oh, my God, no!" The shock of death is something that I cannot even now describe. I put her back gently in the same position, rested her head on her hands, and then ran down the stairs and picked up the telephone. I couldn't remember the emergency number, but I finally got the police and an ambulance. My speech was so fast and probably so incoherent that I had to keep repeating the words until they understood what I was trying to tell them.

"My wife is dead. . . ."

I called Dr. Traherne and Matthew West. Then I ran outside and rang Richard Harris's doorbell. By this time I heard the bell of the ambulance. I rushed back and opened the door for the ambulance staff and the police and pointed to the upstairs.

One of the policemen came down a few minutes later. "I'm sorry, sir. Your wife is dead. She has been for several hours." Then he began asking questions. "Her full name, please." He hadn't recognized her.

"Judy Garland Deans," I said.

"Oh, my God. It can't be." He looked as if he might cry. He asked for a blank sheet of paper and wrote down my answers to his questions. Dr. Traherne arrived. Someone had called Peter Delaney and Bumbles, and now the press was gathering.

The ambulance carried Judy to the morgue at Westminster Hospital. Now my morbid thoughts took over: Judy alone in that dreadful place. It was hard for me to accept the fact that the surgical indignities imposed on that frail, tiny body had nothing to do with Judy. I was in a bad state, and a decision was made that I should drive down to Hazelmere with Matthew for the next twenty-four hours. First I called Charlie Cochran and asked him to notify Sid Luft, so the children wouldn't hear the news over the radio. When I finally got a call through to Liza's apartment, there was no answer. I tracked down her secretary's number, and they located Liza in Southampton. I called Bob Jorgen, asking him to break the news to my family, but they'd already heard it from neighbors. Then I called Liza again.

Liza was considerably upset because I was alone. When we had flown back to London for the last time, Judy had said, almost with a sense of premonition, "Mickey, if anything happens to me, take me home."

I told this to Liza and added, "What do you want?"

"Papa [which is how she referred to Sid Luft] called and wants Mama buried in California. But Mama hated California." So we decided on New York. Frank Campbell's for the funeral.

There was no sleep for me that night, even in the quiet of the country and with the aid of sleeping pills. Judy's final hours came to haunt me. Was she in a daze? Did she awake, forget about the sleeping pills she had taken, and swallow a couple more? And then, as the drugs worked on her system, slowing it down, finally paralyzing the breathing centers, had she cried out? Why had I slept so soundly? The moment between life and death is so delicate, so brief—one moment and the life is saved, another and it flickers into nothingness.

Somehow I managed to endure the next few days. I returned Wednesday, June 25, for the inquest. There were newsmen and photographers everywhere.

During the inquest the pathologist, Dr. Derek Pocock, said the postmortem showed barbiturates in Judy's blood. A high level of barbiturates, sufficient to cause death. "But there is absolutely no evidence to suggest this was a deliberate action by her. There is also no question of alcoholism, and no signs of cirrhosis of the liver." He added that the barbiturate level in her blood was not due to one massive dose but was the result of repeated small doses. Judy had built up too much of a tolerance to the pills.

Accidental death by an incautious dose of barbiturates was the final decision.

I returned to the cottage just long enough to pick up the luggage. I was in a state of shock and confusion, but I remember that Richard Harris and Bumbles Dawson came to the quiet chapel where Judy was lying. It was such a tiny coffin, like a child's. My baby, I thought, what did they do to you?

The plane for New York left at eight in the evening. Father Peter Delaney was with me. Liza had asked that he come to conduct the services.

Just six months ago we'd crossed the Atlantic the other way, going to London with such high hopes. I remembered when we landed at the London airport, the customs officials asked me if we had anything to declare.

"Nothing but four packs of cigarettes," I said.

Then he asked me if we'd brought anything to leave there.

"Just us," I told him. Just Judy and me.

27

Our plane touched down at Kennedy Airport just past midnight on June 26, 1969. I stood to one side and watched the cargo handlers slide the plain brown coffin, wrapped in burlap and tied with heavy cord, onto a cargo lift and into the waiting gray hearse. Then Peter and I joined Liza, Kay Thompson, and Bob Jorgen in a limousine waiting in a small courtyard outside the International Arrivals Building.

The sight of Liza in her dark floppy hat, so like the hats that Judy wore, looking incredibly like Judy at the moment, made me flinch. There was a group of about thirty newsmen, but Peter and I were escorted through the crowd quickly. Bob Jorgen accompanied the P.R. people, who had two cars and a station wagon for the luggage. Kay Thompson, Peter Delaney, and I went with Liza to her apartment on East 57th Street, where we talked until morning.

Liza told me an early will had been found in which Judy had requested cremation. I refused to agree to this, and Liza backed me up. In that will Judy also requested that Gene Hills, her old makeup man from her M.G.M. days, be assigned to prepare her for the funeral. Gene Hills was currently doing

Eva Gabor's makeup for the TV show *Green Acres*, however, and Eva said she could not spare his services. I knew how bad Judy looked toward the end of her life, and since Liza planned to allow the public to view Judy before the interment, I hoped to contact him myself.

Campbell's Funeral Home, on Madison Avenue and 81st Street, has been the scene of final rites for many well-known personages. After leaving Liza's apartment at dawn, I returned to my old apartment to try to get some sleep, but since I couldn't rest, I went over to Campbell's to be near Judy.

Liza and Kay were to choose the coffin. They decided on a small mahogany casket. "But it must be white," Liza insisted.

The funeral director said they had none in white.

Kay Thompson wasn't fazed. "At M.G.M. we'd get a spray gun and paint it white," she said.

The director almost toppled over. Kay, however, was being practical, not irreverent. Kay, who was one of Judy's best friends and Liza's godmother, remained in the background, but you knew all details were being taken care of. You knew also that after the funeral there would be food at Liza's apartment.

Liza had decided upon a yellow-and-white funeral; she had ordered a blanket of yellow roses to drape the coffin and a backdrop of yellow and white mums. The Reverend Peter Delaney would conduct the service, and Liza had asked James Mason, her mother's co-star in *A Star Is Born*, to speak the eulogy. Since Judy was not to be cremated, there was the problem of the burial ground, but none of us could face it at that moment.

Shortly before eleven that morning, I was told that Judy was ready, and I went alone into the chapel. She lay in a white casket, surrounded by the most magnificent flowers I had ever seen. Originally, only the family's flowers were to be in the chapel, but knowing how much Judy loved flowers, I asked the staff to place around her the arrangements others had sent. She wore her chiffon wedding gown, and she was covered to the waist with a fuzzy and uncomfortable-looking blue satin coverlet. She did not resemble at all my proud and lovely wife. I spoke to the funeral director and asked him to change her position and to redo her hair and makeup. He suggested that I leave while they made these arrangements, but I could not. I thought of all the times I'd sat with Judy while she made up for a performance. I told the makeup man what to do, and when they put her gently back in the coffin, her chin high as she always carried it, her hair combed as she always combed it, she ceased to be a corpse and became my sleeping Judy.

The skies were threatening, but a crowd had already gathered outside the funeral parlor. Some carried portable gramophones that were blaring out Judy's old records. I asked the funeral director to ask the fans to stop playing them. A policeman made an announcement, and the mourners acquiesced immediately.

The funeral director told me that he was obliged to prepare for even more demonstrations of Judy's fans' devotion. "We expect Miss Garland's funeral to draw bigger crowds than Rudolph Valentino's," he warned me. At noon there were three thousand fans lined up four deep outside Campbell's.

By the time the first mourners were allowed in, Judy was redressed in the gray crepe gown she had worn at our secret marriage ceremony in January. Her tiny hands were in white gloves and rested on a small Bible. She wore silver slippers and a silver brocaded belt decorated with pearls. She rested on light-blue velvet in the white coffin.

Judy Garland was ready for her final appearance.

Campbell's was to have been open to the public until ten that evening and from eight to eleven the following morning before the funeral. But as twenty-one thousand people began their march past Judy's bier to pay their final respects, I asked that the doors be kept open throughout the night.

That night Lorna and Joey arrived from California with

their father, Sid Luft. I went out to meet them when they came in from the airport. They were so brave, and Liza's presence gave them such great comfort.

The morning of the funeral something happened that would have appealed to Judy's sense of humor. I had breakfast with the Reverend Peter Delaney and James Mason, and we discussed the eulogy Mason was to deliver. Afterward we drove to the funeral parlor in a hired limousine. As we stepped out of the car, a policeman assisted us, first James Mason and then me. Then he saw black patent-leather slippers and full black wool skirts, and he said, offering a helping hand, "Now you, madame. . . ."

It was, of course, Peter in his cassock. The cop's face turned scarlet.

Her death, like her life, made headlines.

Ray Bolger wept when he heard. He and Judy had been devoted friends since the days of *The Wizard of Oz*. "The last time I played the Waldorf, last spring," he said, "Judy came in to see me. It was a very warm, sentimental night for me. Someone in the audience called out, 'Come on, Judy, sing "Over the Rainbow."' I was afraid she would be embarrassed, so I said Judy had already sung herself into their hearts, and she needn't sing if she didn't feel in the mood.

"That pleased her. Her face lit up, and she became beautiful. She looked absolutely marvelous. But then I don't have to tell you about that expression. You've seen it in the movies."

Someone recalled that in the 1950's, when Senator Joseph McCarthy was engaged in a witch hunt, she was one of the five hundred signers of a petition against his practices.

"We loved her when she was happy, and we loved her when she was blue," wrote Rex Reed, "and most of the time she was both. . . . Nobody who ever saw her or listened to her records ever needed a last name. It was always *Judy*."

"She could sing so that it would break your heart," James Mason said.

Alfred de Liagre, the Broadway producer, remembered that Judy was his original choice to star in *The Voice of the Turtle,* one of his great theatrical hits, but the deal couldn't be made. "Judy married Vincente Minnelli at the same time my wife and I were married, and we lived across the street from each other, so we were kind of honeymooning together," he added.

In London Bernard Delfont paid tribute to her. "I think that when she was in form, she was one of the greatest artists. I have seen her in some brilliant performances. Her loss is a great tragedy."

George Cukor, a director of some great films who had worked very closely with Judy, as he had with other great women stars, said sadly, "Judy was obviously a very talented woman, but many people missed the great essence of her— which was that she was an extremely sharp, an extremely intelligent, person. But all her wit and all her intelligence couldn't save her."

She was such a mixture of triumph and despair. A newsman in the crowd remembered her singing "Rock-a-Bye" at the London Palladium charity show and how the audience had wept.

A critic, Burt Korall, who had seen her toward the end, summed up her perennial effectiveness: "That Judy Garland is an entertainer has become secondary to the event. Because of the fanatical response to a Garland performance, one can easily be swept along by the momentum basic to the situation. It's a temptation to ignore the performance and become immersed in the atmosphere."

Perhaps E. Y. Harburg, who wrote the lyrics for "Over the Rainbow" and many other Garland songs, summed it up when he said, "There was never a real world for Judy Garland. It was a phony world right from the word 'go,' when her parents got her into vaudeville at the age of four to sing 'Jingle Bells.' From there on, this little kid was exploited because she had a personality, a little voice, and a talent for the stage. She had no childhood. And then at the age of fourteen she had a bang-up voice; her voice, I think, was one of the greatest in the first part of our century. She went right through bone and flesh into the heart."

A devoted fan, a young woman who was patiently waiting outside the funeral home, said, "We knew she had problems, and we understood. She gave us so much, and yet the world seemed to give her so little."

Among the telegrams and letters was a note from Judy's mother's sister, her aunt, Irene Milne Mathias:

> So often I've wanted to refute some of the reasons printed about Judy not having good balance and equilibrium and forgetting the words to a song, but was in doubt as to how to express the reasons, so I'll explain it to you.
>
> There must be some cause for this failure on the Fitzpatrick side of the family, since several of us suffer the same way. . . .
>
> I cannot ascend and descend steps without something to balance myself.
>
> These lapses of memory or lack of expression are only when we become a little excited or upset. Seem to be an emotional thing.
>
> When Judy appeared here at Cahol Hall last year, her knees crumpled and she dropped to the floor and remained there several minutes. Trouper that she was, she pretended it was part of the performance.

Judy had been aware of this physical weakness; she had mentioned it casually to me when we first arrived in London, but she made nothing of it. There was so much she kept to herself.

She had once said wryly to me, though, in an attempt to analyze her gifts, "Maybe it's because I made a certain sound, a musical sound, a sound that seems to belong to the world. But it also belongs to me because it comes from within me."

The morning of the funeral police closed the block in front of Campbell's to traffic. The chapel was filled to capacity.

Three hundred and fifty of Judy's friends came. Mickey Rooney was there, but he was not the Mickey of the Andy Hardy films, the brash, mischievous, all-American boy. Life had tempered him, as it had Judy. Was he thinking of those young kids, so full of life, who dashed out onto the stage of the Capitol Theater, holding hands, laughing as they sang, inspiring their audience with their joy and zest?

Ray Bolger was there, Lauren Bacall, Jack Benny, Sammy Davis, Jr., Katharine Hepburn (who'd been so kind when Judy needed help), Burt Lancaster, Dean Martin, Lana Turner, Freddie Bartholomew (another child star who had suffered at the hands of his family), Spyros Skouras, Otto Preminger, Pat Lawford, New York City Mayor John Lindsay, and many more. Sid Luft sat with Lorna and Joey, and I sat in a pew with Liza. Loudspeakers had been set up outside so those in the street could hear James Mason's eulogy:

"I traveled in her orbit only for a little while, but it was an exciting while and one during which it seemed that the joys in her life outbalanced the miseries. The little girl whom I knew had a little curl right in the middle of her forehead, and when she was good, she was not only very, very good, she was the most sympathetic, the funniest, the sharpest, and the most stimulating woman I ever knew.

"She was a lady who gave so much and richly both to the vast audience whom she entertained and to the friends around her whom she loved that there was no currency in which to repay her. And she needed to be repaid, she needed devotion and love beyond the resources of any of us. . . .

"The person who probably of all the world knew Judy best is her older daughter, Liza Minnelli. I am going to quote, with her permission, some words attributed to her in the English newspaper I was reading three days ago. Her tribute to Judy was personal and moving.

" 'I wish you could mention the joy she had for life. That's what she gave me. If she was the tragic figure they said she was, I would be a wreck, wouldn't I?

" 'It was her love of life that carried her through everything. The middle of the road was never for her. It bored her. She wanted the pinnacle of excitement. If she was happy, she wasn't just happy. She was ecstatic. And when she was sad, she was sadder than anybody.

" 'She had lived eighty lives in one. And yet I thought she would outlive us all. She was a great star and a great talent, and for the rest of my life I will be proud to be Judy Garland's daughter.' "

Then it was over. Only the family, the Reverend Peter Delaney, and Bob Jorgen drove to Ferncliff Cemetery, in Hartsdale, New York, where Judy was placed in a crypt, pending final burial plans. From the time we left the funeral home, sitting in the dark limousines, an unreal quality took over. Driving in the cortege in the muggy heat, with faces peering into car windows, I felt it was not really happening. On our return we went to Liza's apartment, where Kay Thompson had readied food and drink for us. Kay was taking over, making us feel alive. But there was Joey, and when you looked at Joey, you knew there had been a funeral, although he had the wide-eyed look of a child who doesn't understand death. We persuaded him finally to go to bed.

Sleep had deserted the rest of us. We were overstimulated and yet in shock. The wild, frenetic days, telephones ringing, wires and flowers arriving, doorbells ringing, eighteen hours a day at the funeral home—it had kept us from thinking. But now reality was crushing. Nobody could make conversation. Nobody could relate anymore. We seemed isolated in our numbness. Peter and Bob wanted to do something for me, but there was nothing to do. Liza and Lorna had returned with us to Bob's apartment, which was crowded with Judy's luggage. The tension was growing.

The telephone rang. It was a friend of mine from New Jersey. "Why don't you all come out here?" he suggested. "May do you some good."

We felt a sense of inertia, as though the world had stopped, but Liza decided we should go. We didn't want to use a limousine, since it reminded us too much of the day itself. We went, instead, to a car-rental agency and hired a convertible. I drove, with Lorna in front with me, and Peter and Bob in the back seat with Liza. We started up the East Side Highway, and all I can say is that despite the traffic, it seemed to all of us that there was total silence and no world outside of ourselves. The sky was unbelievably high, brightened by a solitary shining star. Nobody spoke. Even Peter, who was never at a loss for words, was strangely silent. In desperation I switched on the radio. All of a sudden, there was the sound of Judy's voice. I jumped, nearly losing control of the car, reacting with horror for Liza and Lorna.

It was Barry Gray's program, and he was doing the entire Carnegie Hall concert. My hand went to the radio.

"Leave it on," Liza begged in a high, strained voice.

Judy was singing "The Man That Got Away."

It was as though she were here in the car with us. As though she was saying she'd always be with us. We were in another dimension. We seemed to be coming back to life. And we were finding unbelievable comfort. . . .

And then suddenly Liza, with her marvelous instinct for knowing, for being able to turn to something, cried out: "Go, Mama, go!"

The Films
of
Judy Garland

Every Sunday (M.G.M.), 1936.
Pigskin Parade (Twentieth Century Fox), 1936.
Broadway Melody of 1938 (M.G.M.), 1937.
Thoroughbreds Don't Cry (M.G.M.), 1937.
Everybody Sing (M.G.M.), 1938.
Listen Darling (M.G.M.), 1938.
Love Finds Andy Hardy (M.G.M.), 1938.
The Wizard of Oz (M.G.M.), 1939.
Babes in Arms (M.G.M.), 1939.
Andy Hardy Meets Debutante (M.G.M.), 1940.
Strike Up the Band (M.G.M.), 1940.
Little Nelly Kelly (M.G.M.), 1940.
Ziegfeld Girl (M.G.M.), 1941.
Life Begins for Andy Hardy (M.G.M.), 1941.
Babes on Broadway (M.G.M.), 1941.
We Must Have Music (M.G.M.), 1942.
For Me and My Gal (M.G.M.), 1942.
Presenting Lily Mars (M.G.M.), 1943.
Girl Crazy (M.G.M.), 1943.
Thousands Cheer (M.G.M.), 1943.
Meet Me in St. Louis (M.G.M.), 1944.
The Clock (M.G.M.), 1945.
The Harvey Girls (M.G.M.), 1946.
Ziegfeld Follies of 1946 (M.G.M.), 1946.

Till the Clouds Roll By (M.G.M.), 1946.

The Pirate (M.G.M.), 1948.

Easter Parade (M.G.M.), 1948.

Words and Music (M.G.M.), 1948.

In the Good Old Summertime (M.G.M.), 1949.

Summer Stock (M.G.M.), 1950.

A Star Is Born (Warner Brothers Release, Transcona Enterprises Production), 1954.

Pepe (Columbia Pictures), 1960.

Judgment at Nuremberg (United Artists Release, Roxlom Production), 1961.

Gay Purr-ee (Warner Brothers Release, U.P.A. Production), 1962.

A Child Is Waiting (United Artists Release, Stanley Kramer Production), 1962.

I Could Go On Singing (United Artists Release, Barbican Production), 1962.

INDEX